Kindergarten

Teacher's Edition

Senior Authors J. David Cooper, John J. Pikulski
Authors Patricia A. Ackerman, Kathryn H. Au, David J. Chard, Gilbert G. Garcia, Claude N. Goldenberg, Marjorie Y. Lipson, Susan E. Page, Shane Templeton, Sheila W. Valencia, MaryEllen Vogt

Consultants Linda H. Butler, Linnea C. Ehri, Carla B. Ford

HOUGHTON MIFFLIN BOSTON • MORRIS PLAINS, NJ

California • Colorado • Georgia • Illinois • New Jersey • Texas

Literature Reviewers

Consultants: **Dr. Adela Artola Allen**, Associate Dean, Graduate College, Associate Vice President for Inter-American Relations, University of Arizona, Tucson, Arizona; **Dr. Manley Begay**, Co-director of the Harvard Project on American Indian Economic Development, Director of the National Executive Education Program for Native Americans, Harvard University, John F. Kennedy School of Government, Cambridge, Massachusetts; **Dr. Nicholas Kannellos**, Director, Arte Publico Press, Director, Recovering the U.S. Hispanic Literacy Heritage Project, University of Houston, Texas; **Mildred Lee**, author and former head of Library Services for Sonoma County, Santa Rosa, California; **Dr. Barbara Moy**, Director of the Office of Communication Arts, Detroit Public Schools, Michigan; **Norma Naranjo**, Clark County School District, Las Vegas, Nevada; **Dr. Arlette Ingram Willis**, Associate Professor, Department of Curriculum and Instruction, Division of Language and Literacy, University of Illinois at Urbana-Champaign, Illinois

Teachers: **Helen Brooks**, Vestavia Hills Elementary School, Birmingham, Alabama; **Patricia Buchanan**, Thurgood Marshall School, Newark, Delaware; **Gail Connor**, Language Arts Resource Teacher, Duval County, Jacksonville, Florida; **Vicki DeMott**, McClean Science/Technology School, Wichita, Kansas; **Marge Egenhoffer**, Dixon Elementary School, Brookline, Wisconsin; **Mary Jew Mori**, Griffin Avenue Elementary, Los Angeles, California

Program Reviewers

Supervisors: **Judy Artz**, Middletown Monroe City School District, Ohio; **James Bennett**, Elkhart Schools, Elkhart, Indiana; **Kay Buckner-Seal**, Wayne County, Michigan; **Charlotte Carr**, Seattle School District, Washington; **Sister Marion Christi**, St. Matthews School, Archdiocese of Philadelphia, Pennsylvania; **Alvina Crouse**, Garden Place Elementary, Denver Public Schools, Colorado; **Peggy DeLapp**, Minneapolis, Minnesota; **Carol Erlandson**, Wayne Township Schools, Marion County, Indianapolis; **Brenda Feeney**, North Kansas City School District, Missouri; **Winnie Huebsch**, Sheboygan Area Schools, Wisconsin; **Brenda Mickey**, Winston-Salem/Forsyth County Schools, North Carolina; **Audrey Miller**, Sharpe Elementary School, Camden, New Jersey; **JoAnne Piccolo**, Rocky Mountain Elementary, Adams 12 District, Colorado; **Sarah Rentz**, East Baton Rouge Parish School District, Louisiana; **Kathy Sullivan**, Omaha Public Schools, Nebraska; **Rosie Washington**, Kuny Elementary, Gary, Indiana; **Theresa Wishart**, Knox County Public Schools, Tennessee

Teachers: **Carol Brockhouse**, Madison Schools, Wayne Westland Schools, Michigan; **Eva Jean Conway**, R.C. Hill School, Valley View School District, Illinois; **Carol Daley**, Jane Addams School, Sioux Falls, South Dakota; **Karen Landers**, Watwood Elementary, Talladega County, Alabama; **Barb LeFerrier**, Mullenix Ridge Elementary, South Kitsap District, Port Orchard, Washington; **Loretta Piggee**, Nobel School, Gary, Indiana; **Cheryl Remash**, Webster Elementary School, Manchester, New Hampshire; **Marilynn Rose**, Michigan; **Kathy Scholtz**, Amesbury Elementary School, Amesbury, Massachusetts; **Dottie Thompson**, Erwin Elementary, Jefferson County, Alabama; **Dana Vassar**, Moore Elementary School, Winston-Salem, North Carolina; **Joy Walls**, Ibraham Elementary School, Winston-Salem, North Carolina; **Elaine Warwick**, Fairview Elementary, Williamson County, Tennessee

Credits

Cover and Theme Opener
Patrice Briel

Photography
p. i, image copyright © 2000 PhotoDisc, Inc.

Assignment Photography
Joel Benjamin
pp. xiv, T9, T53, T67, T75, T86, T97, T121, T129, T131, T147

Allan Landau
p. T17

Illustration
Gilles Tibo, p. T65; Lily Toy Hong, p. T119

Acknowledgments

Grateful acknowledgment is made for permission to reprint copyrighted material as follows:

Theme 6
What Will the Weather Be Like Today? by Paul Rogers, illustrations by Kazuko. Text copyright © 1989 by Paul Rogers. Illustrations copyright © 1989 by Kazuko. First published in the United States by Greenwillow Books. Reprinted by arrangement with Greenwillow Books, a division of William Morrow & Company Inc.

Printed in the U.S.A.

ISBN: 0-618-07472-4

23456789-B-06 05 04 03 02 01 00

Theme 6

Sunshine and Raindrops

OBJECTIVES

Phonemic Awareness blending and segmenting onset and rime

Phonics sounds for letters *L, l; K, k; Qu, qu*

Decoding *-it* word family

High-Frequency Words recognize two new high-frequency words

Reading Strategies predict/infer; summarize; evaluate; phonics/decoding

Comprehension Skills fantasy/realism; story structure: plot

Vocabulary describing words; weather action words

Writing description; sentences; journals; weather observations; weather report; story; book report

Listening/Speaking/Viewing activities to support vocabulary expansion and writing

Theme 6

Sunshine and Raindrops

Literature Resources

WEEK 1

Teacher Read Aloud
Chicken Soup with Rice
concept book by Maurice Sendak
pages T10–T11

Big Book
What Will the Weather Be Like Today?
fiction by Paul Rogers
pages T18–T19, T28–T33

Science Link
Checking the Weather
nonfiction
pages T40–T41

Decodable **Phonics Library**
Can It Fit?
page T35

WEEK 2

Teacher Read Aloud
The Sun and the Wind
an Aesop's fable
pages T62–T65

Big Book
All to Build a Snowman
fiction by Samuel Tang
pages T72–T73, T82–T87

Social Studies Link
What Can We Do?
nonfiction
pages T94–T95

Decodable **Phonics Library**
Kit
page T89

WEEK 3

Teacher Read Aloud
The Woodcutter's Cap
a traditional Russian tale
pages T116–T119

Revisit the Big Books:
What Will the Weather Be Like Today?
pages T126–T127
All to Build a Snowman
pages T136–T137

Revisit the Links: Science
Checking the Weather
page T144
Social Studies
What Can We Do?
page T145

Decodable **Phonics Library**
Fan
page T139

Big Books for Use All Year

From Apples to Zebras: A Book of ABC's

Higglety Pigglety: A Book of Rhymes

Leveled Books

See Cumulative Listing of Leveled Books.

Phonics Library

Decodable

- Can It Fit?
- Kit
- Fan

Lessons, pages T35, T89, T139

On My Way Practice Reader

Easy / On Level

Here, Kit!

by A. J. Cooper

page T153

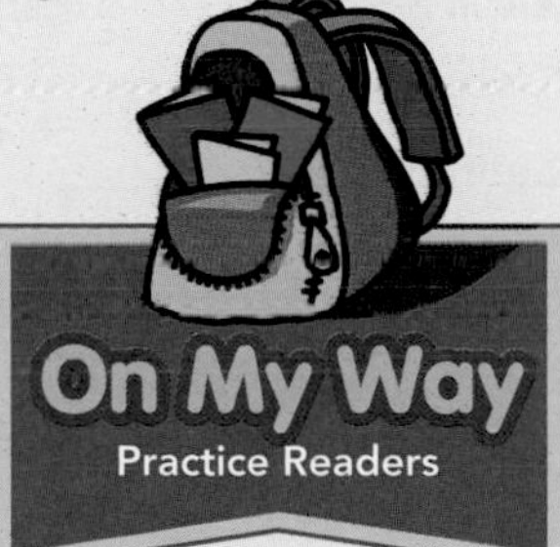

Little Big Books

On Level / Challenge

What Will the Weather Be Like Today?

All to Build a Snowman

Audiotape

Sunshine and Raindrops

Houghton Mifflin Classroom Bookshelf

Level K

Little Readers for Guided Reading

Collection K

Theme 6

Bibliography

Key

- Science
- Social Studies
- Multicultural
- Music
- Math
- Classic
- Art

Books for Browsing

Rabbits and Raindrops
by Jim Arnosky
Putnam 1997 (32p)
Beneath a dry hedge, a mother rabbit and her bunnies wait out a spring rainstorm.

Snowy Flowy Blowy: A Twelve Months Rhyme
by Nancy Tafuri
Scholastic 1999 (32p)
Twelve rhyming words take readers through a family's year in the country.

The Snowy Day
by Ezra Jack Keats
Viking 1962 (32p) also paper
In this Caldecott Medal-winning story, a boy discovers the joys of a snowy day. **Available in Spanish as *Un día de nieve.***

One Hot Summer Day
by Nina Crews
Greenwillow 1995 (24p)
A girl dances her way through a hot summer day until a thunderstorm brings relief.

A Hat for Minerva Louise
by Janet Morgan Stoeke
Dutton 1994 (24p) also paper
On a snowy day, the daffy hen Minerva Louise wears a pair of mittens as hats for her head and tail.

Rain
by Robert Kalan
Greenwillow 1978
(24p) also paper
After a day has gone from sunny to rainy, a beautiful rainbow appears in the sky.

Snowballs
by Lois Ehlert
Harcourt 1995
(32p)
Using buttons, evergreens, bottle caps, and other materials, children create a snow family on a winter day.

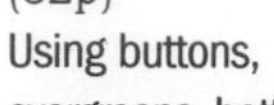

Books for Teacher Read Aloud

The Windy Day
by G. Brian Karas
Simon 1998 (32p)
A blustery breeze upsets the townspeople, but a boy named Bernard loves the windy weather.

Weather
by Lee Bennett Hopkins
Harper 1994 (64p)
also paper
Short poems about all kinds of weather.

Grandmother Winter
by Phyllis Root
Houghton 1999 (32p)
When Grandmother Winter shakes out the quilt she makes from goose feathers, it starts to snow.

Rain Song*
by Lezlie Evans
Houghton 1995
(32p) also paper
Poetic text celebrates the excitement of a summer thunderstorm.

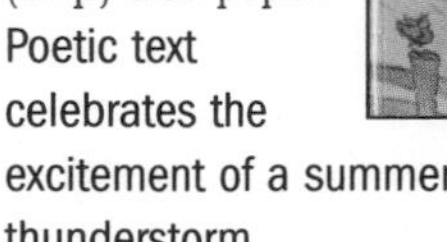

Snow
by Uri Shulevitz
Farrar 1998 (32p)
Despite all predictions to the contrary, a boy is sure it will snow in this Caldecott Honor story.

Can You See the Wind?
by Allan Fowler
Children's 1999
(32p) also paper
Color photos and brief text explain what wind is and how it affects the weather.

April Showers
by George Shannon
Greenwillow 1995 (32p)
Five silly frogs twirl and leap and skip their way through the rain.

A Year for Kiko
by Ferida Wolff
Houghton 1997 (32p)
Throughout the seasons, Kiko enjoys activities from catching snowflakes to cooling off in a pool.

Down Comes the Rain
by Franklyn Branley
Harper 1998 (32p) also paper
An introduction to weather and the water cycle includes easy experiments.

Hide-and-Seek Fog
by Alvin Tresselt
Lothrop 1965 (32p) also paper
For three days in a Cape Cod village, children romp and play in a heavy fog.

Rain Talk
by Mary Serfozo
McElderry 1990 (32p)
also paper
A girl and her dog enjoy the many different sounds rain makes on a summer day.

Elmer Takes Off
by David McKee
Lothrop 1998 (32p)
Elmer the patchwork elephant pretends to be blown away on a windy day.

* = Included in Houghton Mifflin Classroom Bookshelf, Level K

Katy and the Big Snow*
by Virginia Burton
Houghton 1943
(40p)

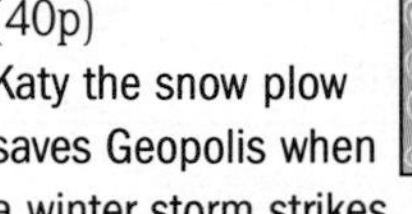

Katy the snow plow saves Geopolis when a winter storm strikes.

When It Starts to Snow
by Phillis Gershator
Holt 1998 (32p)
In rhyming verse, mice, turtles, bears, and other animals tell what they do when it snows.

Books for Shared Reading

Bearsie Bear and the Surprise Sleepover Party*
by Bernard Waber
Houghton 1997
(40p)
Bearsie Bear's animal friends crowd into his house to escape the cold.

The Itsy-Bitsy Spider
by Iza Trapani
Whispering Coyote 1993 (32p)
An extended version of the familiar rhyme in which the weather causes trouble for a spider.

Winter Lullaby
by Barbara Seuling
Harcourt 1998 (32p)
Rhyming verse reveals what different animals do to survive the changing seasons.

A Summery Saturday Morning
by Margaret Mahy
Viking 1998 (32p)
In a rhyming, repetitive story, a group of children set out for a lively summer walk.

In the Cow's Backyard
by Alma Flor Ada
Santillana 1991
(32p) paper

A succession of animals join an ant lying in a hammock in the shade on a hot day.

Books for Phonics Read Aloud

Leo the Late Bloomer
by Robert Kraus
Harper 1971 (32p) also paper
Leo the tiger learns to read and write in his own good time.

A Letter for Amy
by Ezra Jack Keats
Puffin 1998 (32p)

Peter goes out in a thunderstorm to mail a special birthday party invitation to his friend Amy.

Bringing the Rain to Kapiti Plain
by Verna Aardema
Dial 1981 (32p) also paper
In a cumulative Nandi tale, Ki-pat brings rain to the drought-stricken Kapiti Plain.

May I Bring a Friend?
by Beatrice Schenk de Regniers
Atheneum 1964 (32p)
A boy brings his animal friends when he's invited to tea by the king and queen.

The Quilt
by Ann Jonas
Greenwillow 1987 (24p)
A young girl's quilt inspires a dream adventure.

* = Included in Houghton Mifflin Classroom Bookshelf, Level K

Technology

Computer Software Resources

- **Curious George® Learns Phonics**
- **Lexia Quick Phonics Assessment**
- **Lexia Phonics Intervention CD-ROM: Primary**
- **Published by Sunburst Technology***
  Tenth Planet™ Vowels: Short and Long
  Curious George® Pre-K ABCs
  First Phonics
- **Published by The Learning Company**
  Dr. Seuss's ABC™
  Paint, Write & Play!™
  ¡Vamos a Jugar, Pintar y Escribir!
- **Seasons CD-ROM.** *National Geographic*

Video Cassettes

- **A Rainbow of My Own** *by Don Freeman. Weston Woods*
- **Chicken Soup with Rice** *by Maurice Sendak. Weston Woods*
- **Rain** *by Peter Spier. Spoken Arts*
- **Storm!** *National Geographic*
- **Time of Wonder** *by Robert McCloskey. Weston Woods*

Audio Cassettes

- **Henry and Mudge in the Sparkle Days** *by Cynthia Rylant. Live Oak*
- **Gilberto and the Wind** *by Marie Hall Ets. Live Oak*
- **Katy and the Big Snow** *by Virginia Burton. Houghton*
- **The Snowy Day** *by Ezra Jack Keats. Live Oak*
- **The Itsy Bitsy Spider** *by Iza Trapani. Spoken Arts*
- **Audiotapes for *Sunshine and Raindrops*** *Houghton Mifflin Company*

Technology Resources addresses are on page R10.

Education Place
www.eduplace.com *Log on to Education Place for more activities relating to Sunshine and Raindrops.*

Book Adventure
www.bookadventure.org *This Internet reading-incentive program provides thousands of titles for students to read.*

Theme 6

Theme at a Glance

Theme Concept: *Whatever the weather, it affects us every day!*

Learning to Read

✓ Indicates Tested Skills

Week	Selections	Phonemic Awareness and Phonics	High-Frequency Words	Comprehension Skills and Strategies
WEEK 1	**Read Aloud** **Chicken Soup with Rice** **Big Book** **What Will The Weather Be Like Today?** **Science Link** **Checking the Weather** **Phonics Library** *"Can It Fit?"*	✓ Phonemic Awareness: Blending and Segmenting Onset and Rime, *T9, T17, T27, T39, T47* ✓ Initial Consonant *l*, *T12–T13, T20–T21* ✓ Blending *-it* words, *T34, T42–T43* **Phonics Review: Familiar Consonants; *-an, -at, -it* words,** *T13, T20, T36, T44, T50, T52*	✓ High-Frequency Words, *T22–T23, T35, T51* **Word Wall,** *T8, T16, T26, T38, T46*	✓ Comprehension: Fantasy/Realism, *T10, T18, T30, T31, T32, T40, T48* **Strategies: Predict/Infer,** *T10, T18, T29, T40* **Phonics/Decoding,** *T35*
WEEK 2	**Read Aloud** **The Sun and the Wind** **Big Book** **All to Build a Snowman** **Social Studies Link** **What Can We Do?** **Phonics Library** *"Kit"* 	✓ Phonemic Awareness: Blending and Segmenting Onset and Rime, *T61, T71, T81, T93, T101* ✓ Initial Consonant *k*, *T66–T67, T74–T75* ✓ Blending *-it* words, *T88, T96–T97* **Phonics Review: Familiar Consonants; *-at, -an, -it* words,** *T67, T74, T90, T98, T104, T106*	✓ High-Frequency Words, *T76–T77, T89, T105* **Word Wall,** *T60, T70, T80, T92, T100*	✓ Comprehension: Story Structure: Plot, *T62, T72, T83, T84, T102* **Strategies: Summarize,** *T62, T72, T83, T85, T94* **Phonics/Decoding,** *T89*
WEEK 3	**Read Aloud** **The Woodcutter's Cap** **Big Books** **What Will The Weather Be Like Today?** **All to Build a Snowman** **Science and Social Studies Links** **Checking the Weather** **What Can We Do?** **Phonics Library** *"Fan"* 	✓ Phonemic Awareness: Blending and Segmenting Onset and Rime, *T115, T125, T135, T143, T151* ✓ Initial Consonant *q*, *T120–T121, T128–T129* ✓ Blending *-it* words, *T138–T139, T146–T147* **Phonics Review: Familiar Consonants; *-an, -at, -it* words,** *T121, T128, T140, T148, T154, T156*	**High-Frequency Words,** *T130–T131, T139, T155* **Word Wall,** *T114, T124, T134, T142, T150*	✓ Comprehension: Fantasy/Realism, *T116, T126, T152* ✓ Story Structure: Plot, *T136, T137, T152* **Strategies: Predict/Infer,** *T144, T145* **Evaluate,** *T116, T126, T136, T145* **Phonics/Decoding,** *T139*

Pacing

- This theme is designed to take approximately 3 weeks, depending on your students' needs.

Multi-age Classroom

Related theme—

- **Grade 1:** *We Can Work It Out*

Education Place: www.eduplace.com Log on to Education Place for more activities relating to *Sunshine and Raindrops.*

Lesson Planner CD-ROM: Customize your planning for *Sunshine and Raindrops* with the Lesson Planner.

Word Work		Writing & Language			Centers
High-Frequency Word Practice	**Building Words**	**Oral Language**	**Writing**	**Listening/ Speaking/Viewing**	**Content Areas**
Matching Words, *T14* **Building Sentences,** *T24*	**Word Family** ***-it,*** *T36* **Word Families** ***-it, -an, -at,*** *T44, T52*	**Using Describing Words** • describing weather, *T15* **Vocabulary Expansion** • using describing words, *T25*	**Shared Writing** • writing a description, *T37* **Interactive Writing** • writing sentences, *T45* **Independent Writing** • Journals, *T53*	**Listening,** *T25* **Viewing and Speaking,** *T37, T45*	**Book Center,** *T11* **Phonics Center,** *T13, T21, T43* **Writing Center,** *T15, T45* **Science Center,** *T19* **Art Center,** *T25, T33*
Matching Words, *T68* **Building Sentences,** *T78*	**Word Family** ***-it,*** *T90* **Word Families** ***-it, -an, -at,*** *T98, T106*	**Using Weather Action Words** • action words for weather, *T69* **Vocabulary Expansion** • using weather action words, *T79*	**Shared Writing** • weather observations, *T91* **Interactive Writing** • a weather report, *T99* **Independent Writing** • Journals, *T107*	**Listening and Speaking,** *T69* **Viewing and Speaking,** *T79, T91, T99*	**Book Center,** *T63, T87* **Phonics Center,** *T67, T75, T97* **Writing Center,** *T69, T79, T99* **Dramatic Play Center,** *T63* **Math Center,** *T73, T87* **Art Center,** *T87*
Matching Words, *T122* **Building Sentences,** *T132*	**Word Family** ***-it,*** *T140* **Word Families** ***-it, -an, -at,*** *T148, T156*	**Action Words** • action words for outdoor activities, *T123* **Vocabulary Expansion** • describing words, *T133*	**Shared Writing** • writing a story, *T141* **Interactive Writing** • writing a story, *T149* **Independent Writing** • Journals, *T157*	**Listening and Speaking,** *T123, T141, T149* **Viewing and Speaking,** *T133*	**Book Center,** *T127* **Phonics Center,** *T121, T129, T147* **Writing Center,** *T123, T133, T149* **Dramatic Play Center,** *T117* **Art Center,** *T137* **Science Center,** *T145*

Planning for Assessment

Use these resources to meet your assessment needs. For additional information, see the *Teacher's Assessment Handbook.*

Emerging Literacy Survey

Lexia CD-ROM

Diagnostic Planning

Emerging Literacy Survey

- If you have used this survey to obtain baseline data on the skills children brought with them to kindergarten, this might be a good time to re-administer all or parts of the survey to chart progress, to identify areas of strength and need, and to test the need for early intervention.

Lexia Quick Phonics Assessment CD-ROM

- Can be used to identify students who need more help with phonics.

Ongoing Assessment

Phonemic Awareness:

- **Practice Book,** pp. 165–166, 175–176, 185–186

Phonics:

- **Practice Book,** pp. 167, 170–171, 177, 180–181, 187, 190–191

Comprehension:

- **Practice Book** Reading Responses, pp. 163–164, 169, 173–174, 179, 183–184, 189

Writing:

- Writing samples for portfolios

Informal Assessment:

- **Diagnostic Checks**, pp. T23, T33, T43, T51, T77, T86, T97, T105, T131, T147, T155

Integrated Theme Test

Theme Skills Test

End-of-Theme Assessment

Integrated Theme Test:

- Assesses children's progress as readers and writers in a format that reflects instruction. Simple decodable texts test reading skills in context.

Theme Skills Test:

- Assesses children's mastery of specific reading and language arts skills taught in the theme.

Kindergarten Benchmarks

For your planning, listed here are the instructional goals and activities that help develop benchmark behaviors for kindergartners. Use this list to plan instruction and to monitor children's progress. See the Checklist of skills found on T159.

Theme Lessons and Activities:	Benchmark Behaviors:
Oral Language • songs, rhymes, chants, finger plays • shared reading	• can listen to a story attentively • can participate in the shared reading experience
Phonemic Awareness • blending and segmenting onset and rime • beginning sounds	• can blend sounds into meaningful units
Phonics • initial consonants *l, k, qu* • word family *-it*	• can name single letters and their sounds • can decode some common CVC words
Concepts of Print • capital at the beginning of sentence • end punctuation (period, question mark, exclamation point) • quotation marks	• can recognize common print conventions
Reading • decodable texts • high-frequency words *is, here*	• can read and write a few words • can select a letter to represent a sound
Comprehension • fantasy/realism • elements of plot (problem, solution)	• can think critically about a text • can use effective reading strategies
Writing and Language • drawing and labeling images • writing simple phrases or sentences • journal writing	• can label pictures using phonetic spellings • can write independently

Theme 6

Launching the Theme

Sunshine and Raindrops

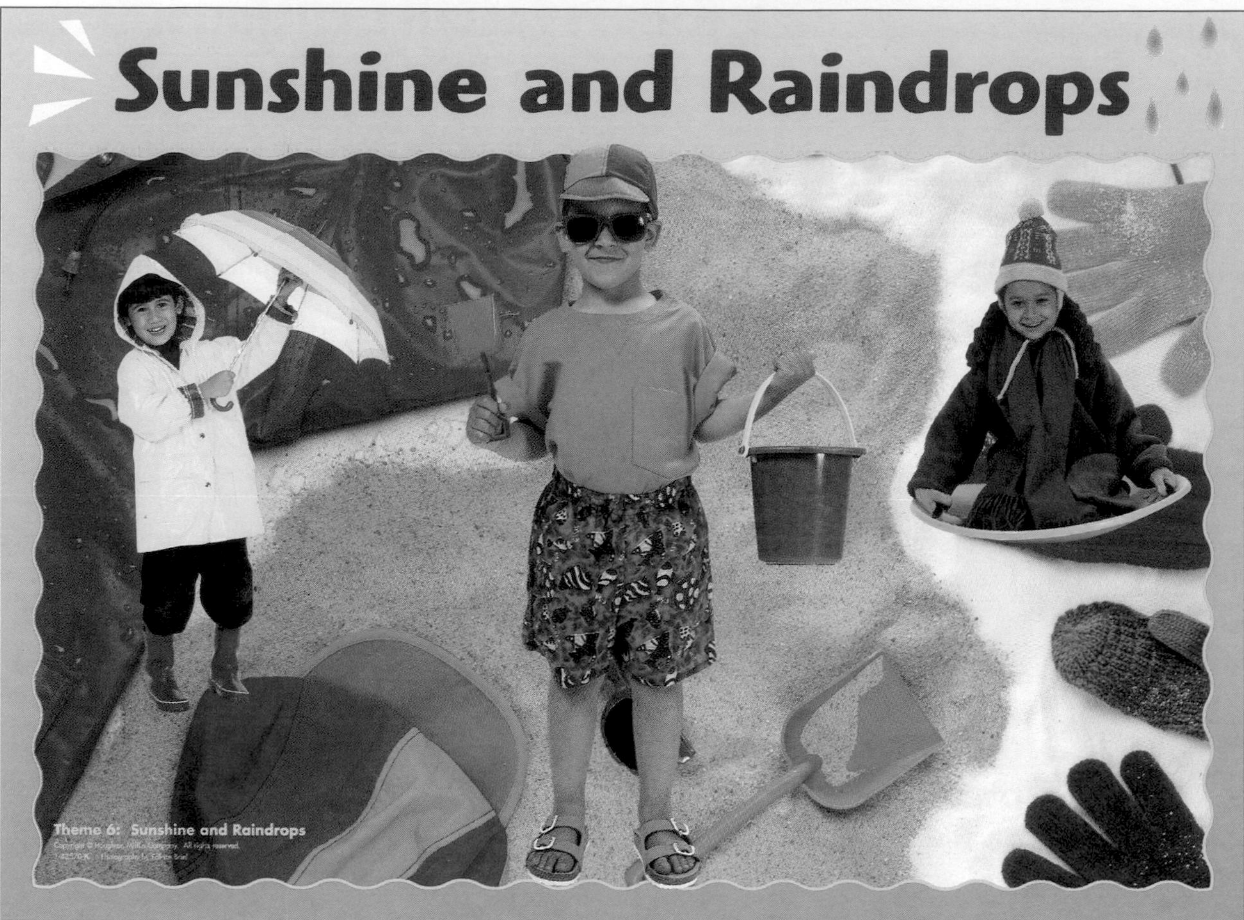

Theme Poster: Sunshine and Raindrops

Using the Theme Poster

Explain that this theme is about all kinds of weather. ***What things did you notice about the weather on the way to school?*** Explain that in many places, the weather at different times of the year can be steamy hot, icy cold, or wild and stormy! Display the Theme Poster and discuss what weather each child is dressed for.

Hang the Poster near a table where you can set up a Weather Station for the On-Going Project. Display children's writing and drawings to extend the Poster.

- **Week 1** After reading *Chicken Soup with Rice*, display a yearly calendar. They can write about someone in the Poster having fun in a favorite month.
- **Week 2** Use *Checking the Weather* to inspire young weather-watchers! Children can record day-to-day changes in their science weather journals.
- **Week 3** After reading *What Can We Do?*, children can write new scenes with the same question/answer format and display them.

Multi-age Classroom

Related themes:

Grade 1 . . . We Can Work It Out

Grade K . . . Sunshine and Raindrops

Theme Poem: "First Snow"

Read the poem "First Snow," asking children to think of what a snowy day would look like. What would a snow-covered car or mailbox look like? Why does the poet say familiar places "look like somewhere else today?"

THEME 6
First Snow
Snow makes whiteness where it falls.
The bushes look like popcorn-balls.
And places where I always play,
Look like somewhere else today.
by Marie Louise Allen
26

Higglety Pigglety: A Book of Rhymes, page 26

On-Going Project

Materials • weather maps • simple weather instruments • special weather gear • pictures and picture books showing all kinds of weather

Weather Station

Display the Theme Poster as a backdrop for a Weather Station. Encourage children to add all kinds of weather-related items to the display.

Weather Center
Week 1
Monday
Tuesday
Wednesday
Thursday
Friday
Sunny
Cloudy
Rainy
Snowy

- Graph the weather each day. Help children keep a pictograph, or running record, counting days that are sunny, rainy, snowy, and so on. Children can take turns being the "weather forecaster," broadcasting daily weather reports from the Weather Station.
- Share picture books or show a video about weather. Children who are interested in unusual types of weather such as blizzards or tornados can ask the librarian to help them learn more.
- Invite a meterologist from a local television station to visit. Help children prepare good questions to ask the visitor.
- In the last week, have children report weather trends they observed during the theme.

Technology

www.eduplace.com

Log onto *Education Place* for more activities relating to *Sunshine and Raindrops.*

Lesson Planner CD-ROM

Customize your planning for *Sunshine and Raindrops* with the Lesson Planner.

Book Adventure

www.bookadventure.org

This Internet reading-incentive program provides thousands of titles for students to read.

Home Connection

Send home the theme newsletter for *Sunshine and Raindrops* to introduce the theme and suggest home activities **(Blackline Masters 89–90).**

Home
Community
Connection

For other suggestions relating to *Sunshine and Raindrops,* see **Home/Community Connections.**

Theme 6

Classroom Routines

Sunshine and Raindrops

To introduce a routine...

1. Demonstrate the routine for the class.
2. Cycle every child through the routine at least once with supervision.
3. Establish ground rules for acceptable work products.
4. Check children's work.
5. Praise children's growing independence.

Instructional Routines

Phonics Center

Because the routine changes slightly in this theme, as children begin building sentences, reintroduce the routine, establishing the same rules for good work habits.

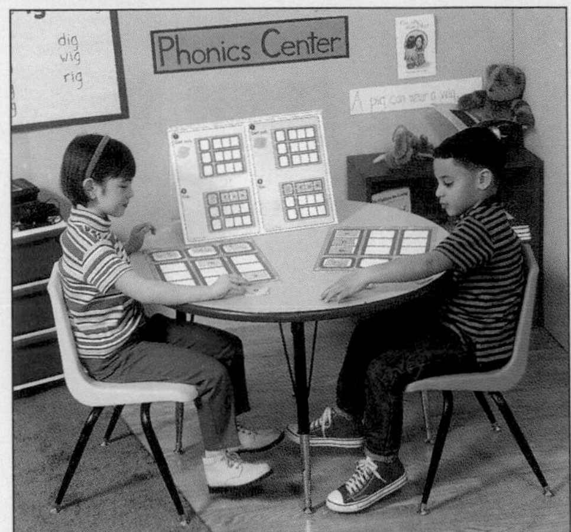

Blending Buckets

Materials • 2 coffee cans • 5" x 7" index cards • letter cards • a letter tray

To extend your Building Words activities during Word Work in this theme, set up a blending game for partners to play. Make two blending buckets from coffee cans. In one, place individual letter cards for the week's target sound. Add a few cards for review sounds, too. In the other bucket, place word family cards. Put a letter tray between the buckets. Partners take turns drawing a card from each bucket to make a word in the tray and then write the words on individual index cards. For a challenge, have partners sort the index cards by initial sound or word family and then read them aloud to another pair of partners.

Management Routines

Date Stamp

Buy a date stamp and have children stamp their own papers, or simply write the date on children's writings and drawings. Organize samples of children's work chronologically to track their progress.

Alphabetical Journal File

Label hanging file folders alphabetically and hang them in a cardboard carton. Use the carton to store portfolios, journals, and other dated samples of children's writing. Teach children how to find and store their work independently. This is a hands-on way for children to learn about alphabetical order, reading their own names, and getting organized. Samples of children's work will be readily available for parent conferences.

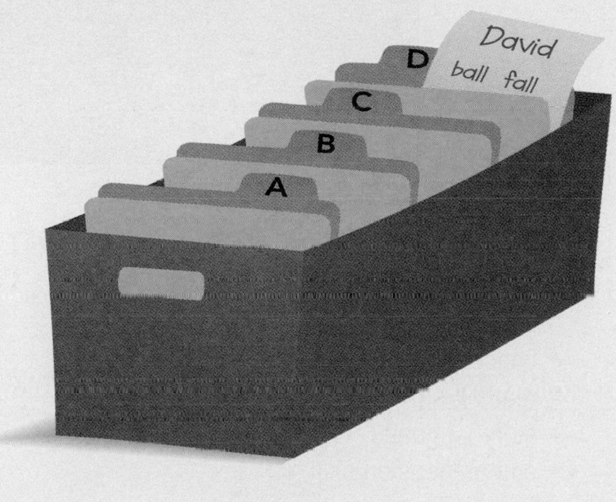

When you introduce a routine, hang a clipboard or a notebook in a handy place. Make notes to yourself to follow up with children who may need extra help with the routine. Also note children who understand and can help guide a friend.

Week 1

Literature for Week 1

Different texts for different purposes

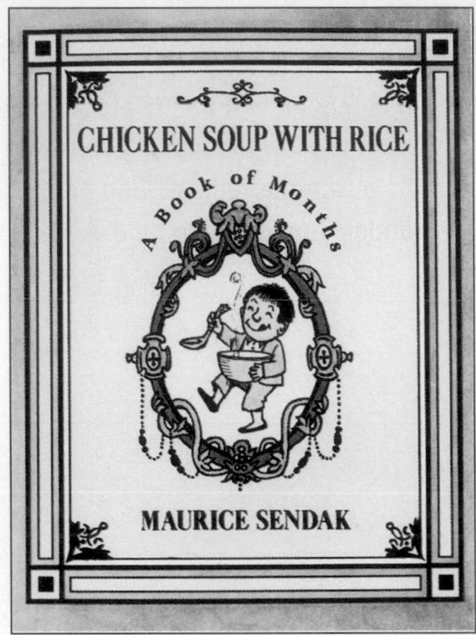

Teacher Read Aloud

Purposes

- oral language
- listening strategy
- comprehension skill

Awards

- ALA Notable Children's Books, 1940–1970
- Best Books for Children

Big Books:

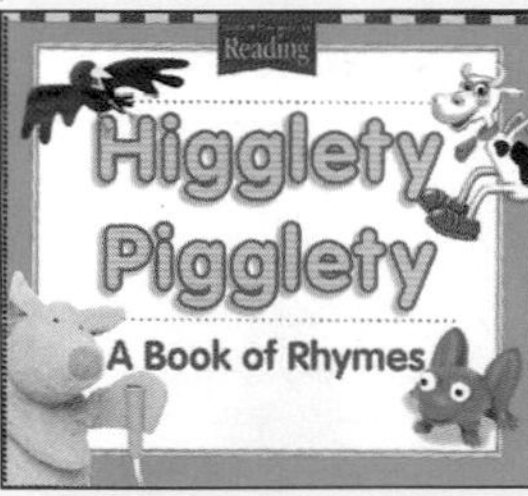

Higglety Pigglety: A Book of Rhymes

Purposes

- oral language development
- phonemic awareness

From Apples to Zebras: A Book of ABC's

Purposes

- alphabet recognition
- letters and sounds

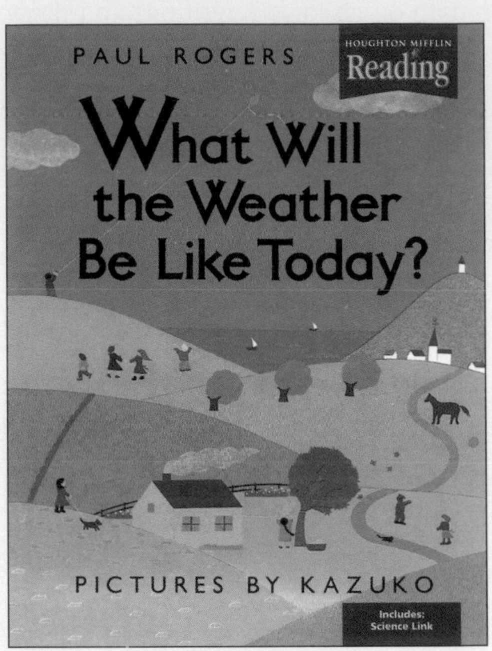

Big Book: Main Selection

Purposes

- concepts of print
- reading strategy
- story language
- comprehension skill

Also available in Little Big Book and audiotape

Also in the Big Book:
- Science Link

Purposes

- reading strategies
- comprehension skills
- concepts of print

Phonics Library

Also available in Take-Home version

Purpose

- applying phonics skills and high-frequency words

Leveled Books

On My Way Paperback

Here, Kit!
by ***A. J. Cooper***
page T153

Little Readers for Guided Reading
Collection K

Houghton Mifflin Classroom Bookshelf
Level K

www.eduplace.com
Log on to *Education Place* for more activities relating to *Sunshine and Raindrops*

www.bookadventure.org
This free Internet reading incentive program provides thousands of titles for students to read.

Week 1

Suggested Daily Routines

Instructional Goals	Day 1	Day 2
Learning to Read ✓ *Phonemic Awareness:* Blending and Segmenting Onset and Rime *Strategy Focus:* Predict/Infer ✓ *Comprehension Skill:* Fantasy/Realism ✓ *Phonics Skills* *Phonemic Awareness:* Beginning Sound /l/ Initial Consonant *L, l* *Compare and Review:* Initial Consonants: *g, v* ✓ *High-Frequency Word: is* ✓ *Concepts of Print:* Question Mark, Word Spacing	**Opening Routines,** *T8–T9* Word Wall • **Phonemic Awareness:** Blending and Segmenting Onset and Rime **Teacher Read Aloud** *Chicken Soup with Rice, T10–T11* • **Strategy:** Predict/Infer • **Comprehension:** Fantasy/Realism Phonics **Instruction** • Phonemic Awareness, Beginning Sound /l/, *T12–T13; **Practice Book,** 165–166*	**Opening Routines,** *T16–T17* Word Wall • **Phonemic Awareness:** Blending and Segmenting Onset and Rime **Sharing the Big Book** *What Will the Weather Be Like Today?, T18–T19* • **Strategy:** Predict/Infer • **Comprehension:** Fantasy/Realism Phonics **Instruction, Practice** • Initial Consonant *l, T20–T21* • ***Practice Book,** 167* **High-Frequency Word** • New Word: *is, T22–T23* • ***Practice Book,** 168*
Word Work *High-Frequency Word Practice:* Word Families: *-it, -an, -at*	**High-Frequency Word Practice** • Words: *like, and, I, see, T14*	**High-Frequency Word Practice** • Building Sentences, *T24*
Writing & Language *Vocabulary Skill:* Using Describing Words *Writing Skills:* Writing a Description, Writing Sentences	**Oral Language** • Using Describing Words, *T15*	**Vocabulary Expansion** • Using Describing Words, *T25* • Listening, *T25*

✓ = tested skills

Managing Small Groups (Day 1)	Managing Small Groups (Day 2)
Teacher-Led Group • Reread familiar **Phonics Library** selections **Independent Groups** • Finish ***Practice Book,*** *163–166* • ***Phonics Center:*** Theme 6, Week 1, Day 1 • Book, Writing, other Centers	**Teacher-Led Group** • Begin ***Practice Book,*** *167–168* and handwriting **Blackline Masters 168 or 194.** **Independent Groups** • Finish ***Practice Book*** *167–168* and handwriting **Blackline Masters 168 or 194.** • ***Phonics Center:*** Theme 6, Week 1, Day 2 • Science, Art, other Centers

Leveled Books

Have children read in appropriate levels daily.

Phonics Library
On My Way Practice Readers
Little Big Books
Houghton Mifflin Classroom Bookshelf

Lesson Planner CD-ROM: Customize your planning for *Sunshine and Raindrops* with the Lesson Planner.

Day 3

Opening Routines, *T26–T27*

- **Phonemic Awareness:** Blending and Segmenting Onset and Rime

Sharing the Big Book
What Will the Weather Be Like Today?, T28–T32
- **Strategy:** Predict/Infer
- **Comprehension:** Fantasy/Realism, *T29; **Practice Book,** 169*
- **Concepts of Print:** Question Mark, *T29*

Phonics
Practice, Application
- Review Consonant *l, T34–T35*

Instruction
- Blending *-it, T34–T35; **Practice Book,** 170*
- **Phonics Library:** "Can It Fit?," *T35*

Building Words
- Word Family: *-it, T36*

Shared Writing
- Writing a Description, *T37*
- Viewing and Speaking, *T37*

Managing Small Groups

Teacher-Led Group
- Read **Phonics Library** selection "Can It Fit?"
- Write letters *I, i;* begin **Blackline Masters 165 or 191.**
- Begin ***Practice Book,** 169–170*

Independent Groups
- Finish **Blackline Masters 165 or 191** and ***Practice Book,** 169–170*
- Art, other Centers

Day 4

Opening Routines, *T38–T39*

- **Phonemic Awareness:** Blending and Segmenting Onset and Rime

Sharing the Big Book
Science Link: "Checking the Weather," *T40–T41*
- **Strategy:** Predict/Infer
- **Comprehension:** Fantasy/Realism
- **Concepts of Print:** Word Spacing

Phonics
Practice
- Review Initial Consonant *l, T42–T43; **Practice Book,** 171*

Building Words
- Word Families: *-it, -an, -at, T44*

Interactive Writing
- Writing Sentences, *T45*
- Viewing and Speaking, *T45*

Managing Small Groups

Teacher-Led Group
- Reread **Phonics Library** selection "Can It Fit?"
- Begin ***Practice Book,** 171*

Independent Groups
- Finish ***Practice Book,** 171*
- ***Phonics Center:*** Theme 6, Week 1, Day 4
- Writing, other Centers

Day 5

Opening Routines, *T46–T47*

- **Phonemic Awareness:** Blending and Segmenting Onset and Rime

Revisiting the Literature
Comprehension: Fantasy/Realism, *T48*
Building Fluency
- **Phonics Library:** "Can It Fit?," *T49*

Phonics
Review
- Consonants, Word Families, *T50*

High-Frequency Word Review
- Words: *I, see, my, like, a, to, and, go, is, T51; **Practice Book,** 172*

Building Words
- Word Families: *-at, -an, -it, T52*

Independent Writing
- Journals: Favorite Type of Weather, *T53*

Managing Small Groups

Teacher-Led Group
- Reread familiar **Phonics Library** selections
- Begin ***Practice Book,** 172,* **Blackline Master 36.**

Independent Groups
- Reread **Phonics Library** selections
- Finish ***Practice Book,** 172,* **Blackline Master 36.**
- Centers

Week 1

Setting up the Centers

Teacher's Note

Management Tip Encourage children to select different Centers. Post a sign-up sheet outside each Center so you can keep track of who has worked in each one during the week. You may wish to write each child's name on a clothespin and attach it to the sign-up sheet of the appropriate Center.

Phonics Center

Materials • Phonics Center materials for Theme 6, Week 1

This week children sort pictures whose names begin with /g/, /h/, or /l/. They make words with the letters *b, l, s,* and the word family *-it.* Children also begin to build sentences with Word and Picture Cards.

Prepare materials for Days 1, 2, and 4. Cut apart the letter grids and put them in plastic bags by color. Put out the Workmats and open the Direction Chart to the appropriate day. On Day 4, explain how children are to build words and a sentence using the new Workmat. See pages T13, T21, and T43 for this week's Phonics Center activities.

Book Center

The Snowy Day *by Ezra Jack Keats*
Katy and the Big Snow *by Virginia Lee Burton*
The Itsy Bitsy Spider *by Iza Trapani*
Rain *by Robert Kalan*

Materials • books about weather

In addition to the weather books listed in the Theme 6 Bibliography, put copies of classic favorites and fresh new titles in the Book Center after you've read them aloud. See page T11 for this week's Book Center suggestion.

Materials • crayons • markers • lined and unlined writing paper

To begin the theme, children copy and illustrate a sentence containing a describing word about their favorite kind of weather. Later they copy and illustrate sentences from the Shared Writing activity about their weather observations. See pages T15 and T45 for this week's Writing Center activities.

Science Center

Materials • lined and unlined paper • crayons or markers • microphone made from foil-covered cardboard tube • tennis ball

Children write or draw weather reports and broadcast them from the Weather Station using a microphone. See page T19 for this week's Science Center activity.

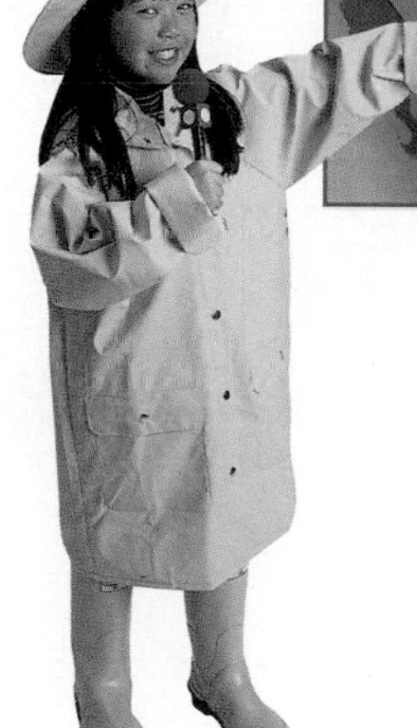

Materials • paper • crayons or colored chalk • prisms • flashlights • paint

Children draw a picture to complete a sentence comparing snow to something else. Later they make rainbows with a prism and a flashlight, compare the colors they see, and paint their own rainbows. See pages T25 and T33 for this week's Art Center activities.

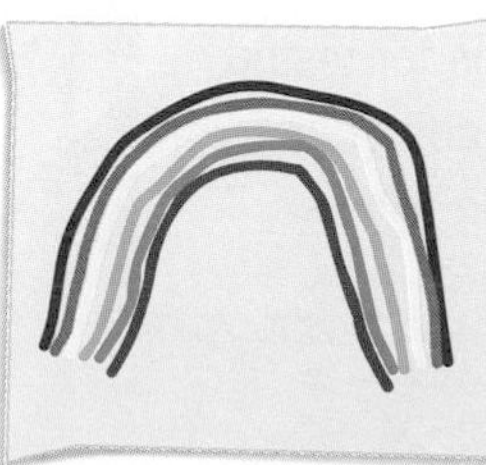

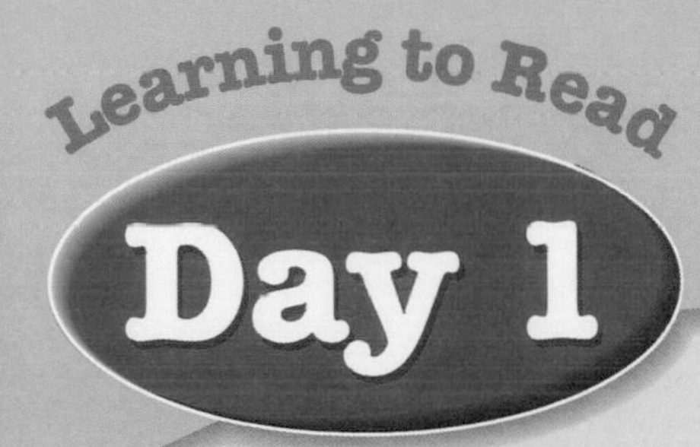

Opening

Day at a Glance

Learning to Read

Read Aloud:

Chicken Soup with Rice

✓ **Learning About /l/,** *page T12*

Word Work

✓ **High-Frequency Word Practice,** *page T14*

Writing & Language

Oral Language, *page T15*

Half-Day Kindergarten

✓ Indicates lessons for tested skills. Choose additional activities as time allows.

Calendar

Sunday	Monday	Tuesday	Wednesday	Thursday	Friday	Saturday
			1	2	3	4
5	6	7	8	9	10	11
12	13	14	15	16	17	18
19	20	21	22	23	24	25
26	27	28	29	30	31	

Use rich describing language for today's weather: *cold, windy, cool, breezy, blustery.*

Daily Message

Modeled Writing Model how to write the sounds you hear. Also talk about punctuation. For example: ***Who will remind me what mark to put at the end of this sentence?***

Today is Jennifer's birthday.
Happy birthday, Jennifer!

Have children chant the spelling of each word on the wall today: **a-n-d spells *and;* g-o *spells* go*!***

Routines

Daily Phonemic Awareness
Blending and Segmenting Onset and Rime

- Read "As I Was Walking" on page 28 of *Higglety Pigglety.*
- Play a guessing game. ***I'll say some sounds. You put them together to make words from the poem: /l/.../ake/** (lake)**; /m/.../et/** (met)**; /c/.../ake/** (cake)**.***
- Give other one-syllable examples from the poem.
- Continue by having partners decide on a word. Partners separate the beginning sound from the rest of the word, the rest of then the class blends the sounds.

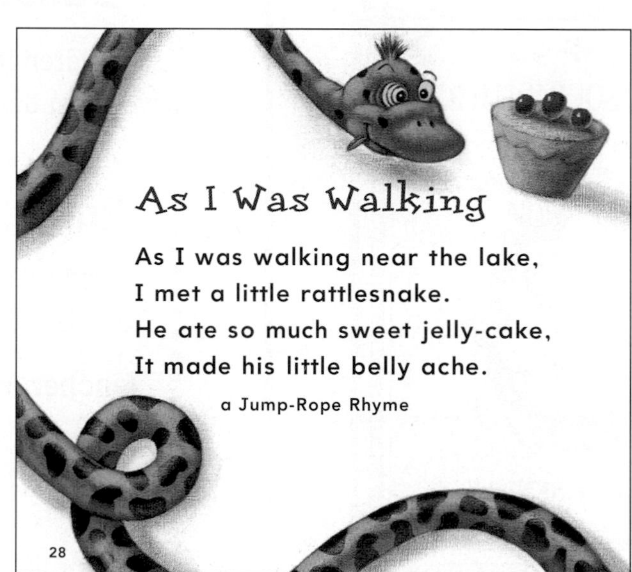
As I Was Walking

As I was walking near the lake,
I met a little rattlesnake.
He ate so much sweet jelly-cake,
It made his little belly ache.

a Jump-Rope Rhyme

28

***Higglety Pigglety: A Book of Rhymes*, page 28**

Getting Ready to Learn

To help plan their day, tell children that they will

- listen to a story called *Chicken Soup with Rice.*

- meet a new Alphafriend, Larry Lion.

- read, write, and explore more about weather in the Book Center.

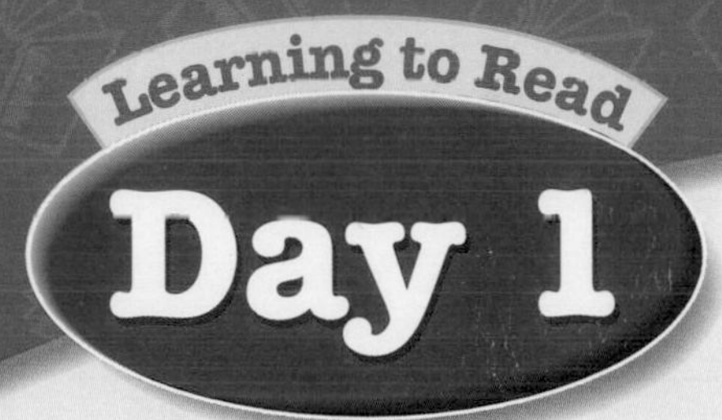

Teacher Read Aloud

Oral Language/Comprehension

Building Background

Ask children if they like chicken soup. If they've had chicken soup with rice, have them describe the taste and texture.

Strategy: Predict/Infer

Introduce *Chicken Soup with Rice: A Book of Months* by author/illustrator Maurice Sendak. Share the title and cover illustration.

Teacher Modeling Model the strategy as you share a few illustrations.

How can I tell what Chicken Soup with Rice is about?

- *Part of the title says A Book of Months. Here's January, when it's cold, and children are ice skating.*
- *Maybe there's something for every month's weather. We'll see what happens.*

Comprehension Focus: Fantasy/Realism

Teacher Modeling Tell children that some books are about things that could really happen and some are about things that are make-believe. Good readers know how to tell the difference.

Think Aloud

I see a turtle stirring a pot of soup. Real turtles don't make soup! This story must be make-believe.

Read Aloud

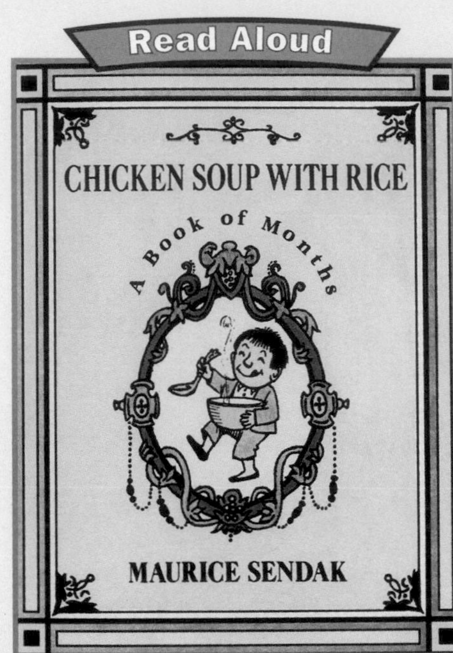

Purposes • oral language • listening strategy • comprehension skill

Selection Summary
In this book of imaginative rhymes, a young boy tells why his favorite food is the best choice for every month of the year.

Key Concept
Months of the year

English Language Learners

Review the names for the months of the year and the kind of weather children can expect to experience during that month. Then, to help children recognize the humor of the book, talk about the kinds of food one might enjoy each month, for example, ice cream in July and hot chocolate or soup in December.

Listening to the Story

Read aloud with expression. The rhyme is so infectious that children will want to chime in right away.

Responding

Retelling the Story Help children summarize parts of the story.

- ***What did the boy in the story do in January?***
- ***What was the same about the scenes for every month of the year?***
- ***What part of this story could really happen?***
- ***Which month was your favorite? Why?***

Practice Book pages 163–164 Children will complete the pages at small group time.

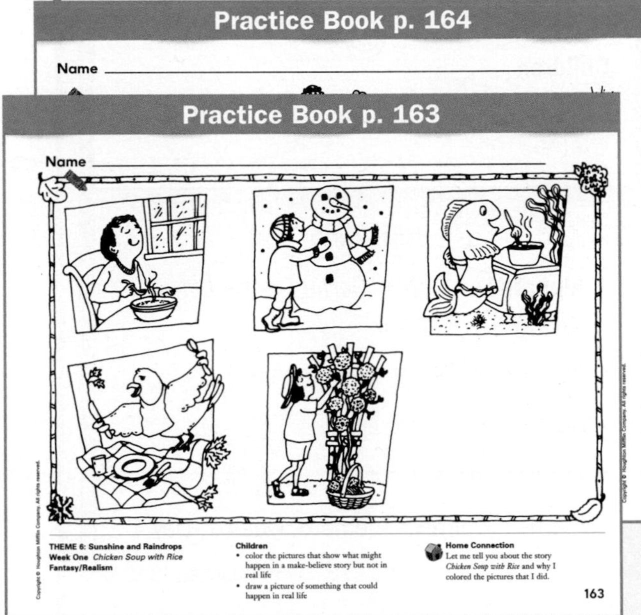

Practice Book p. 164

Name

Practice Book p. 163

Name

THEME 6: Sunshine and Raindrops
Week One *Chicken Soup with Rice*
Fantasy/Realism

Children
- color the pictures that show what might happen in a make-believe story but not in real life
- draw a picture of something that could happen in real life

Home Connection
Let me tell you about the story *Chicken Soup with Rice* and why I colored the pictures that I did.

163

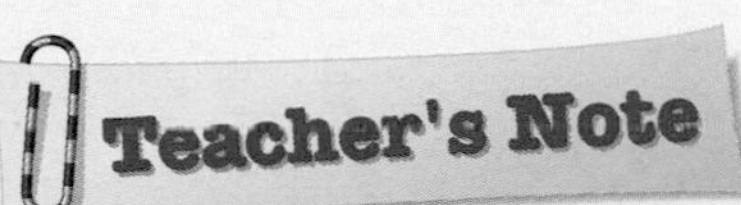

Teacher's Note

Post the names of the months on the Writing Center bulletin board, grouping them by season. This will help children who want to use the words in their writing and remind them of the weather in different seasons.

At Group Time
Book Center

Fill your Book Center with books about weather. Include such favorites as *The Snowy Day* by Ezra Jack Keats, *Katy and the Big Snow* by Virginia Lee Burton, *The Itsy-Bitsy Spider* by Iza Trapani, and *Rain* by Robert Kalan. Children can browse through the books and talk about the different types of weather they see.

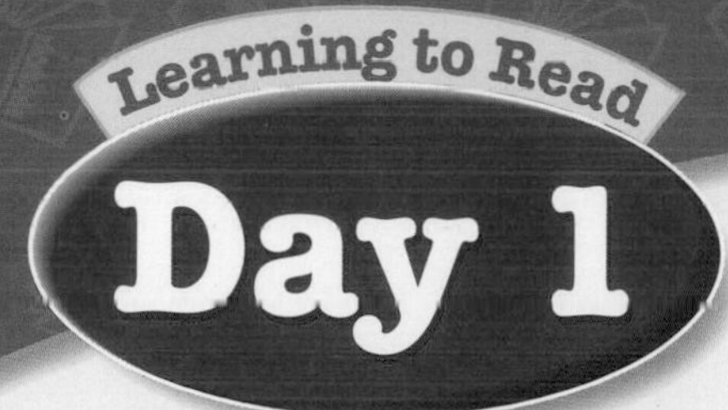

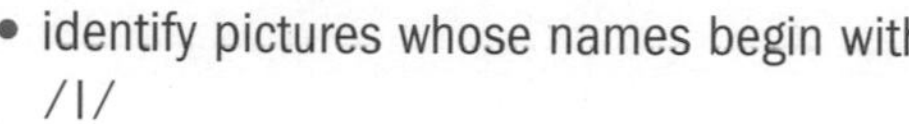

Children

- identify pictures whose names begin with /l/

MATERIALS

- **Alphafriend Cards** *Gertie Goose, Larry Lion, Vinny Volcano*
- **Alphafriend Audiotape** Theme 6
- **Alphafolder** *Larry Lion*
- **Picture Cards** for *g, l, v*
- **Phonics Center:** Theme 6, Week 1, Day 1

Home Connection

A take-home version of song Larry Lion's is an **Alphafriends.** Children can share the song with their families.

English Language Learners

Make sure children can hear and understand all the words in Larry Lion's song. If possible, bring in examples of lollipops, lemon drops, lentils, and lettuce. Explain that liver is a type of meat.

Phonemic Awareness

Introducing the Alphafriend: Larry Lion

Use the Alphafriend routine below to introduce Larry Lion.

1. **Alphafriend Riddle** Read these clues:
   - *This Alphafriend's sound is /l/. Say it with me: /l/.*
   - *This* lllarge *animal* lllives *in the grasslands.*
   - *He* lllikes *his* lllong *mane and* lllong *tail. He* llloves *to roar!*

When most hands are up, call on children until they guess *lion.*

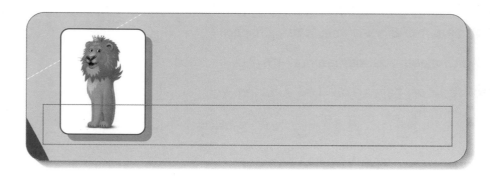

2. **Pocket Chart** Display Larry Lion in a pocket chart. Say his name, stretching the /l/ sounds slightly, and have children echo.
3. **Alphafriend Audiotape** Play Larry Lion's song. Listen for words that start with /l/.
4. **Alphafolder** Have children look at the scene and name all the /l/ pictures.
5. **Summarize**
   - *What is our Alphafriend's name? What is his sound?*
   - *What words in our Alphafriend's song start with /l/?*
   - *Each time you look at Larry this week, remember the /l/ sound.*

Larry Lion's Song
(tune: Twinkle, Twinkle, Little Star)

Larry Lion likes lollipops.
Larry Lion likes lemon drops.
Larry Lion likes lentil stew.
Larry Lion likes lasagna, too.
Larry Lion likes liver for lunch,
Topped with lettuce,
crunch, crunch, crunch!

Listening for /l/

Compare and Review: /g/, /v/ Display Alphafriends *Gertie Goose* and *Vinny Volcano* opposite *Larry Lion.* Review each character's sound.

Tell children you'll name some pictures and they should signal "thumbs up" for each one that begins like Larry's name. Volunteers put those cards below Larry's picture. For "thumbs down" words, volunteers put the cards below the correct Alphafriends.

Pictures: *lemon, van, leash, lamp, goat, leaf, guitar, vase, log, game*

Tell children that they will sort more pictures in the Phonics Center today.

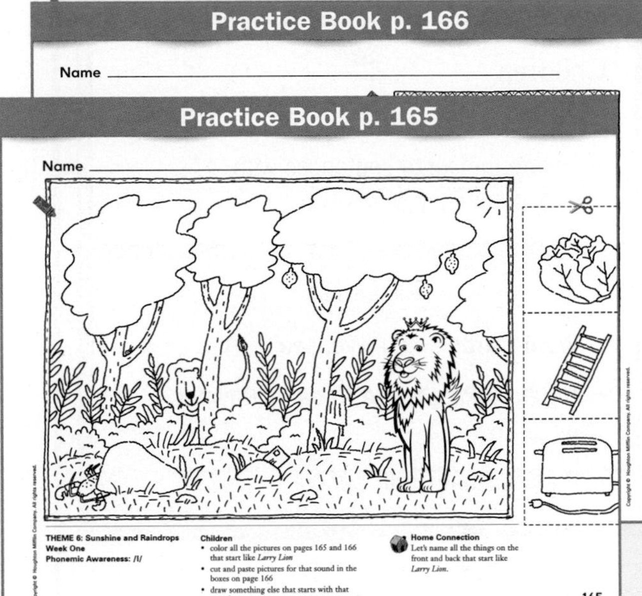

Practice Book p. 166

Name

Practice Book p. 165

Name

THEME 6: Sunshine and Raindrops
Week One
Phonemic Awareness: /l/

Children
- color all the pictures on pages 165 and 166 that start like *Larry Lion*
- cut and paste pictures for that sound in the boxes on page 166
- draw something else that starts with that sound

Home Connection
Let's name all the things on the front and back that start like *Larry Lion*.

165

Apply

Practice Book pages 165–166 Children will complete the pages at small group time.

At Group Time
Phonics Center

Use the Phonics Center materials for **Theme 6, Week 1, Day 1.**

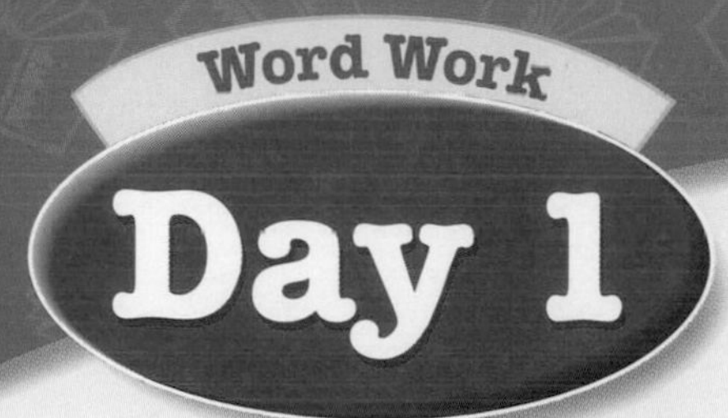
Word Work
Day 1

High-Frequency Word Practice

OBJECTIVES

Children
- read high-frequency words
- create and write sentences with high-frequency words

MATERIALS

- **Word Cards** *and, I, like, see*
- ***Higglety Pigglety: A Book of Rhymes,*** page 26
- **Punctuation Card:** period

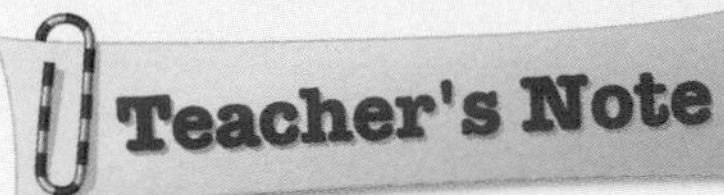
Teacher's Note

You will need a word card for the word *can* to build the sample sentence.

Matching Words

- Display cards for the high-frequency words *like, and, I* in a pocket chart. Ask children to identify each word and match it on the Word Wall.
- Remind children that these words are often found in books. Ask them to listen for the words as you read "First Snow."
- Have children match the Word Cards *like, and, I* to those words in the poem "First Snow."

THEME 6
First Snow
Snow makes whiteness where it falls.
The bushes look like popcorn-balls.
And places where I always play,
Look like somewhere else today.
by Marie Louise Allen
26

***Higglety Pigglety: A Book of Rhymes,* page 26**

Writing Opportunity Place the Word Cards *I can see* in the pocket chart. Read them together, and review the *-an* in *can.* Ask children to use weather words to finish the sentence in different ways. Then select one of the words, draw a picture for it, and place it in the pocket chart. Children can copy the sentence, adding their own drawings.

like
and
I

I
can
see
.

Oral Language

Using Describing Words

On chart paper, write the sentence *I like* ______ *days.* Help children read the sentence. If necessary, point out *I* and *like* on the Word Wall as a prompt.

- Say that a describing word is missing from the sentence. Explain that describing words tell how something looks, smells, sounds, feels, or tastes. Brainstorm words that describe weather, writing children's ideas on the chart.
- Volunteers can reread the sentence and choose a word from the list to complete it.

I like______days.

hot	cold
sunny	cool
warm	snowy
windy	rainy
blustery	stormy

OBJECTIVES

Children
- use describing words

Materials • index cards • paper • crayons or markers

Put the chart from above in the Writing Center. Children can try reading it on their own or with a partner. Each child can write a favorite describing word or draw a picture on an index card to complete the sentence. Some children will be able to copy and illustrate their sentences.

English Language Learners

Make sure English language learners know the verbs for the senses: looks, smells, feels, sounds, tastes. Use realia—graphics, perfume or spices, fabrics, tactile objects, noises, foods—to provide practice using the verbs. Help children use adjectives to describe the objects you have used.

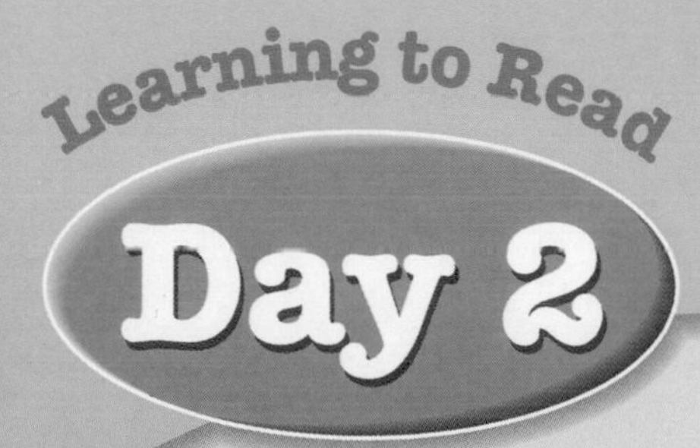

Opening

Day at a Glance

Learning to Read

Big Book:

What Will the Weather Be Like Today?

✓ **Phonics: Initial Consonant *l*,** *page T20*

✓ **High-Frequency Word: *is*,** *page T22*

Word Work

High-Frequency Word Practice, *page T24*

Writing & Language

Vocabulary Expansion, *page T25*

Half-Day Kindergarten

✓ Indicates lessons for tested skills. Choose additional activities as time allows.

Calendar

Sunday	Monday	Tuesday	Wednesday	Thursday	Friday	Saturday
			1	2	3	4
5	6	7	8	9	10	11
12	13	14	15	16	17	18
19	20	21	22	23	24	25
26	27	28	29	30	31	

Write a weather word for today on an index card, add a symbol, and post it near the calendar. A child can make the symbol on a self-stick note and put it on today's date.

Daily Message

Modeled Writing Write about something that happened yesterday. Compare yesterday and today on the calendar. Do this all week to help children with the concepts.

Yesterday we read a book about chicken soup. Today we will read about the weather.

Choose children to take turns finding Word Wall words with a pointer as you call them out.

Routines

Daily Phonemic Awareness
Blending and Segmenting Onset and Rime

Tell children that you are thinking of a weather word and ask them to guess it. Say the word, segmenting it by onset and rime: /h//ot/ (*hot*); /c//old/ (*cold*); /r//ain/ (*rain*); /w//ind/ (*wind*); /f//og/ (*fog*). Give children time to think, then hold up corresponding weather cards so they can check their responses.

Then say the words one at a time. Call on volunteers to segment each word by isolating the beginning sound and then saying the end of the word.

DAY 2

Getting Ready to Learn

To help plan their day, tell children that they will

- listen to a Big Book: *What Will the Weather Be Like Today?*

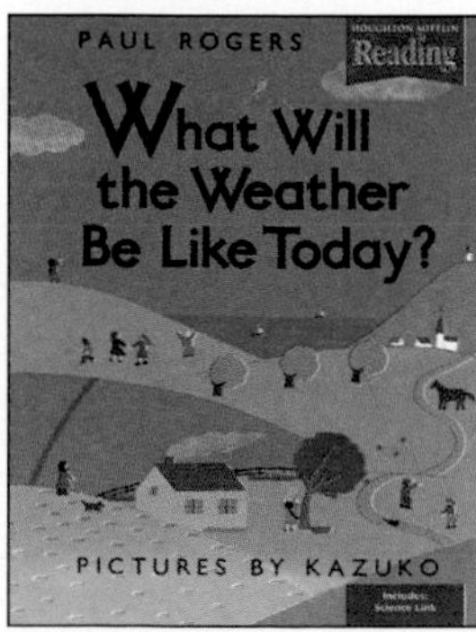

- learn the new letters *L* and *l*, and sort words that begin with *l*.

- broadcast a weather report from the class "weather station."

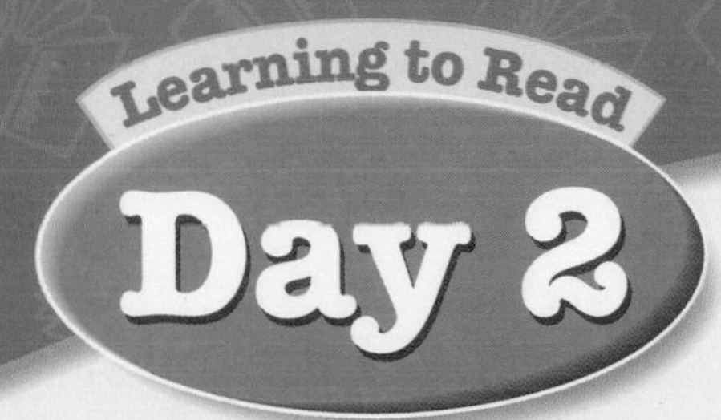

Sharing the Big Book

Oral Language/Comprehension

Building Background

Introduce the Big Book by reading the title and author's and illustrator's names. Tell children that the title is a question. (Point out the question mark.) Then talk about how children might answer it.

Begin a graphic organizer, writing the words children suggest for each category. Save the chart and add to it throughout the theme.

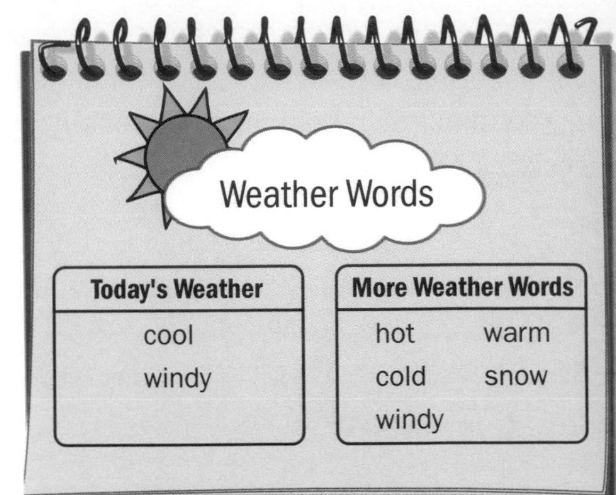

Weather Words
Today's Weather
cool
windy
More Weather Words
hot
warm
cold
snow
windy

Strategy: Predict/Infer

Teacher Modeling Model how to predict what the story will be about.

Think Aloud

The first thing I notice about a book is its title and the illustrations. Let's look through this book. I notice that the title is a question about weather and the illustrations show lots of different places. So I think the book is about weather in those places. Let's read and see if I'm right.

Comprehension Focus: Fantasy/Realism

Teacher Modeling Remind children that good readers and listeners think about what happens in the story.

Think Aloud

When I read, I also think about what could be real or what's make-believe. You think about that too.

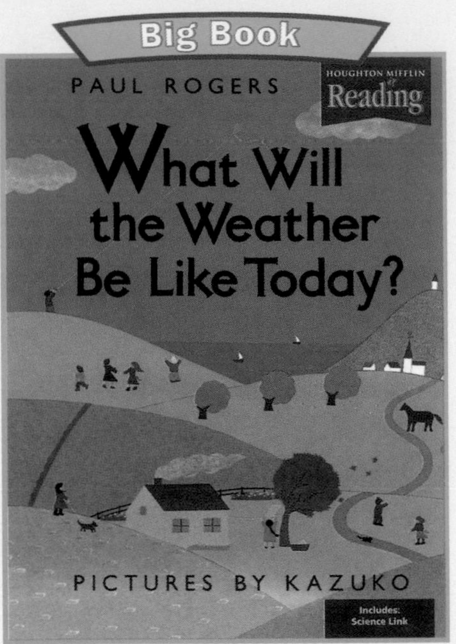

Big Book
PAUL ROGERS
HOUGHTON MIFFLIN
Reading
What Will the Weather Be Like Today?
PICTURES BY KAZUKO
Includes: Science Link

Purposes • concepts about print • story language • reading strategy • comprehension skill

Selection Summary
A host of animals in different parts of the world talk about the day's weather, in rhyming text.

Key Concepts
Types of weather
Animal environments

Sharing the Story

Read the selection aloud, emphasizing the rhyme and the rhythm and tracking the print with a pointer or your hand. Pause often for children to supply a rhyming word.

Responding

Personal Response Encourage children to use the language of the story as they react to it.

- ***What did you like best about the story? What did you learn?***
- ***What parts of the world did you notice? Did you see a desert? a pond? What else?***
- ***How will you answer the question, "What is the weather where you are today?"***

Materials • "microphone" from foil-covered tennis ball and cardboard tube

Have children observe today's weather: ***Are there clouds? What do they look like? What is the temperature? Has the weather changed since yesterday?*** Children can draw or write reports and "broadcast" them from the "weather station."

DAY 2

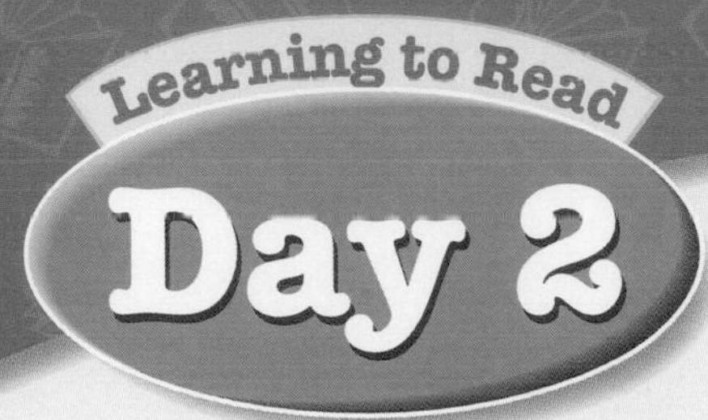

Phonics

Initial Consonant l

OBJECTIVES

Children

- identify words that begin with /l/
- identify pictures whose names start with the letter *l*
- form the letters *L, l*

MATERIALS

- **Alphafriend Card** *Larry Lion*
- **Letter Cards** *g, l, v*
- **Picture Cards** for *g, l, v*
- **Blackline Master 168**
- **Phonics Center:** Theme 6, Week 1, Day 2

Develop Phonemic Awareness

Beginning Sound Read the lyrics to Larry Lion's song aloud and have children echo it line-for-line. Have them listen for the /l/ words and "leap" for each one.

Larry Lion's Song
(tune: Twinkle, Twinkle, Little Star)

Larry Lion likes lollipops.
Larry Lion likes lemon drops.
Larry Lion likes lentil stew.
Larry Lion likes lasagna, too.
Larry Lion likes liver for lunch,
Topped with lettuce,
crunch, crunch, crunch!

Connect Sounds to Letters

Beginning Letter Display the *Larry Lion* card and have children name the letter on the picture. Say: ***The letter* l *stands for the sound /l/, as in* lion. *When you see an* l, *remember* Larry Lion. *That will help you remember the sound /l/.***

Write *lion* on the board. Underline the *l*. ***What is the first letter in the word* lion?** (*l*) ***Lion starts with /l/, so* l *is the first letter I write for* lion.**

Compare and Review: *g, v* In a pocket chart, display the Letter Cards as shown and the Picture Cards in random order. Review the sounds for *l, v,* and *g.* In turn, children can name a picture, say the beginning sound, and put the card below the right letter.

Tell children that they will sort more pictures in the Phonics Center today.

Extra Support

To help children remember the sound for *l*, point out that the letter's *name* gives a clue to its sound: *l*, /l/.

Handwriting

Writing *L, l* Tell children that now they'll learn to write the letters that stand for /l/: capital *L* and small *l*. Write each letter as you recite the handwriting rhymes. Chant each rhyme as children "write" the letter in the air.

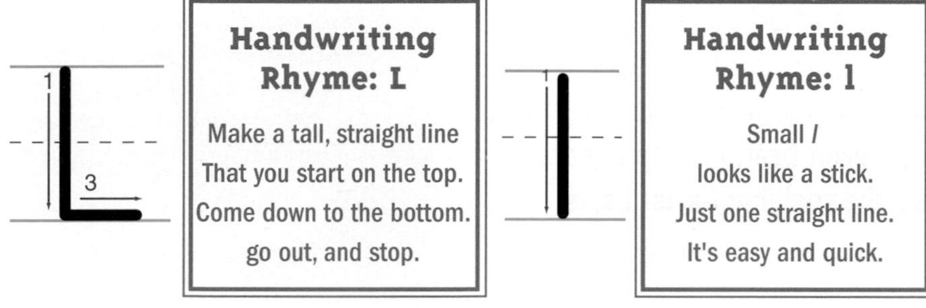

1
3
Handwriting Rhyme: L
Make a tall, straight line
That you start on the top.
Come down to the bottom.
go out, and stop.
Handwriting Rhyme: l
Small *l*
looks like a stick.
Just one straight line.
It's easy and quick.

Apply

Practice Book page 167 Children can complete this page at small group time.

Blackline Master 168 This page provides additional handwriting practice.

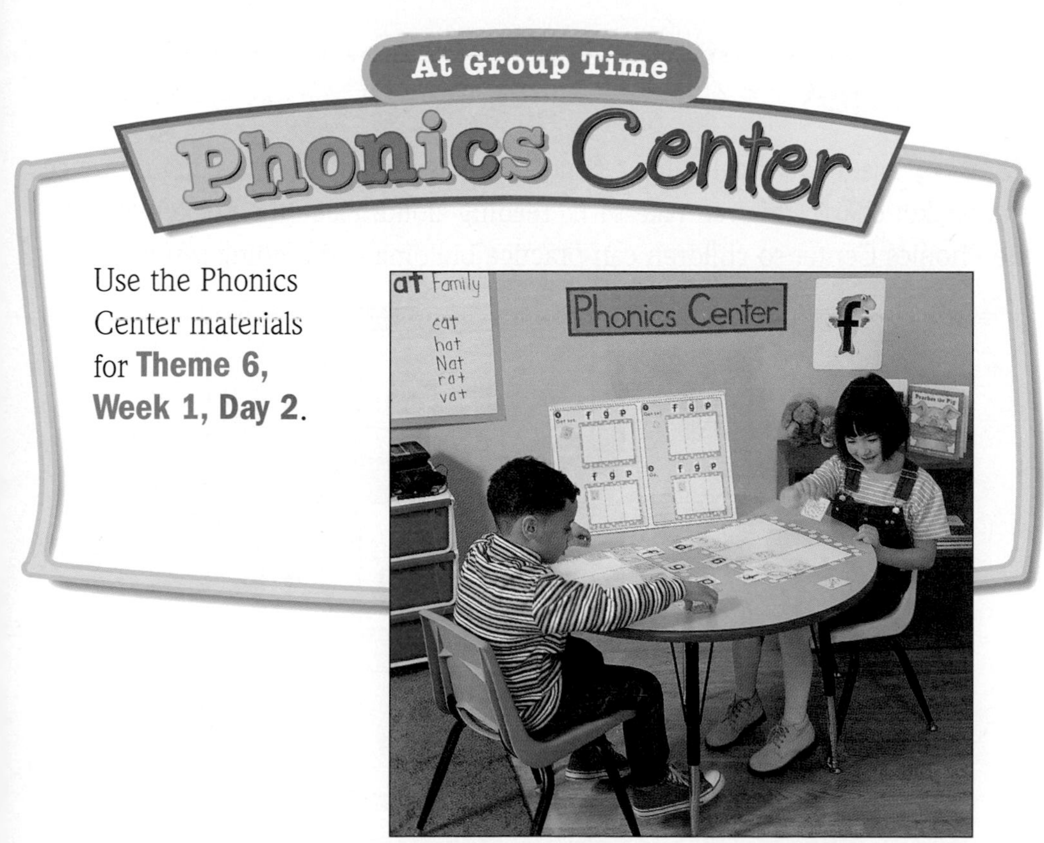

Use the Phonics Center materials for **Theme 6, Week 1, Day 2.**

Practice Book p. 167

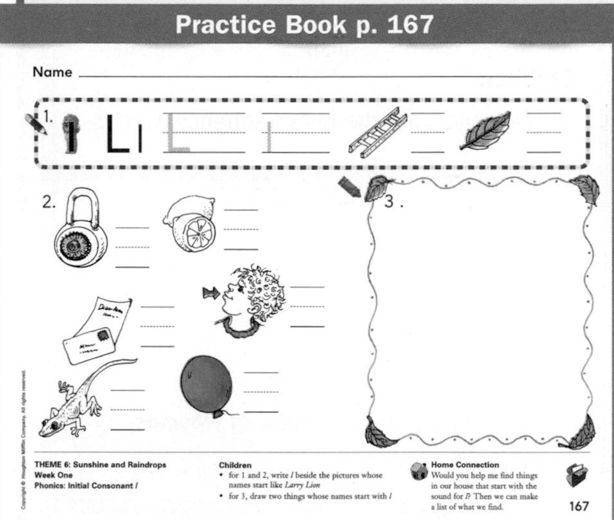

Handwriting practice for the continuous stroke style is available on **Blackline Master 194.**

Portfolio Opportunity

Save the Practice Book page to show children's grasp of the letter-sound association.

Save **Blackline Master 168** for a handwriting sample.

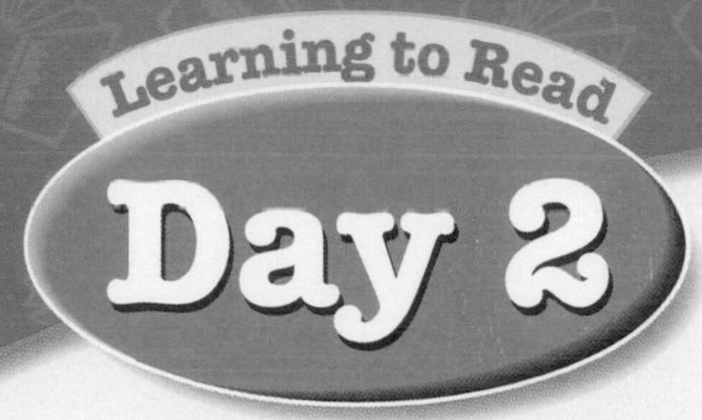

OBJECTIVES

Children

- read and write the high-frequency word *is*

MATERIALS

- **Word Cards** *A, is, My*
- **Picture Cards** *dog, hat, hen*
- **Punctuation Card:** period
- ***Higglety Pigglety: A Book of Rhymes,*** page 13

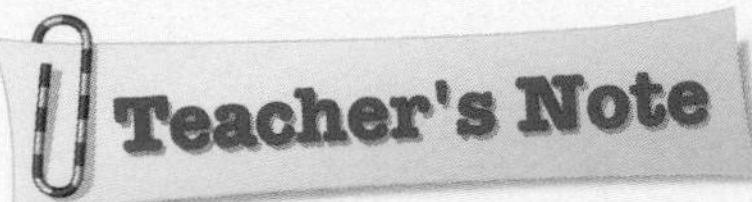

You will also need to make word cards for the words *fat* and *tan* to complete the lesson.

High-Frequency Word

New Word: is

Teach

Tell children that today they will learn to read and write a word that they will often see in stories. Say *is* and use it in context.

A lion *is* big. A mouse *is* small. A lion *is* loud. A mouse *is* quiet.

Write *is* on the board and have children spell it as you point to the letters. Say: ***Spell* is *with me,* i-s, is.** Then lead a cheer, clapping on each beat, to help children remember the spelling: **i-s, is! i-s, is!**

Word Wall Post *is* on the Word Wall and remind children to look there when they need to remember how to write the word.

Practice

Reading Make word cards for *fat* and *tan.* Then build the following sentences in a pocket chart. Children take turns reading aloud. Place the pocket chart in the Phonics Center so children can practice building and reading sentences.

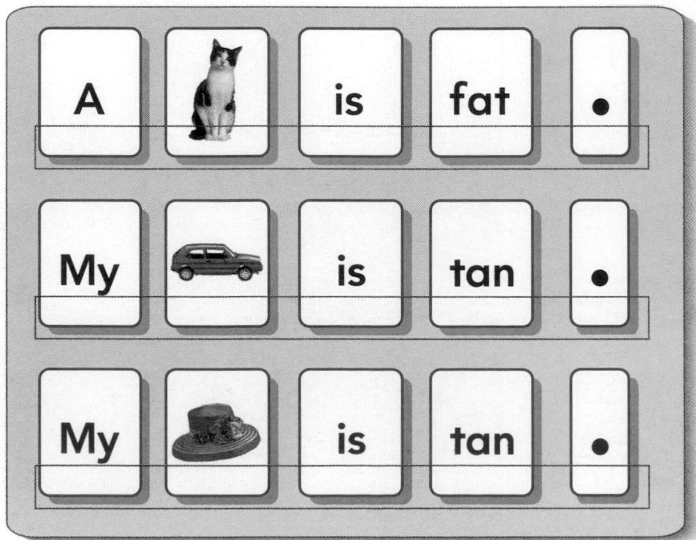

Display *Higglety Pigglety,* page 13.

- Share the poem "Rainy Day" aloud.
- Reread the second line of the poem and recite it, tracking the print. Have children point to the word is both times it appears.

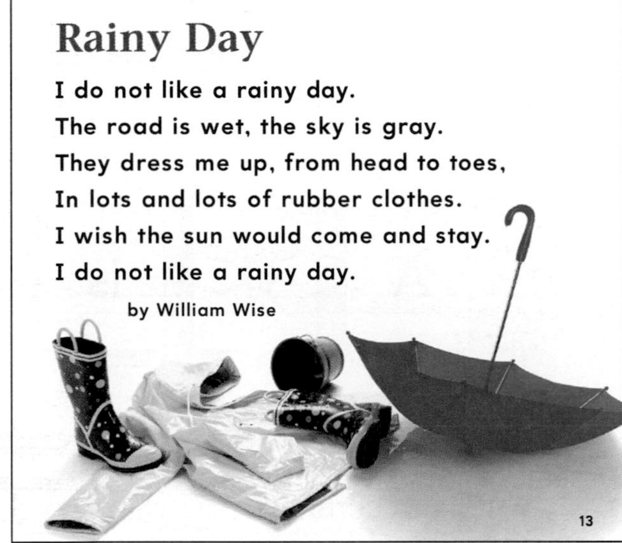

Rainy Day

I do not like a rainy day.
The road is wet, the sky is gray.
They dress me up, from head to toes,
In lots and lots of rubber clothes.
I wish the sun would come and stay.
I do not like a rainy day.

by William Wise

13

***Higglety Pigglety: A Book of Rhymes,* page 13**

Apply

Practice Book page 168 Children will read and write *is* as they complete the Practice Book page. On Day 3, they will practice reading *is* in the **Phonics Library** story "Can It Fit?"

Practice Book p. 168

Name ____________

Is

1. Is a man a pan?

2. ______ a cat a hat?

3. ______ Nat a cat?

4. ______ Dan a man?

THEME 6: Sunshine and Raindrops
Week One
High-Frequency Word: *is*

168

Children
- read the questions and look at the pictures
- write *is* to complete 2, 3, and 4
- mark yes (smile) or no (frown) to show their answers to the questions

Home Connection
Ask me to read these questions to you. Then we can take turns asking other questions like these about things in this room.

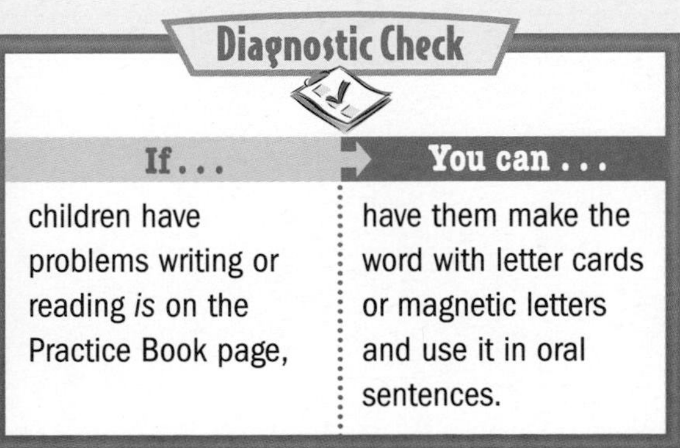

Diagnostic Check

If . . .	You can . . .
children have problems writing or reading *is* on the Practice Book page,	have them make the word with letter cards or magnetic letters and use it in oral sentences.

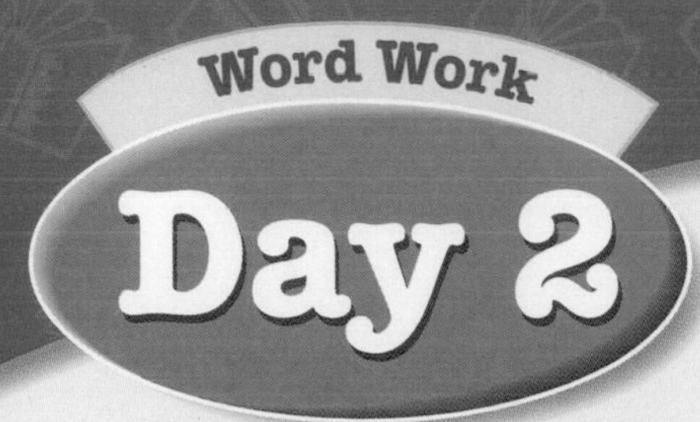

High-Frequency Word Practice

OBJECTIVES

Children

- read high-frequency words
- create and write sentences with high-frequency words

MATERIALS

- **Word Cards** *A, is*
- **Punctuation Card:** period

For this activity, prepare index cards on which rebus pictures for weather words have been drawn: *sun, rain, wind, clouds*.

Building Sentences

Tell children you want to build a sentence about the weather.

- Display the Word Cards in random order. Review the words together. Tell children that you are ready to build the sentence.
- ***I want the first word to be*** **A.** ***Who can find that word?***
- Continue building a sentence about the sun, incorporating the word *is*.
- Read the completed sentence together, then continue with a new one.

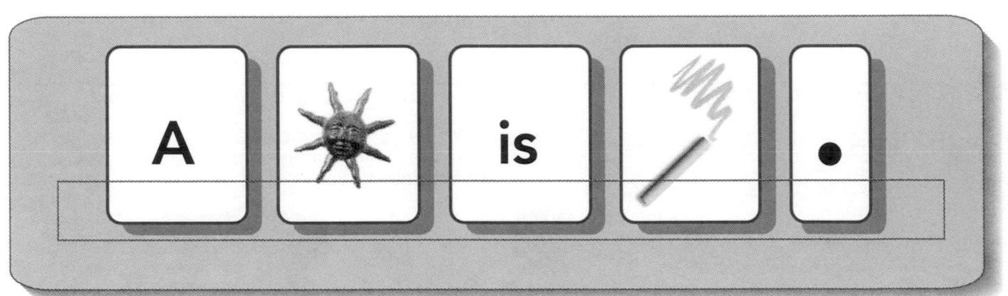

Writing Opportunity Have children write a sentence from the pocket chart and illustrate it.

Vocabulary Expansion

Using Describing Words

Remind children that they have talked about *describing words*, words that tell how something looks, smells, sounds, feels, or tastes. Explain that another way to describe a thing is to compare it to something else.

***Higglety Pigglety: A Book of Rhymes*, page 26**

Listening Reread the poem "First Snow," pointing out that "The bushes look like popcorn-balls." Ask what the poet is comparing the bushes to and why. Talk about other things a snow-covered bush might look like.

On chart paper, write the stem *Snow looks like . . .* and help children brainstorm comparisons. List their ideas.

At Group Time
Art Center
Materials • paper • crayons or colored chalk
On a few sheets of paper, write the stem Snow looks like ______.
Put them in the Art Center. At small group time, children can complete the sentence with an illustration.
Snow looks like ______ .

OBJECTIVES

Children

- use describing words
- brainstorm comparisons

MATERIALS

- ***Higglety Pigglety: A Book of Rhymes*,** page 26

DAY 2

Opening

Day at a Glance

Learning to Read

Big Book:

What Will the Weather Be Like Today?

✓ **Phonics: Blending *l* -*it*, *page T34***

Word Work

Building Words, ***page T36***

Writing & Language

Shared Writing, ***page T37***

Half-Day Kindergarten

✓ Indicates lessons for tested skills. Choose additional activities as time allows.

Calendar

Sunday	Monday	Tuesday	Wednesday	Thursday	Friday	Saturday
			1	2	3	4
5	6	7	8	9	10	11
12	13	14	15	16	17	18
19	20	21	22	23	24	25
26	27	28	29	30	31	

Continue weather words in your calendar routine. Count the number of days you used the same word (*sunny,* for example). Look for the small words *sun* in *sunny, rain* in *rainy, wind* in *windy.*

Daily Message

Modeled Writing Continue to compare *yesterday* and *today.* Focus on comparing weather, using weather symbols in the daily message.

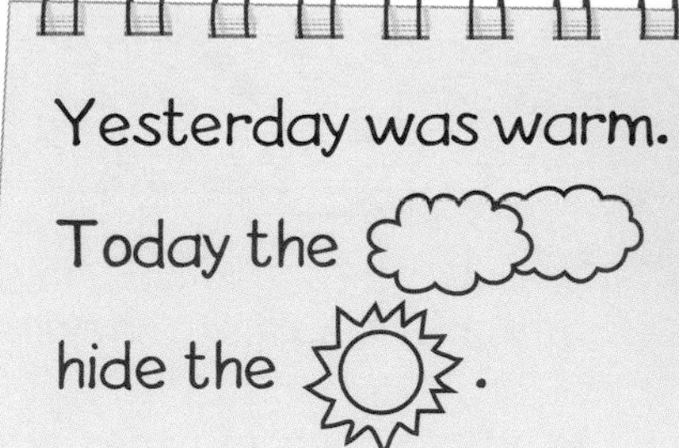

Choose a volunteer to point to and read the two words that were added to the wall this week. *(is, it)* ***Is and it are in the same column because they both begin with i. Who can read all the words that start with a?*** Continue reading the remaining groups of words.

Routines

Daily Phonemic Awareness
Blending and Segmenting Onset and Rime

Play "Pat, Pat, Clap."

- Show how to pat your knees in a slow 2, 1 rhythm. (*Pat, pat, clap.*)
- Blend onset and rime in a slow rhythm: */ c / / at / cat; / f / / at / fat.* You give the sounds, and children will pat, pat, clap as they say the word on the third beat.
- As children catch on, try whispering a word to a volunteer to segment into sounds. The rest of the class will then pat, pat the sounds and clap to say the word.

Words for Pat, Pat, Clap

fat	pet	ten
met	Ben	wet
sit	nut	lit
cut	sun	bat
bun	win	run
pig	fun	wig

DAY 3

Getting Ready to Learn

To help plan their day, tell children that they will

- reread and talk about the Big Book: *What Will the Weather Be Like Today?*

- read a story called "Can It Fit?"

- learn about rainbows in the Science Center.

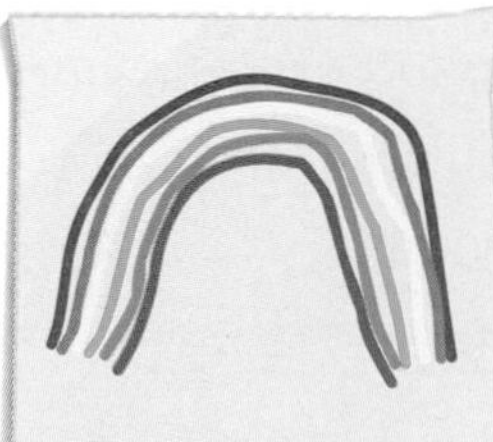

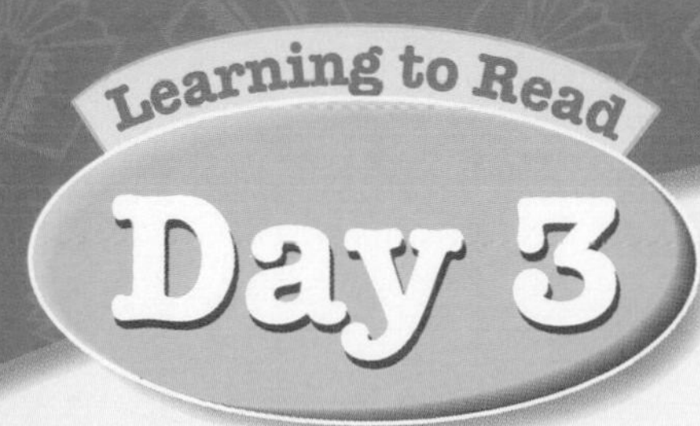
Learning to Read
Day 3

Sharing the Big Book

OBJECTIVES

Children

- identify realistic and make-believe elements in the story
- tell the purpose of a question mark

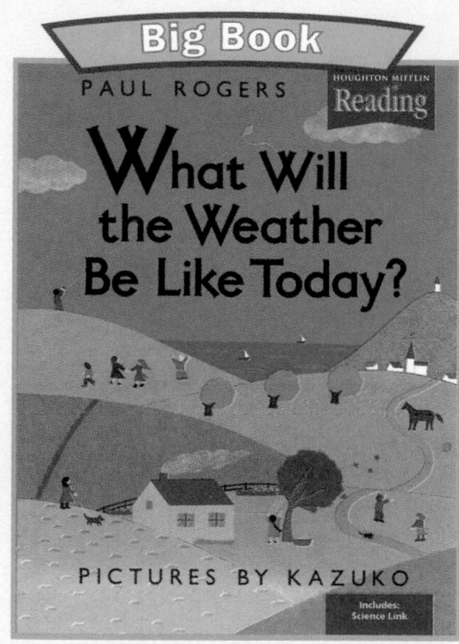
Big Book
PAUL ROGERS
Reading
What Will the Weather Be Like Today?
PICTURES BY KAZUKO

Reading for Understanding Reread the story, emphasizing the rhyme and rhythm. Pause for Supporting Comprehension points.

MEETING INDIVIDUAL NEEDS

Extra Support

Move your hand to help children track the print from left to right. Ask a volunteer to show where the sentence begins on page 6 and where it ends. Repeat with a few more pages.

Just at the moment
when night becomes day,
when the stars in the sky
begin fading away,

pages 2–3

you can hear all the birds
and the animals say,
"What will the weather
be like today?"

pages 4–5

Will it be windy?

pages 6–7

Will it be warm?
8
9

pages 8–9

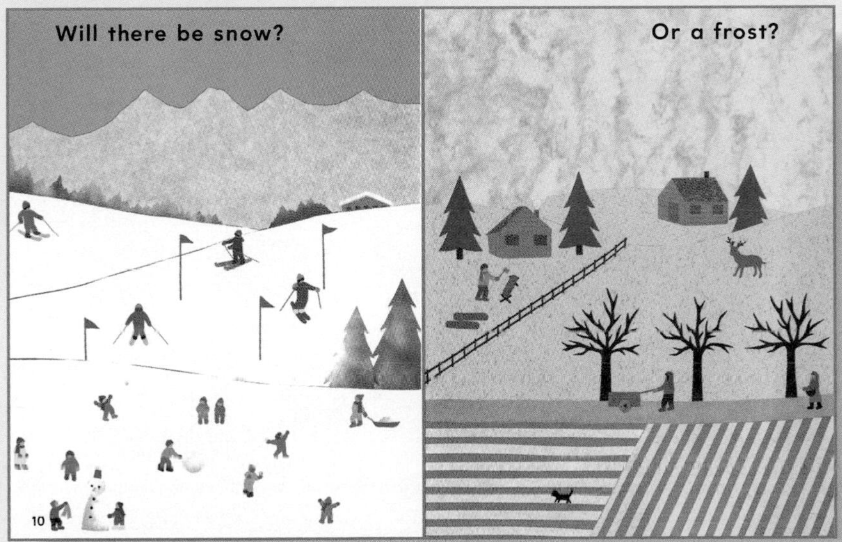

Will there be snow?
Or a frost?
10

pages 10–11

pages 12–13

Supporting Comprehension

title page

Strategy: Predict/Infer

Teacher-Student Modeling Review how you made predictions before reading yesterday. Prompts:

- *What did the title and pictures tell us about the story?... Did we read about weather in many places?*

pages 2–5

Drawing Conclusions

- *When does this story start?* (early in the morning) *What do all the animals want to know?* (what today's weather will be)

pages 12–13

Noting Details

- *What helps you know this picture shows a storm?* (lightning, umbrellas)

DAY 3

Revisiting the Text

page 6

Concepts of Print

 **Question Mark**

- Point to the question mark. *This mark shows that a sentence asks something.* Read the question. Then read page 8 and point to the question mark. *What does this mark tell you?*

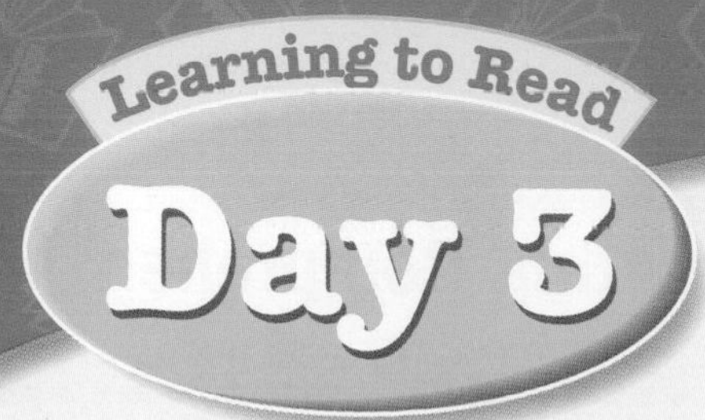

Supporting Comprehension

page 15

Drawing Conclusions

- *Why do you think the frog hopes it will rain?* (Frogs like water.)

page 17

Cause/Effect

- *Why doesn't the mole know if it's raining or not?* (The mole is underground.)

page 19

Comprehension Focus: Fantasy/Realism

Teacher-Student Modeling *Let's name the animals we've read about. Are these ducks and bees real animals or make-believe? What can these animals do that real ones cannot?* (talk)

Oral Language

On a rereading, note interesting words.

complain: To *complain* means to grumble about something. The lizard says he won't *complain* if the weather is dry.

bog: A *bog* is wet, squishy ground. Why is a *bog* a good place for a frog?

pages 14–15

pages 16–17

pages 18–19

"Weather? What's that?"
say the fish in the sea.
21

pages 20–21

The world has awakened.
The day has begun,

pages 22–23

and somewhere it's cloudy,
and somewhere there's sun,

pages 24–25

Supporting Comprehension

pages 20–21

Drawing Conclusions

- ***Why don't the fish know about the weather?*** (They live under the water.)

pages 24–25

Making Judgments

- ***Tell about the weather in these illustrations. What do you see?*** (People on page 24 are dressed warmly; the sky is gray. People on page 25 are covered from the hot sun.) ***In which place would you rather live? Why?***

pages 24–25

Comprehension Focus: Fantasy/Realism

Student Modeling *Is this part of the story about real things or make-believe things? How do you know?*

DAY 3

Challenge

Some children will be able to find words with specific patterns, such as rhyming words with similar spellings (*frog, bog*), or words with the same initial sound (*weather, wet*).

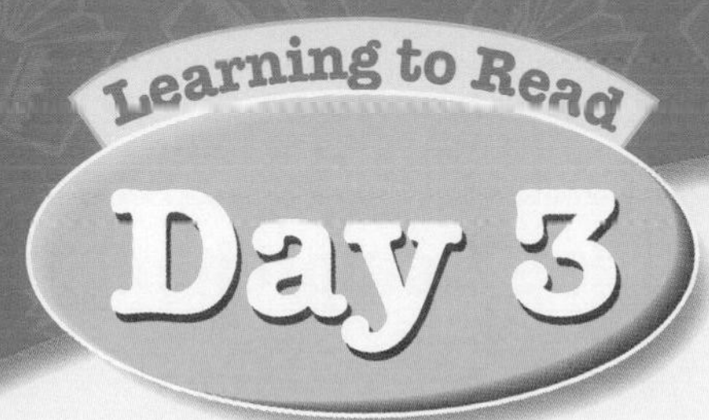

Supporting Comprehension

page 30

Gathering Information

- ***Can you answer the author's question? How do you find out about the day's weather?*** (Look at the sky; listen to the radio; see what clothing others are wearing.)

page 19

Comprehension Focus: Fantasy/Realism

Student Modeling Have children browse through the book. ***Which things could really happen? Which are make-believe things?*** Use two colors of self-stick notes to mark some of the realistic and make-believe elements. Discuss children's decisions.

Language Patterns

Rhyme This book contains a strong rhyme scheme. As you reread it, point out the rhyming pairs.

and somewhere the sun
and the rain meet to play,

pages 26–27

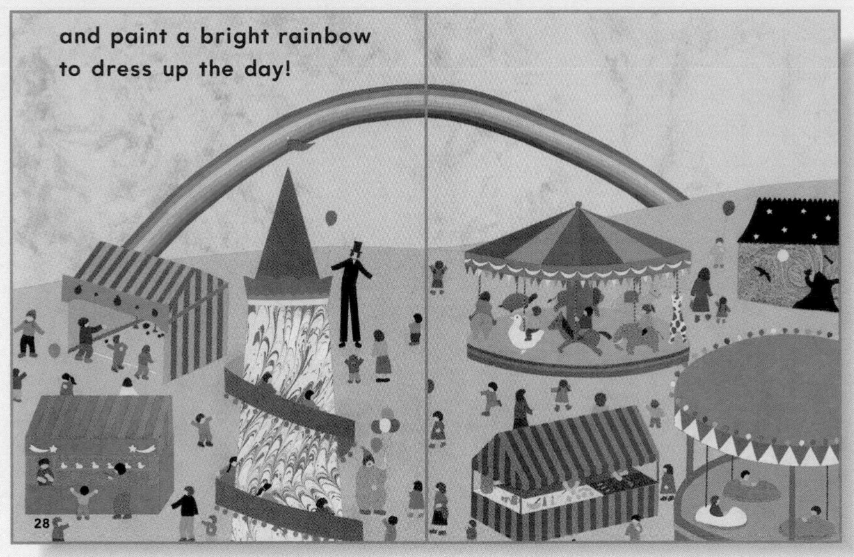

and paint a bright rainbow
to dress up the day!

pages 28–29

How is the weather
where *you* are today?
30

page 30

Responding to the Story

Retelling Use these prompts to help children summarize the selection:

- ***What kinds of weather did we read about in this story?***
- ***What kinds of animals told us about the weather?***
- ***What real things did we read about? what make-believe things?***

Literature Circle Have small groups discuss the places or weather shown in the book and vote for their favorites.

Practice Book page 169 Children will complete the page at small group time.

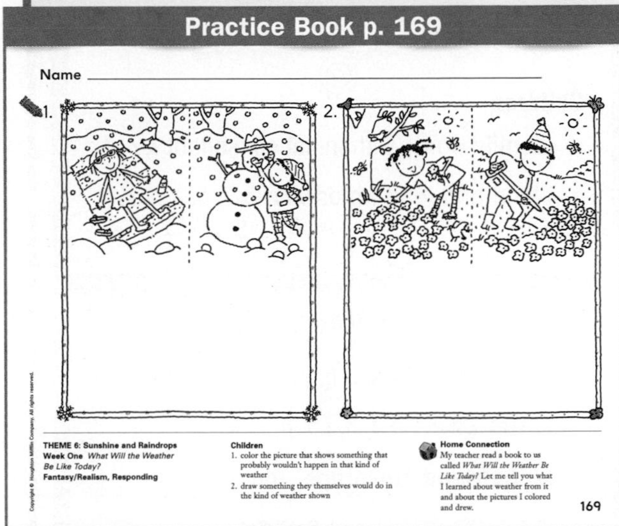
Practice Book p. 169

Name ________________

1.

2.

THEME 6: Sunshine and Raindrops
Week One *What Will the Weather Be Like Today?*
Fantasy/Realism, Responding

Children
1. color the picture that shows something that probably wouldn't happen in that kind of weather
2. draw something they themselves would do in the kind of weather shown

Home Connection
My teacher read a book to us called *What Will the Weather Be Like Today?* Let me tell you what I learned about weather from it and about the pictures I colored and drew.

169

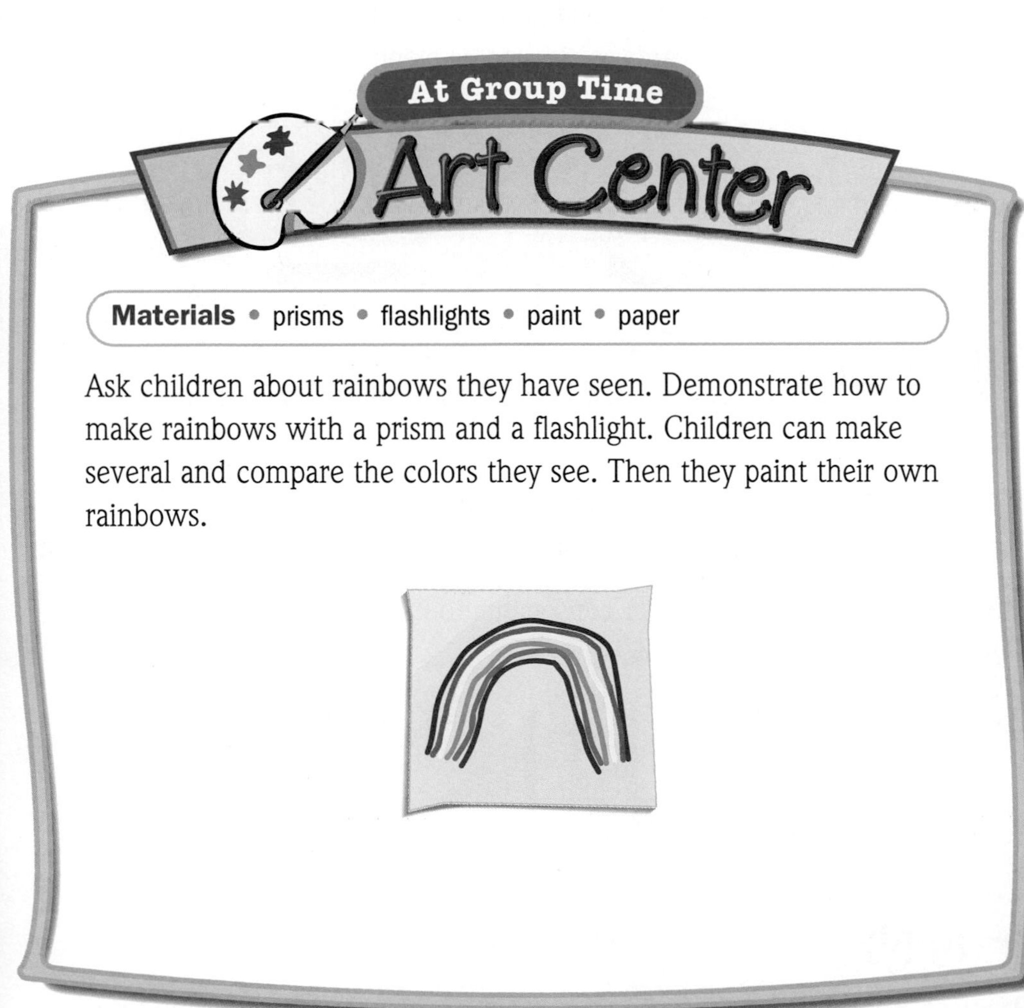

At Group Time
Art Center

Materials • prisms • flashlights • paint • paper

Ask children about rainbows they have seen. Demonstrate how to make rainbows with a prism and a flashlight. Children can make several and compare the colors they see. Then they paint their own rainbows.

Diagnostic Check

If . . .	You can . . .
children need more practice recognizing the difference between fantasy and realism,	help those children review a few library books at group time and tell what is make-believe or realistic.

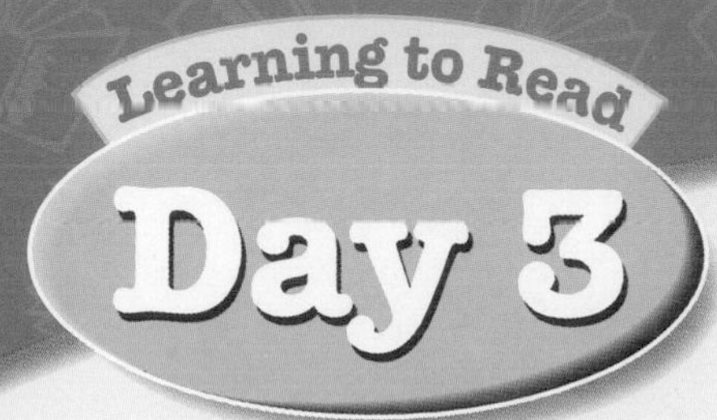

OBJECTIVES

Children

- identify words with initial consonant *l*, /l/
- blend and read words with *b, f, h, l, p, s,* and *-it*

MATERIALS

- **Alphafriend Cards** *Iggy Iguana, Larry Lion*
- **Letter Cards** *b, f, h, i, l, p, s, t*
- **Alphafriend Audiotape** Theme 6

Practice Book p. 170

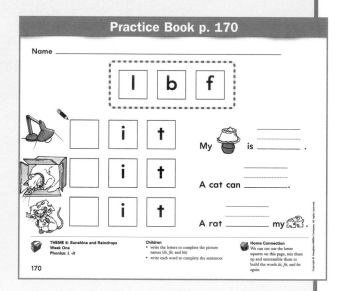

Name ______________________

l b f

☐ i t — My ☐ is ______.

☐ i t — A cat can ______.

☐ i t — A rat ______ my ☐.

THEME 6: Sunshine and Raindrops
Week One
Phonics: *l, -it*

Children
- write the letters to complete the picture names (*lit, fit,* and *bit*)
- write each word to complete the sentences

Home Connection
We can cut out the letter squares on this page, mix them up and unscramble them to build the words *lit, fit,* and *bit* again.

170

Extra Support

Read a line from "As I Was Walking," *Higglety Pigglety: A Book of Rhymes* on page 28. Children name the word that starts with /l/ and find it on the page by looking for the initial *l*.

Phonics

✓ *Blending* l -it

Connect Sounds to Letters

Review Consonant *l* Play Larry Lion's song and have children clap for each /l/ word. Write *L* and *l* on the board and list words from the song.

Blending *–it* Tell children they'll build a word with *l*, but first they'll learn about a vowel ("helper letter"). Introduce Alphafriend *Iggy Iguana.*

This animal is an iguana. Say* Iggy Iguana *with me. Iggy's letter is the vowel* i*, and the sound* i *stands for is /ĭ/. Hold up the Letter Card *i*. ***You say /ĭ/. Listen for the /ĭ/ sound in these words: /ĭ/* in*, /ĭ/* if*, /ĭ/* it*, /ĭ/* imagine.**

Hold up Letter Cards *i* and *t*. Remind children that they know the sound for t. Model blending the sounds as you hold the cards apart and then together: ***/ĭ/ /t/, it. I've made the word* it*. The sound for* i *is first, and the sound for* t *is last.*** Have volunteers move the cards as classmates blend.

Add *it* to the Word Wall. Children will use *it* to make other words.

Blending *-it* Words Build *it* in a pocket chart. Then put *l* in front of *it,* and model blending /l/ /it/, *lit.* Have volunteers blend the sounds while you point.

Model blending *-it* with familiar consonants to make *lit, sit, fit, bit, pit, hit.*

Apply

Practice Book page 170 Children complete the page at small group time.

Phonics in Action

Applying Phonics Skills and High-Frequency Words

Phonics/Decoding Strategy

Teacher-Student Modeling Discuss using the Strategy to read words in the **Phonics Library** story "Can it Fit?"

The title begins with capital C. *The sound for* C *is /k/. I know the sounds for* a, n: */ă//n/,* on. *Let's blend: /c//an/,* Can *is the first word in the title. I also know the sounds for* i, t, */ĭ//t/,* it. *The last word begins with capital* F. *The sound for* f *is /f/. The last word is /f//it/,* fit. *I think the story is about something that might not fit.*

Do a picture walk. Show children that on page 2 there is a van. There is a dog on page 3. Ask: ***Can the dog fit?*** Write *fit* on the board; model saying the three sounds and then blending /f//it/, *fit.* Ask one child to point and model blending. Then read the story with children.

Coached Reading

Have children read each page silently before reading with you. Prompts:

page 1 *Do you think anything else can fit in the back of this van?*

page 2 *The man is sitting in his van. Who else do you think can fit in the van?*

page 3 Together, blend *sit*. Ask: ***Can you find a word that rhymes with*** sit? (*fit*) ***What letters are the same in those rhyming words?*** (*i, t* as in *it*)

page 5 *Who is trying to fit into the van now?*

page 6 *The van is very full. Do you think the driver can fit?*

page 7 *Everyone finally fit into the van! Could this story really happen? Why or why not?*

Now let's go back to find things that begin with Larry Lion's sound /l/. (lights, ladder, logs, license)

Phonics Library

Purposes
- apply phonics skills
- apply high-frequency words

Can It Fit?
by Amy Griffin
illustrated by Mike Gordon

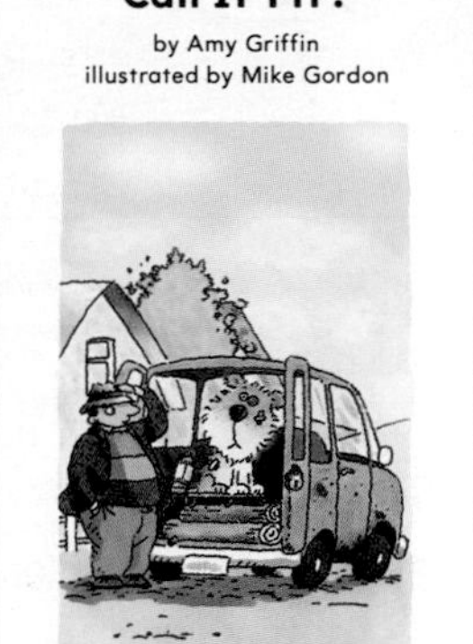

1

It is my van.
I can sit.

2

can fit.
Sit, , sit!

3

can fit.
Sit, , sit!

4

can fit.
Sit, , sit!

5

Can a man fit?
Can a man sit?

6

A man can fit.
Go!

7

DAY 3

Home Connection

Children can color the pictures in the take-home version of "Can It Fit?" After rereading on Day 4, children can take it home to read to family members.

OBJECTIVES

Children

- blend initial consonants with *–it* to read words

MATERIALS

- **Letter Cards** *b, f, h, i, l, p, s, t*

Building Words

Word Family: *–it*

- Using the Letter Cards, model how to build *it*.
- ***First I'll stretch out the sounds: /i/... /t/. How many sounds do you hear? The first sound is /ĭ/. I'll put up an* i *to spell that. The last sound is /t/. What letter should I choose for that?***
- Blend /ĭ/ and /t/ to read *it.* Then ask which letter you should add to build *lit*. Model how to read *lit* by blending /l/ with /it/.
- Then replace *l* with s and say: ***Now what happens if I change /l/ to /s/?*** Continue making and blending *-it* words by substituting *s, b, h, p, f.*

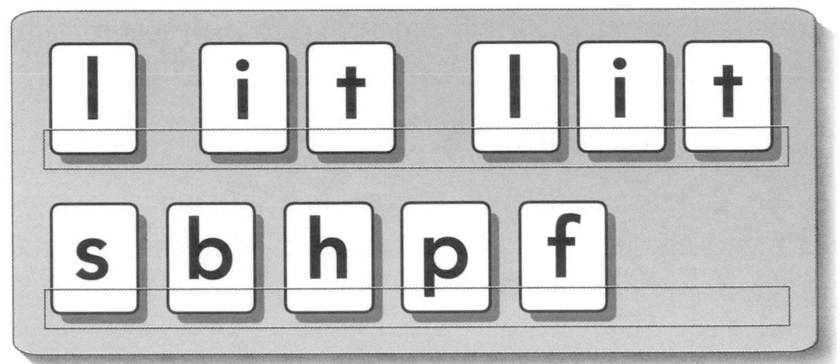

- Have small groups work together to build *-it* words. They can use magnetic letters or other manipulatives in your collection.

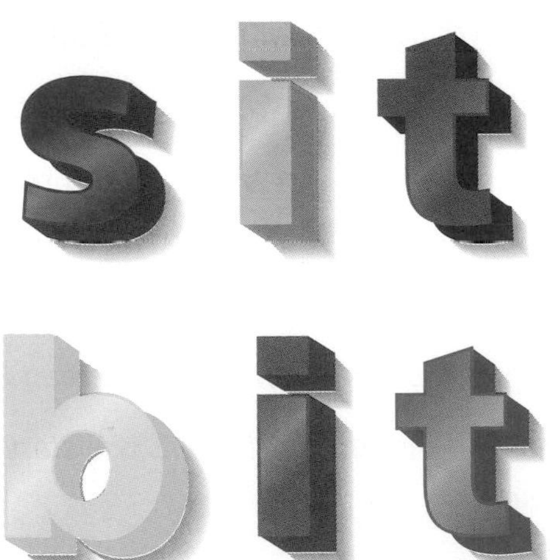

Shared Writing

Writing a Description

Viewing and Speaking Show children pages from *What Will the Weather Be Like Today?* along with any other pictures of winter scenes. Remind them that describing words tell how something looks, feels, smells, sounds, or tastes.

- Tell children to think about a winter scene. Ask what things they would see. On chart paper, start a graphic organizer and record their naming words on the right-hand side as shown.
- Read the list of winter things. Now ask children to use describing words to tell how these things look, sound, or feel. Record their suggestions on the left side of the chart.

Incorporate new vocabulary into a description of a winter scene for a shared writing activity.

- Write the stem *I see* _______. Call on volunteers to suggest words to complete the sentence, using the graphic organizer for ideas. Continue with another stem: *I feel* _______.
- Point out the period at the end of each sentence.

OBJECTIVES

Children

- think of descriptive weather words

MATERIALS

- **Big Book:** *What Will the Weather Be Like Today?*

DAY 3

Learning to Read

Day 4

Day at a Glance

Learning to Read

Big Book:

Checking the Weather

 **Phonics: Reviewing /l/; Blending *-it words, page T42***

Word Work

Building Words, *page T44*

Writing & Language

Interactive Writing, *page T45*

 **Half-Day Kindergarten**

 Indicates lessons for tested skills. Choose additional activities as time allows.

Opening

Calendar

Sunday	Monday	Tuesday	Wednesday	Thursday	Friday	Saturday
			1	2	3	4
5	6	7	8	9	10	11
12	13	14	15	16	17	18
19	20	21	22	23	24	25
26	27	28	29	30	31	

Help children find today's weather word card. For example: ***We need the card that says*** rainy. ***Show me "thumbs up" if*** rainy ***begins with /r/. What letter stands for /r/? Can you find the right card? Point to it.***

Daily Message

Modeled Writing Use some words that begin with *l* in today's message. Then talk about what the words mean.

Mrs. Baker's
kitten roars
like a lion.

Remind children that the words on the Word Wall are in ABC order. ***I will say the alphabet, and you raise your hand when I come to a letter that begins a word on the wall.*** **A... *are there any words that begin with* a*? Who will point to them and read them?***

Routines

Daily Phonemic Awareness
Blending and Segmenting Onset and Rime

- Reread "As I Was Walking" on page 28 of *Higglety Pigglety.*
- Play a guessing game. ***Let's put some sounds together to make words from the poem:*** **/m/ /et/** (met); **/l/ /ake/** (lake); **/m/ /uch/** (much).
- ***Now let's play another game. This time, I will say a word from the poem and you tell me the beginning sound and the sounds at the end.***

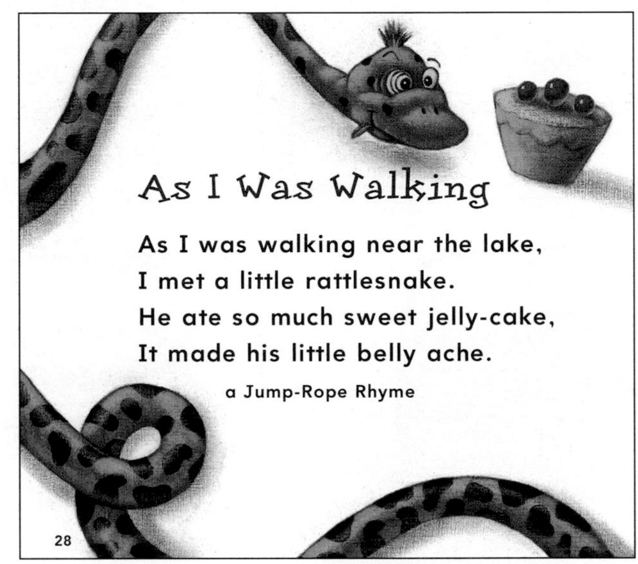
As I Was Walking

As I was walking near the lake,
I met a little rattlesnake.
He ate so much sweet jelly-cake,
It made his little belly ache.

a Jump-Rope Rhyme

28

***Higglety Pigglety: A Book of Rhymes*, page 28**

Getting Ready to Learn

To help plan their day, tell children that they will

- read the Science Link: *Checking the Weather.*

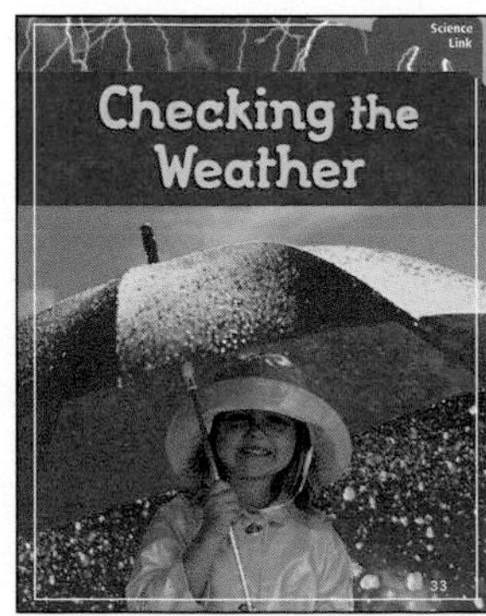

- build words with *l* and other letters in the Phonics Center.

- reread a story called "Can It Fit?"

DAY 4

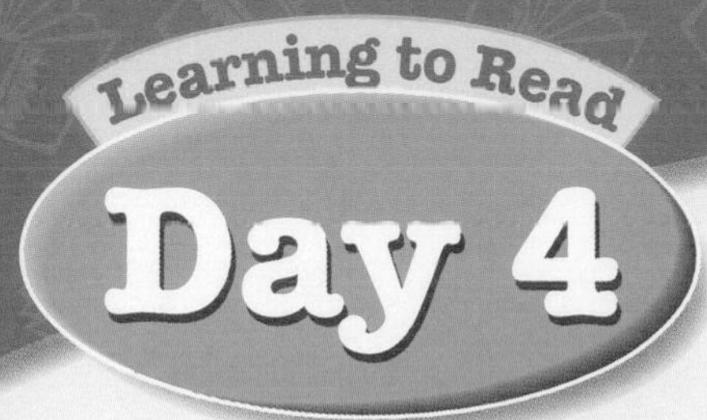

Sharing the Big Book

Science Link

Children

- identify realistic elements in the selection
- match words and spaces on separate pages

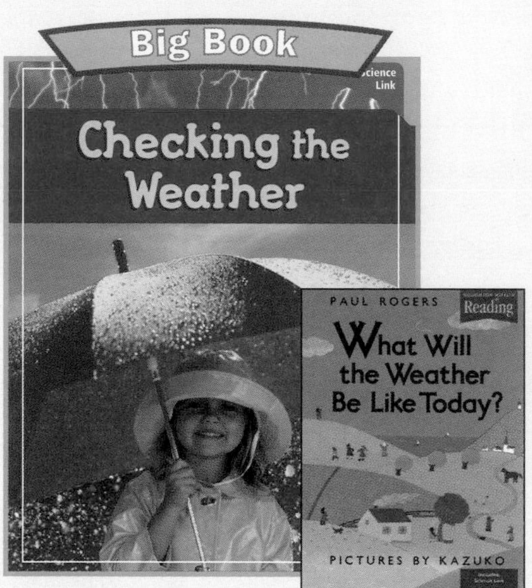

pages 33–38

Oral Language

sandcastle: We've read about castles in fairy tales. This is a *sand*castle. Tell us about a sandcastle.

English Language Learners

Help English Language learners use the pictures to predict what the article is about and to review any vocabulary needed to understand the text. In particular, review the weather instruments, what they are used for, and how they work.

Building Background

Suppose you woke up and wanted to know how hot or cold it was outside. How would you know what to wear? What could help you know the temperature? Read the title, and discuss a few pictures. Explain that we can use different weather tools, *Checking the Weather,* or instruments, to tell what the weather is like.

Reading for Understanding Pause for discussion as you share the selection.

page 34

Strategy: Predict/Infer

Student Modeling Say that each page begins with a question. Read the first line, pointing as you read. Ask: ***What kind of weather do you think we'll read about? What clues help you to know that?***

Comprehension Focus: Fantasy/Realism

Student Modeling ***Do the pictures look real or make-believe? Could these types of weather really happen? How do you know?***

page 35

Drawing Conclusions

- ***How can you tell that it is a sunny, warm day?***

pages 36–37

Cause-Effect

- ***Why is a windy day a good day to fly a kite? Why are these children standing with their mouths open?***

What is the weather
like today?
How can we find out?

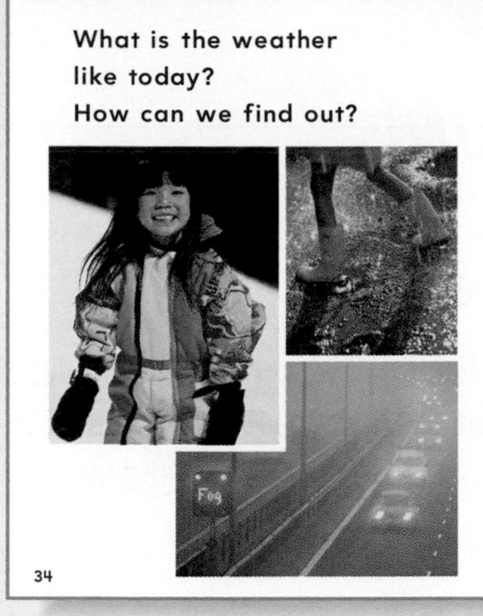

34

Is it hot or cold today?
How hot or cold is it?
A thermometer will show us.

35

pages 34–35

Is it windy today?
How windy is it?
A wind gauge will show us.

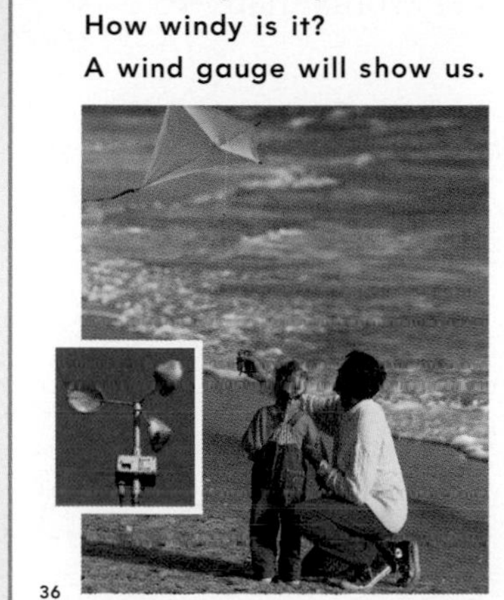

36

Is it rainy today?
How rainy is it?
A rain gauge will show us.

37

pages 36–37

How else can we find out?
We can go outside and see!

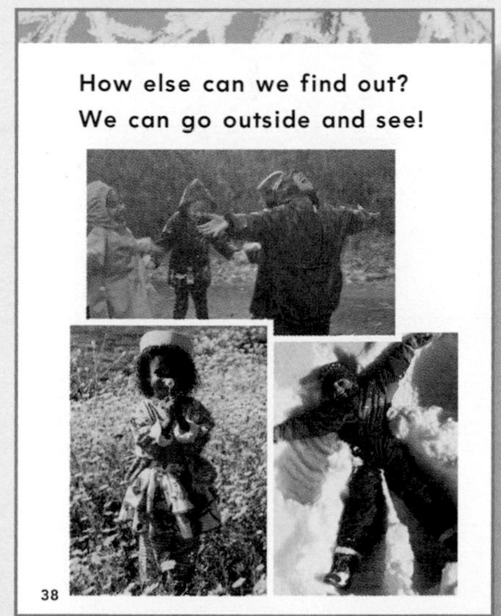

38

page 38

Revisiting the Text

pages 36-37

Concepts of Print

 **Word Spacing**

- Cover the words *A wind*. Then point to *gauge will show us*. Ask: ***How many words do you see? The spaces separate words. Where are the same words on the next page?***

Responding

Retelling Talk about the article together. Ask children to tell what type of weather they like best. Have volunteers retell the selection, using the photographs as prompts and acting out activities they see on each page.

Challenge

For children who are ready for a challenge, prepare cards for the words and end mark in one or two sentences in the selection. One child builds a sentence and then challenges a partner to find it in the book.

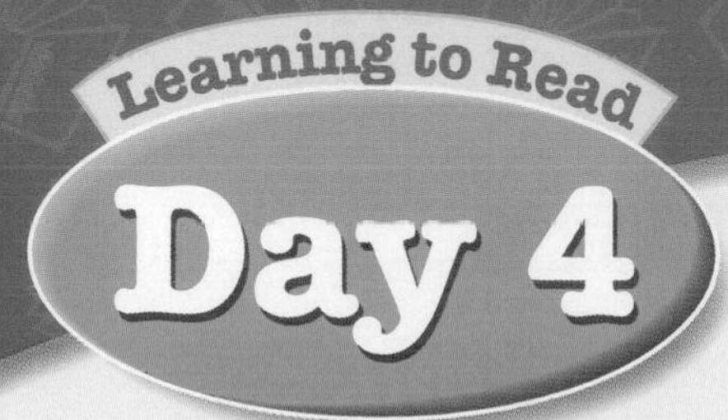

OBJECTIVES

Children

- identify initial *l* for words that begin with /l/
- blend *l* and other initial consonants with *-it*

MATERIALS

- ***From Apples to Zebras: A Book of ABC's,*** page 13
- **Alphafriend Card** *Iggy Iguana*
- **Letter Cards** *b, f, h, i, l s, t*
- **Word Cards** *A, a, I, is*
- **Picture Cards** *ball, lamp*
- **Phonics Center:** Theme 6, Week 1, Day 4

Teacher's Note

During writing, children may ask how to spell words from the *-it* family. Help children find *it* on the Word Wall and add the appropriate initial consonant(s).

English Language Learners

The short *i* sound does not occur in Spanish, Khmer, or Vietnamese. In Spanish and Vietnamese, the letter *i* elicits the long *e* sound. Lao does not distinguish between short *i* and long *e*. Give children practice with short *i* by having them repeat pairs of words: *hit/heat; fit/feet; mitt/meet.*

Phonics

Blending -it words

Connect Sounds to Letters

Review Consonant *l* On page 13 of *From Apples to Zebras,* cover the words with self-stick notes. Then display the page. Ask children what letter they expect to see first in each word and why. Uncover the words so children can check their predictions.

Reviewing *-it* Remind children that to build some words with *l,* they also need a vowel ("helper letter") because every word has at least one of those. Ask which Alphafriend stands for the vowel sound /ĭ/. (Iggy Iguana) Display Iggy and have children think of other words that start with /ĭ/. (*igloo, if, icky, in*)

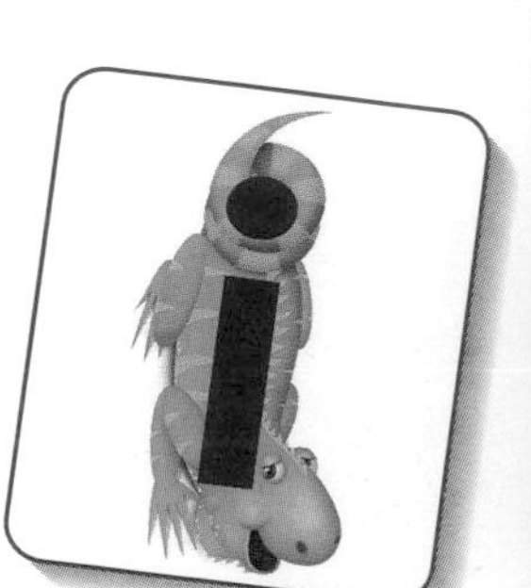

Hold up Letter Cards *i* and *t*. ***Watch and listen as I build a word from the Word Wall: /ĭ/ /t/,*** **it.** ***/ĭ/ /t/,*** **it.**

Blending *-it* Words Put Letter Card *l* in front of *it*. ***Now let's blend my new word: /l/ /it/,*** **lit.** Continue, having volunteers build and blend *sit, fit, bit, hit.*

Apply

Build a sentence with the cards shown. Then have a volunteer read the sentence.

Repeat the activity with *I hit a <ball>*. Then have volunteers read the sentences and blend the *-it* words. Tell children they will build more sentences today in the Phonics Center.

Practice Book page 171 Children will complete this page at small group time.

Phonics Library In groups today, children will also read *-it* words as they reread the **Phonics Library** story, "Can It Fit?" See suggestions, page T35.

Use the Phonics Center materials for **Theme 6, Week 1, Day 4**.

Practice Book p. 171

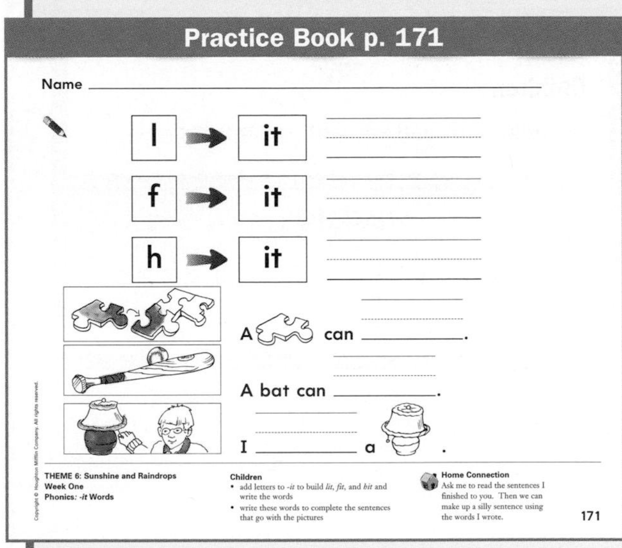

Name ____________

l → it ____
f → it ____
h → it ____

A [puzzle] can ________.

A bat can ________.

I ________ a [lamp].

THEME 6: Sunshine and Raindrops
Week One
Phonics: *-it* Words

Children
- add letters to *-it* to build *lit*, *fit*, and *hit* and write the words
- write these words to complete the sentences that go with the pictures

Home Connection
Ask me to read the sentences I finished to you. Then we can make up a silly sentence using the words I wrote.

171

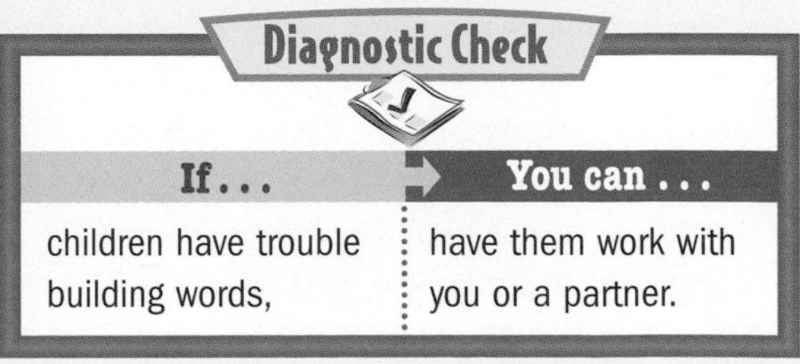

Diagnostic Check

If . . .	You can . . .
children have trouble building words,	have them work with you or a partner.

DAY 4

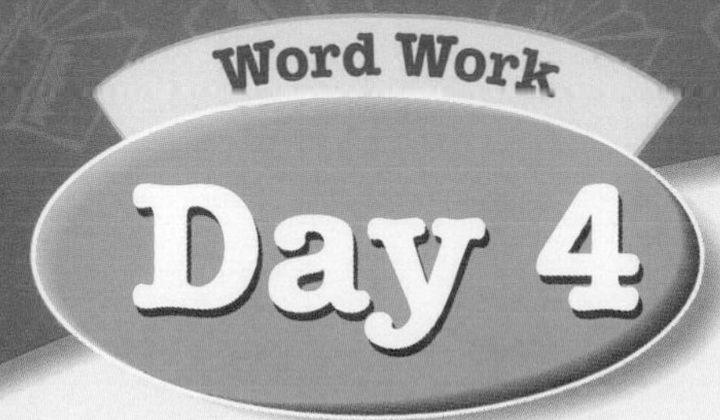

OBJECTIVES

Children

- build and read *–it, –an, –at* words

MATERIALS

- **Letter Cards** *a, b, c, f, h, i, l, m, n, p, r, s, t, v*

Building Words

Word Families: *-it, -an, -at*

Model how to build *it* in a pocket chart, stretching out the sounds. ***Let's build the word*** **lit*****. Which letter should I put in front of*** **it*****?*** Now use known consonants to replace *l*, building other *-it* words.

Next, use letter cards to build *an*. ***First I'll stretch out the sounds: /ă/... /n/. How many sounds do you hear? The first sound is /ă/. I'll put up an a to spell that. The last sound is /n/. What letter should I choose for that?*** Blend /a/ and /n/ to read *an*.

Continue building words with initial consonants:

- Ask which letter you should add to build *pan*. Model how to read *pan* by blending /p/ with /an/.
- Replace *p* with *f*. ***What happens if I change /p/ to /f/?*** Continue making and blending *-an* words by substituting *c, m, r, t, v*.
- Repeat, this time building *-at* and making new words by substituting initial consonants *b, f, h, m, p, r, s*.

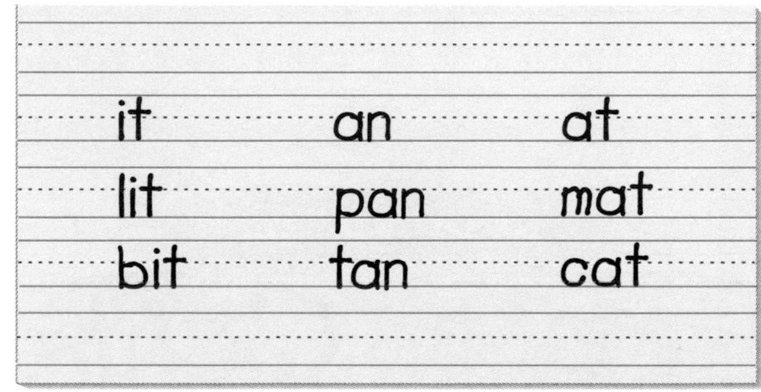

Have children write some *-it, -an,* and *-at* words on white boards or paper. They can read their lists of words to a partner.

Writing & Language

Day 4

Interactive Writing

Writing Sentences

Viewing and Speaking Show children pages from *Checking the Weather* and *Chicken Soup with Rice* along with any other pictures of winter scenes. Remind them that describing words tell how something looks, feels, smells, sounds, or tastes.

Display the graphic organizer from yesterday's shared writing. (See page T37.) Review the list of objects and describing words, and invite children to suggest new ones.

- Continue adding sentences to the chart, using the stems *I see* ______ ______ and *I feel* ______ ______. Together, brainstorm words to fill in the blanks.
- If a suggested word begins or ends with a known consonant, have a volunteer write the letter. For any word that rhymes with *an, at,* or *it,* ask a child to write the last two letters. Choose another volunteer to write the period at the end of each sentence.

At Group Time

Writing Center

Put the chart paper from the previous activity in the Writing Center. Children "read" it on their own or with a partner. They can copy and illustrate their own sentence.

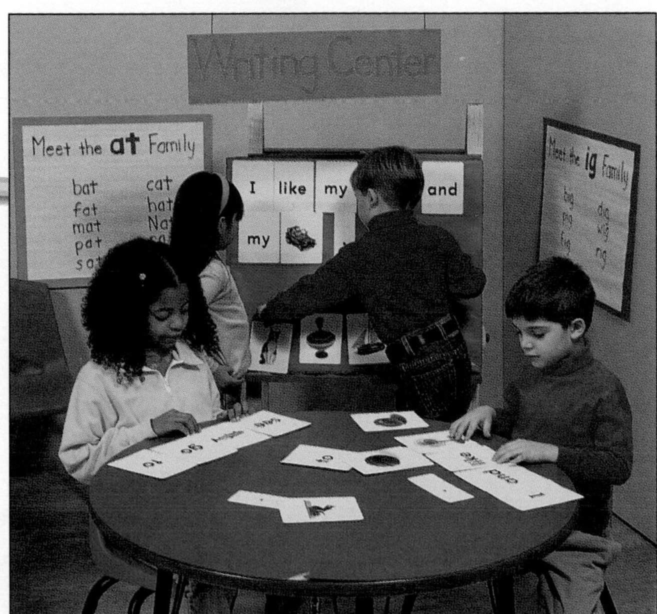

OBJECTIVES

Children

- use describing words in an oral context
- write letters or words for an interactive writing activity

MATERIALS

- **Read Aloud:** *Chicken Soup with Rice*
- **Big Book:** *Checking the Weather*

Portfolio Opportunity

Save children's work as samples of their use of describing words.

DAY 4

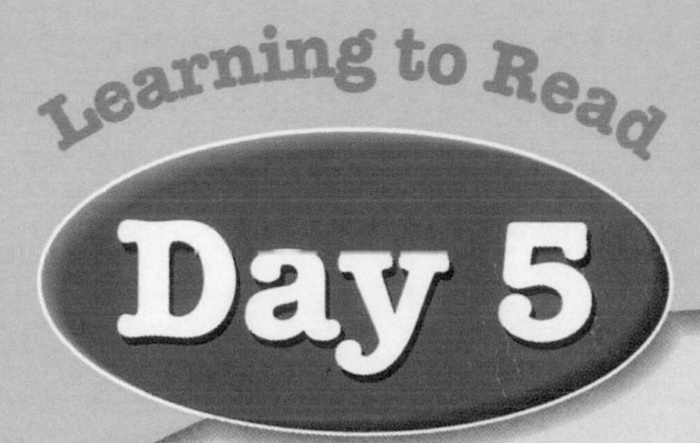

Opening

Day at a Glance

Learning to Read

Revisiting the Literature:

Chicken Soup with Rice, What Will the Weather Be Like Today?, Checking the Weather, "Can It Fit?"

✓ **Phonics Review: Initial Consonants *b, f, l, m, r; –an, –it* Words,** ***page T50***

Word Work

Building Words, *page T52*

Writing & Language

Independent Writing, *page T53*

Half-Day Kindergarten

✓ Indicates lessons for tested skills. Choose additional activities as time allows.

Calendar

Sunday	Monday	Tuesday	Wednesday	Thursday	Friday	Saturday
			1	2	3	4
5	6	7	8	9	10	11
12	13	14	15	16	17	18
19	20	21	22	23	24	25
26	27	28	29	30	31	

Review the week's weather and have volunteers describe it in their own words. (Sample answers: It was sunny on Monday and Tuesday. It was rainy yesterday. Today it is warm.)

Daily Message

Interactive Writing Share the pen: In the daily message, occasionally ask volunteers to contribute letters and/or words they can read and write.

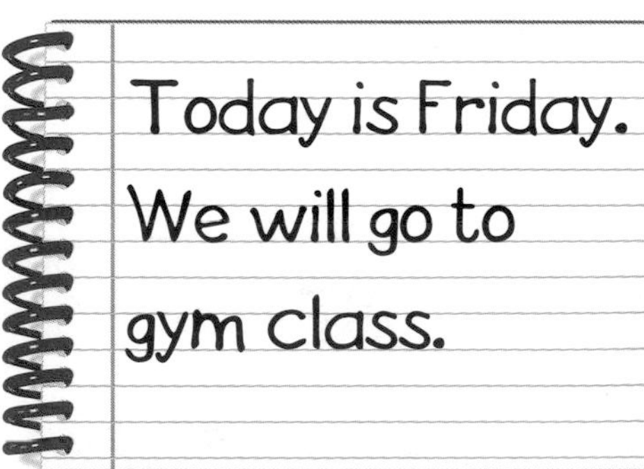

Today is Friday.
We will go to
gym class.

Read the Word Wall together, and then play a rhyming game: ***I'm going to find a word on the wall that rhymes with* sky. Sky *rhymes with...* I. *Now raise your hand when you find a word that rhymes with* he.**

Routines

Daily Phonemic Awareness
Blending and Segmenting Onset and Rime

- Read "Itsy Bitsy Spider" on page 27 of *Higglety Pigglety.*
- Play a guessing game. ***Let's put some sounds together to make words from the poem: /d/ /own/*** (down)***; /k/ /ame/*** (came)***; /r/ /ain/*** (rain)***; /s/ /un/*** (sun)***.***
- ***Now I will say a word from the poem and you tell me the beginning sound and the sounds at the end.***

The Itsy Bitsy Spider

The itsy bitsy spider
Climbed up the waterspout.

Down came the rain
And washed the spider out.

Out came the sun
And dried up all the rain,

And the itsy bitsy spider
Climbed up the spout again.

27

***Higglety Pigglety: A Book of Rhymes,* page 27**

Getting Ready to Learn

To help plan their day, tell children that they will

- reread and talk about all the books they've read this week.

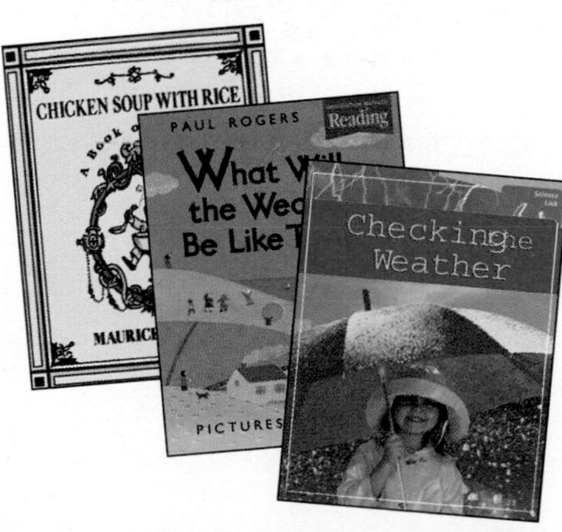

- take home a story they can read, "Can It Fit?"

Can It Fit?
by Amy Griffin
illustrated by Mike Gordon

- describe something in their journals.

DAY 5

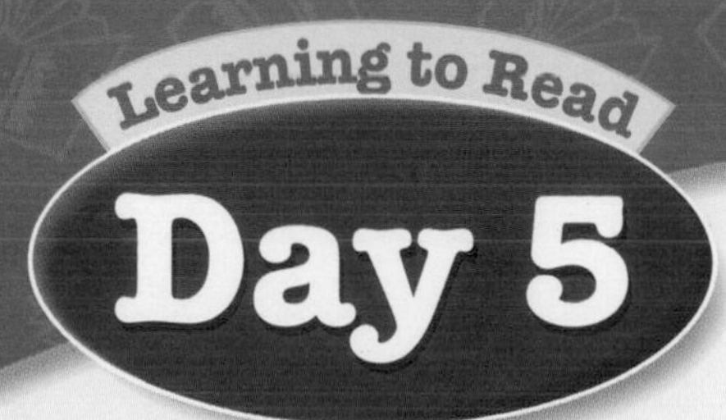

Revisiting the Literature

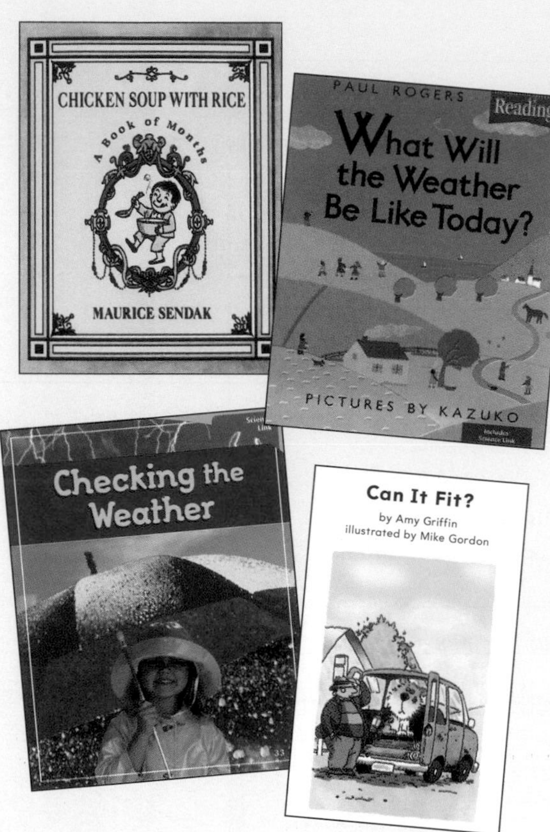

Literature Discussion

Today children will compare the different books you shared this week: *Chicken Soup with Rice, What Will the Weather Be Like Today?, Checking the Weather,* and "Can It Fit?" First, use these suggestions to help children recall the selections:

- Have volunteers show and tell what happened during their favorite months in *Chicken Soup with Rice.*
- Read pages 2–12 of *What Will the Weather Be Like Today?* Have children name the weather words.
- Read *Checking the Weather* and invite children to name the different types of weather instruments they learned about.
- Together, read page 3 from "Can It Fit?" Ask volunteers how they blended *fit.*
- Ask children to vote for their favorite book of the week, and then read the text of the winner aloud.

Comprehension Focus: Fantasy/Realism

Comparing Books Remind children that they have learned to think about which things are real and make-believe in books. Browse through each selection, inviting comment about things that can or cannot happen in real life. Ask children if some selections seemed more realistic than others and why. You might introduce the terms *fiction* and *nonfiction.*

www.eduplace.com

Log on to **Education Place** for more activities relating to Sunshine and Raindrops.

www.bookadventure.org

This Internet reading-incentive program provides thousands of titles for children to read.

Building Fluency

Rereading Familiar Texts

Phonics Library: "Can It Fit?" Remind children that this week they've learned the new word *is*, and they've learned to read words with *-it*. As they reread the **Phonics Library** story "Can It Fit?," have them look for words with *-it*.

Review Feature several familiar **Phonics Library** titles in the Book Corner. Have children demonstrate their growing skills by choosing one to reread aloud, alternating pages with a partner. From time to time ask children to point out words or pages that they can read more easily now.

Oral Reading Frequent rereadings of familiar texts help children develop a less word-by-word and more expressive style in their oral reading. Model often how to read in phrases, pausing for end punctuation. Then have children try it.

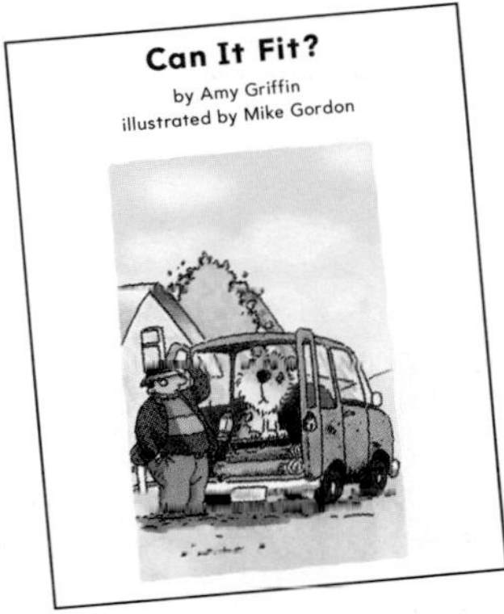

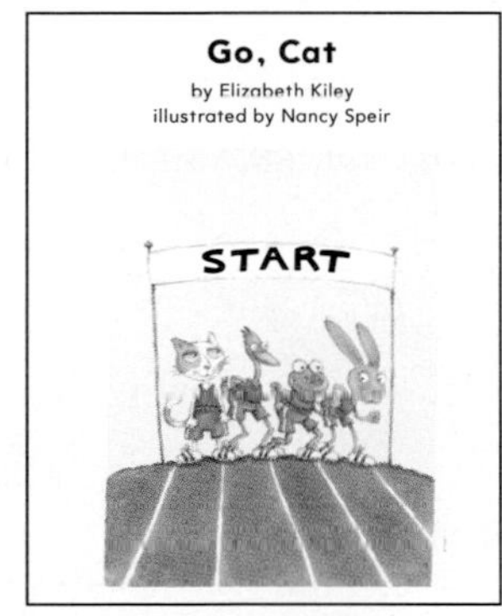

Blackline Master 36 Children complete the page and take it home to share their reading progress.

Leveled Books

The materials listed below provide reading practice for children at different levels.

Little Big Books

Little Readers for Guided Reading

Houghton Mifflin Classroom Bookshelf

Home Connection

Remind children to share the **take-home** version of "Can It Fit?" with their families.

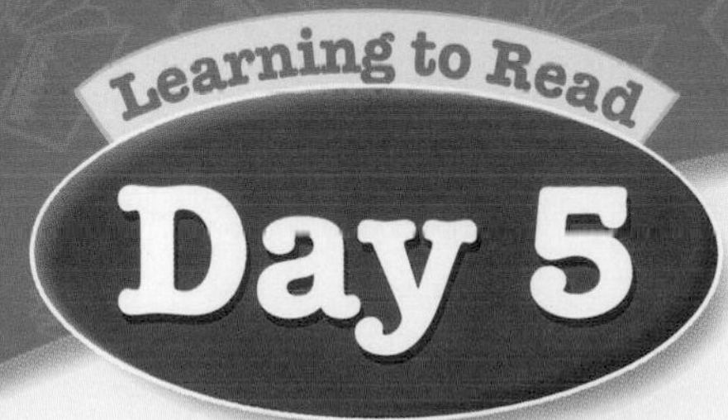

Phonics Review

Consonants, Word Families

OBJECTIVES

Children

- build and read words with initial consonants and short *a* + *t*, short *i* + *t*, short *a* + *n*
- make sentences with high-frequency words

MATERIALS

- **Word Cards** *a, and, go, I, is, like, my, see, to*
- **Punctuation Cards:** period, question mark
- **Picture Cards** choose for sentence building

Review

Tell children they will take turns being word builders and word readers today. Have a group of word builders stand with you at the chalkboard.

- ***Let's build* an. *First, count the sounds... I know a stands for* /ă/ *and* n *stands for* /n/.** Write the letters.
- Children copy an on the board and blend the sounds.
- ***Add* t *in front of your letters.*** Children copy and ask the rest of the class (word readers) what new word they've made.
- A new group changes places with the first one. At your direction they erase the *t,* write *f,* and ask the word readers to say the new word.
- Continue until everyone builds a word by replacing one letter. Examples: *pan, van, can, Nan, ran; rat, hat, cat, Nat, sat; sit, lit, fit, pit, hit, bit.*

High-Frequency Word Review

 *I, see, my, like, a, to, and, go, is*

Review

Give each small group the Word Cards, Picture Cards, and Punctuation Card needed to make a sentence. Each child holds one card. Children stand and arrange themselves to make a sentence.

Apply

Practice Book page 172 Children can complete the page independently and read it to you during small group time.

Phonics Library Have children take turns reading aloud to the class. Each child might read one page of "Can It Fit?" or a favorite **Phonics Library** selection from the previous theme. Remind readers to share the pictures! Discussion questions:

- ***Did you hear any rhyming words in either story? What letters are the same in those words?***
- ***This week we added* is *to the Word Wall. Find it in "Can It Fit?"***

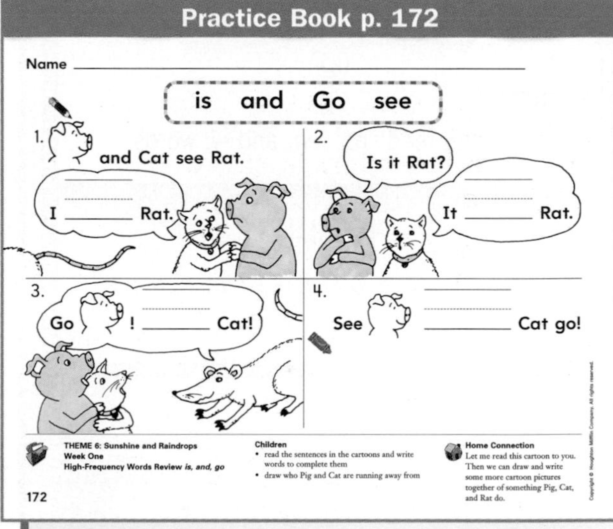

Practice Book p. 172

Name ______________________

is and Go see

1. ______ and Cat see Rat.
I ______ Rat.

2. Is it Rat?
It ______ Rat.

3. Go ______ ! ______ Cat!

4. See ______ ______ Cat go!

THEME 6: Sunshine and Raindrops
Week One
High-Frequency Words Review *is, and, go*

Children
- read the sentences in the cartoons and write words to complete them
- draw who Pig and Cat are running away from

Home Connection
Let me read this cartoon to you. Then we can draw and write some more cartoon pictures together of something Pig, Cat, and Rat do.

172

Portfolio Opportunity

Save the Practice Book page to show children's recognition of high-frequency words.

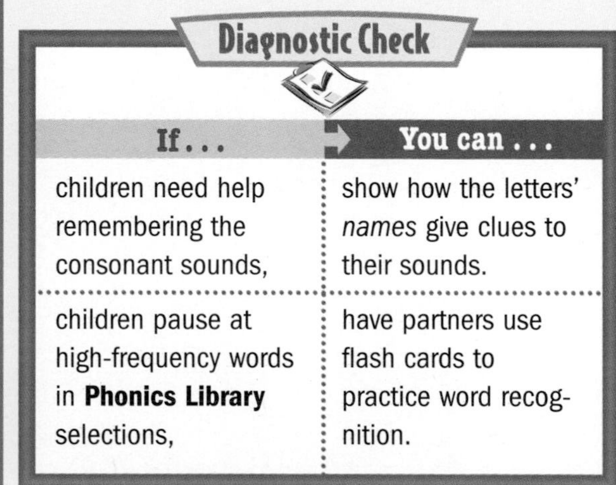

Diagnostic Check

If . . .	You can . . .
children need help remembering the consonant sounds,	show how the letters' *names* give clues to their sounds.
children pause at high-frequency words in **Phonics Library** selections,	have partners use flash cards to practice word recognition.

DAY 5

OBJECTIVES

Children

- build and read *–at, –an,* and *–it* words

MATERIALS

- **Letter Cards** *a, b, c, f, h, i, l, m, n, p, r, s, t, v*

Building Words

Word Families: *-at, -an, -it*

Model how to build *at.* Along the bottom of a pocket chart, line up the letters *s, m, r, b, h, v, c, p,* and *f.* ***Let's build the word*** **bat.** ***Who can tell me which letter I should take from here, to make*** **bat?** Have a volunteer take the letter *b* and place it in front of *-at.* Continue building *-at* words, using the remaining initial consonants. On chart paper, keep a list of all the *-at* words you make and reread it together.

Continue the activity with *-an* words and *-it* words. Examples: *an, can, fan, man, pan, ran, tan, van; it, bit, fit, hit, lit, pit, sit.*

Have small groups work together to build *-at, -an,* and *-it* words with magnetic letters or other materials. This time, they can write some of the new words in the Word Bank section of their journals and add appropriate pictures.

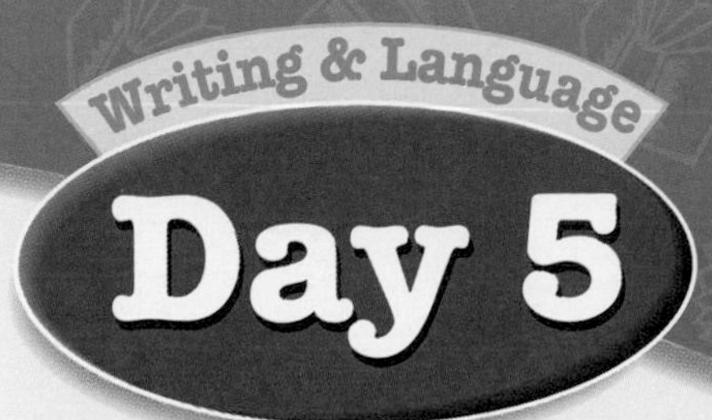

Independent Writing

Journals

Together, reread the charts from this week's shared and interactive writing. Point out all the describing words that were used to talk about weather. Tell children today they'll write about their favorite type of weather.

- Pass out the journals.
- ***Let's discuss what we've learned about weather this week. What are some new weather facts you could put in your journal? What are some describing words for your favorite weather?***
- Remind children that they can use the posted describing words and weather words as they write.
- If time permits, allow children to share what they've written with the class.

OBJECTIVES

Children

- write independently

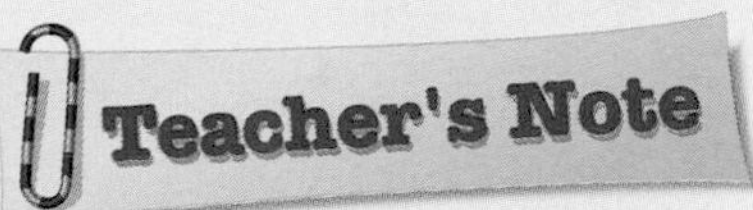

Writing ability varies greatly among children in a kindergarten classroom. Use plain paper for journals to accommodate those children who are not ready for writing on lined paper, as well as those who will be drawing as much as writing in their journals.

DAY 5

Week 2

Literature for Week 2

Different texts for different purposes

The Sun and the Wind

Teacher Read Aloud

Purposes

- oral language
- listening strategy
- comprehension skill

Big Books:

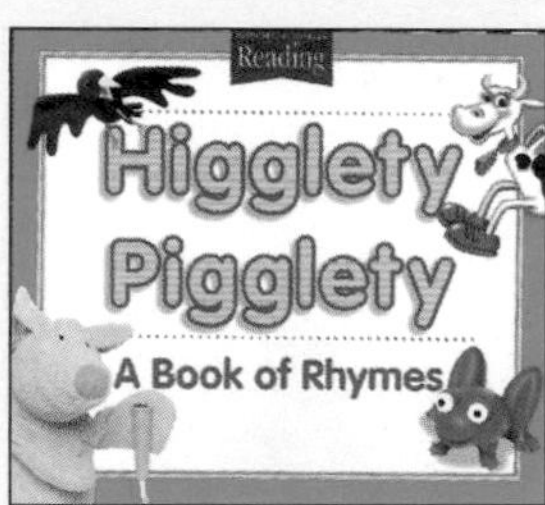

Higglety Pigglety: A Book of Rhymes

Purposes

- oral language development
- phonemic awareness

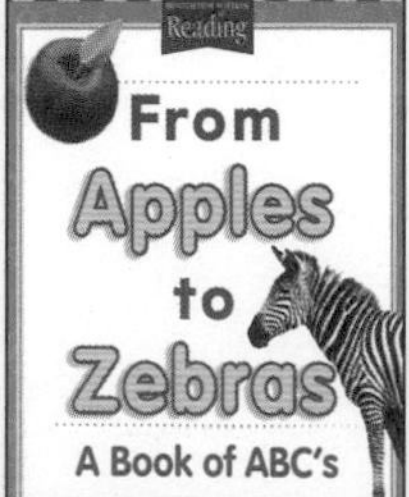

From Apples to Zebras: A Book of ABC's

Purposes

- alphabet recognition
- letters and sounds

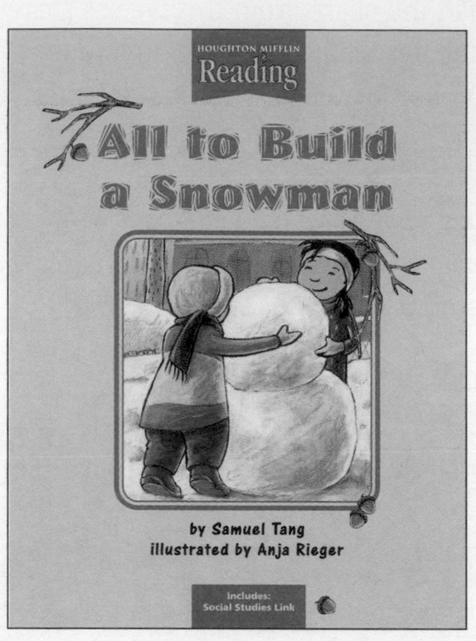

Big Book: Main Selection

Purposes

- concepts of print
- reading strategy
- story language
- comprehension skills

Also available in Little Big Book and audiotape

Leveled Books

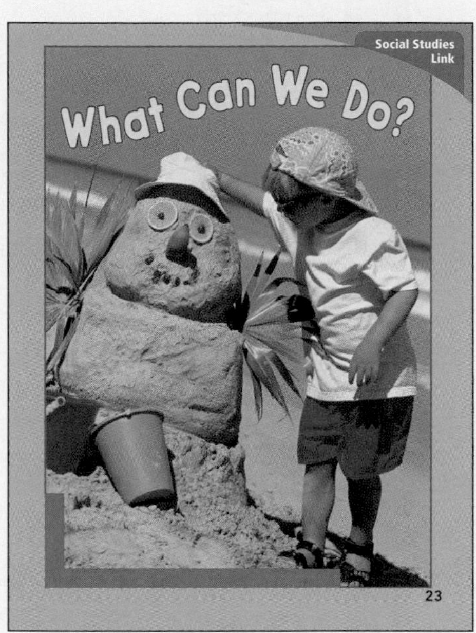

Also in the Big Book:
- Social Studies Link

Purposes

- reading strategies
- comprehension skills
- concepts of print

Phonics Library

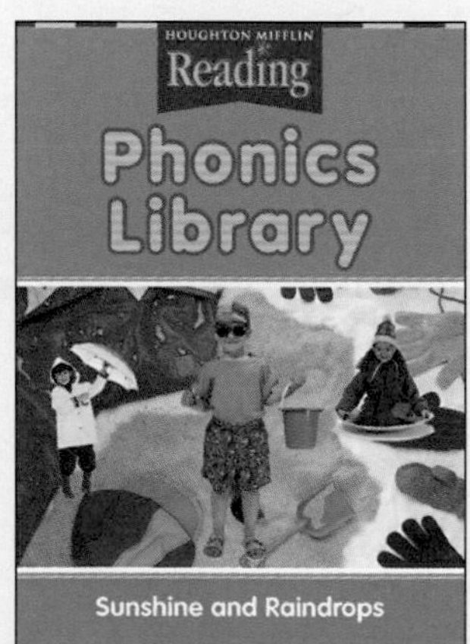

Also available in Take-Home version

Purpose

- applying phonics skills and high-frequency words

On My Way Paperback

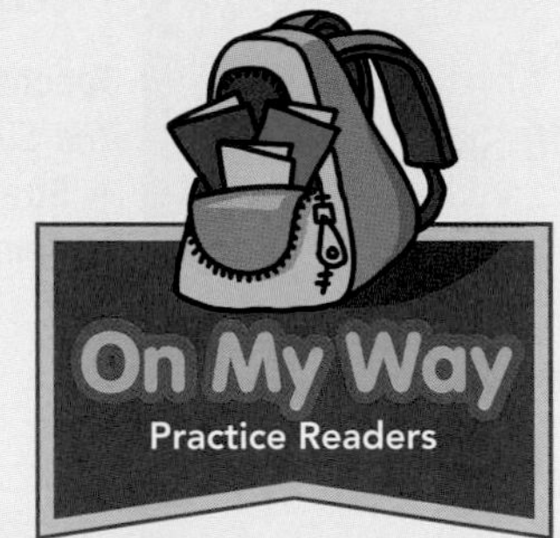

Here, Kit!
by A. J. Cooper
page T153

Little Readers for Guided Reading
Collcction K

Houghton Mifflin Classroom Bookshelf
Level K

www.eduplace.com
Log on to *Education Place* for more activities relating to *Sunshine and Raindrops*.

www.bookadventure.org
This free Internet reading incentive program provides thousands of titles for students to read.

Week 2

Suggested Daily Routines

Instructional Goals	Day 1	Day 2
Learning to Read ✓ *Phonemic Awareness:* Blending and Segmenting Onset and Rime *Strategy Focus:* Summarize ✓ *Comprehension Skill:* Story Structure: Plot ✓ *Phonics Skills* *Phonemic Awareness:* Beginning Sound /k/ Initial Consonant *K, k* *Compare and Review:* Initial Consonants: *k, f, t* ✓ *High-Frequency Word:* here ✓ *Concepts of Print:* Quotation Marks, End Punctuation	**Opening Routines,** *T60–T61* Word Wall • **Phonemic Awareness:** Blending and Segmenting Onset and Rime **Teacher Read Aloud** *The Sun and the Wind, T62–T65* • **Strategy:** Summarize • **Comprehension:** Story Structure: Plot Phonics **Instruction** • Phonemic Awareness, Beginning Sound /k/, *T66–T67; **Practice Book,** 175–176*	**Opening Routines,** *T70–T71* Word Wall • **Phonemic Awareness:** Blending and Segmenting Onset and Rime **Sharing the Big Book** *All to Build a Snowman, T72–T73* • **Strategy:** Summarize • **Comprehension:** Story Structure: Plot Phonics **Instruction, Practice** • Initial Consonant *k, T74–T75* • ***Practice Book,** 177* **High-Frequency Word** • New Word: *here, T76–T77* • ***Practice Book,** 178*
Word Work *High-Frequency Word Practice:* Word Families: *-it, -an, -at*	**High-Frequency Word Practice** • Words: *and, I, is, like, my, to, T68*	**High-Frequency Word Practice** • Building Sentences, *T78*
Writing & Language *Vocabulary Skill:* Using Weather Action Words *Writing Skills:* Weather Observations, A Weather Report	**Oral Language** • Using Weather Action Words, *T69* • Listening and Speaking, *T69*	**Vocabulary Expansion** • Using Weather Action Words, *T79* • Viewing and Speaking, *T79*

✓ = tested skills

Managing Small Groups (Day 1)

Teacher-Led Group
- Reread familiar **Phonics Library** selections

Independent Groups
- Finish ***Practice Book,** 173–176*
- ***Phonics Center:*** Theme 6, Week 2, Day 1
- Book, Dramatic Play, Writing, other Centers

Managing Small Groups (Day 2)

Teacher-Led Group
- Begin ***Practice Book,** 177–178* and handwriting **Blackline Masters 163 or 189.**

Independent Groups
- Finish ***Practice Book,** 177–178* and handwriting **Blackline Masters 163 or 189.**
- ***Phonics Center:*** Theme 6, Week 2, Day 2
- Math, Writing, other Centers

Leveled Books

Have children read in appropriate levels daily.

Phonics Library
On My Way Practice Readers
Little Big Books
Houghton Mifflin Classroom Bookshelf

Lesson Planner CD-ROM: Customize your planning for *Sunshine and Raindrops* with the Lesson Planner.

Day 3

Opening Routines, *T80–T81*

Word Wall

- **Phonemic Awareness:** Blending and Segmenting Onset and Rime

Sharing the Big Book
All to Build a Snowman, T82–T85

- **Strategy:** Summarize
- **Comprehension:** Story Structure: Plot, *T83; **Practice Book,** 179*
- **Concepts of Print:** Quotation Marks, End Punctuation, *T84*

Phonics

Practice, Application

- Review Consonant *k, T88–T89*

Instruction

- Blending *-it, T88–T89; **Practice Book,** 180*
- **Phonics Library:** "Kit," *T89*

Building Words

- Word Family: *-it, T90*

Shared Writing

- Weather Observations, *T91*
- Viewing and Speaking, *T91*

Day 4

Opening Routines, *T92–T93*

Word Wall

- **Phonemic Awareness:** Blending and Segmenting Onset and Rime

Sharing the Big Book
Social Studies Link: "What Can We Do?," *T94–T95*

- **Strategy:** Summarize
- **Comprehension:** Story Structure: Plot
- **Concepts of Print:** End Punctuation

Phonics

Practice

- Review Initial Consonant *k, T96–T97; **Practice Book,** 181*

Building Words

- Word Families: *-it, -an, -at, T98*

Interactive Writing

- A Weather Report, *T99*
- Viewing and Speaking, *T99*

Day 5

Opening Routines, *T100–T101*

Word Wall

- **Phonemic Awareness:** Blending and Segmenting Onset and Rime

Revisiting the Literature
Comprehension: Story Structure: Plot, *T102*
Building Fluency

- **Phonics Library:** "Kit," *T103*

Phonics

Review

- Consonants, Word Families, *T104*

High-Frequency Word Review

- Words: *I, see, my, like, a, to, and, go, is, here, T105; **Practice Book,** 182*

Building Words

- Word Families: *-at, -an, -it, T106*

Independent Writing

- Journals: Weather Report, *T107*

Managing Small Groups (Day 3)

Teacher-Led Group

- Read **Phonics Library** selection "Kit"
- Write letters *l, i;* begin **Blackline Masters 165 or 191.**
- Begin ***Practice Book,*** *179–180*

Independent Groups

- Finish **Blackline Masters 165 or 191** and ***Practice Book,*** *179–180*
- Art, Math, other Centers

Managing Small Groups (Day 4)

Teacher-Led Group

- Reread **Phonics Library** selection "Kit"
- Begin ***Practice Book,*** *181*

Independent Groups

- Finish ***Practice Book,*** *181*
- ***Phonics Center:*** Theme 6, Week 2, Day 4
- Writing, other Centers

Managing Small Groups (Day 5)

Teacher-Led Group

- Reread familiar **Phonics Library** selections
- Begin ***Practice Book,*** *182,* **Blackline Master 36.**

Independent Groups

- Reread **Phonics Library** selections
- Finish ***Practice Book,*** *182,* **Blackline Master 36.**
- Centers

Week 2

Setting up the Centers

Management Tip Children who take a particular interest in the subject may be able to work on independent projects in the Weather Station after they've completed work in the Centers.

Phonics Center

Materials • Phonics Center materials for Theme 6, Week 2

Children make words with the letters *f, k, p,* and the word family *-it* this week. They also build sentences with Word Cards. See pages T67, T75, and T97 for this week's Phonics Center activities.

Book Center

Materials • books of Aesop's fables

Put retellings of Aesop's fables in the Book Center after you've read them aloud. See the Teacher's Note on page T63 for this week's Book Center suggestion.

Once in a Wood: Ten Tales from Aesop *by Eve Rice*
Seven Blind Mice *by Ed Young*
The Lion and the Mouse *by Bernadette Watts*
Two Mice in Three Fables *by Lynn Reiser*

Writing Center

Materials • crayons • markers • lined and unlined writing paper

Children draw a picture of their favorite weather and use action words to write about it. Later they describe and write about weather using more action words. Finally they illustrate a sentence from the class weather report. See pages T69, T79, and T99 for this week's Writing Center activities.

Dramatic Play Center

Materials • large paper sun • "blowing" cloud • overcoat or large wrap

Groups of three children act out *The Sun and the Wind.* See page T63 for this week's Dramatic Play Center activity.

Math Center

Materials • magazines & catalogs • paper • scissors • glue • white paper • circles in three sizes (12-, 8-, 4-inch) • buttons • ribbon or strips of fabric

Children sort pictures by season and paste them onto art paper labeled *Winter, Spring, Summer,* and *Fall.* Later they make snow people using small, medium, and large circles of paper. See pages T73 and T87 for this week's Math Center activities.

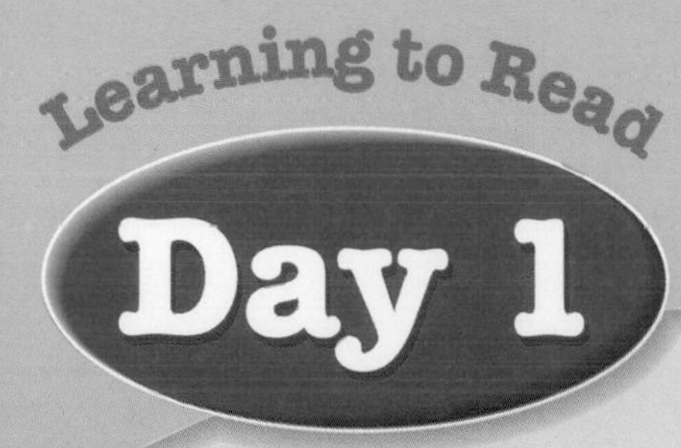

Day at a Glance

Learning to Read

Read Aloud:

The Sun and the Wind

✓ Learning About /k/, *page T66*

Word Work

✓ **High-Frequency Word Practice,** *page T68*

Writing & Language

Oral Language, *page T69*

Half-Day Kindergarten

✓ Indicates lessons for tested skills. Choose additional activities as time allows.

Opening

Calendar

Sunday	Monday	Tuesday	Wednesday	Thursday	Friday	Saturday
			1	2	3	4
5	6	7	8	9	10	11
12	13	14	15	16	17	18
19	20	21	22	23	24	25
26	27	28	29	30	31	

If you have not yet done so, display a thermometer, talk about it, and post it outside a window. Record the temperature next to the calendar each day. Ask: ***Is the temperature warmer* (a higher number) *or cooler* (a lower number) *than yesterday's temperature?***

Daily Message

Interactive Writing Invite children to contribute news to the daily message. They can share the pen to write their own names or familiar words.

Tina found her lost cat. It was staying cool in the basement!

Distribute cards for the posted words. Then have children take turns matching their card to the same word on the Wall, chanting the spelling, and saying the word: **i-s *spells* is.**

Routines

Daily Phonemic Awareness

Blending and Segmenting Onset and Rime

Teach this familiar cheer from sporting events, adapted for word play.

Teacher: *I'll say /r/. You say /ain/.*
I'll say /r/. You say /ain/:
/r/!

Children: */ain/!*

Teacher: */r/!*

Children: */ain/!*

Teacher: *What's the word?*

Children: Rain!

Repeat with other one-syllable words. Then have partners choose a word to segment and take turns leading the cheer.

Getting Ready to Learn

To help plan their day, tell children that they will

- listen to a Read Aloud story called *The Sun and the Wind.*

- meet a new Alphafriend, Keely Kangaroo.

- act out a story in the Dramatic Play Center.

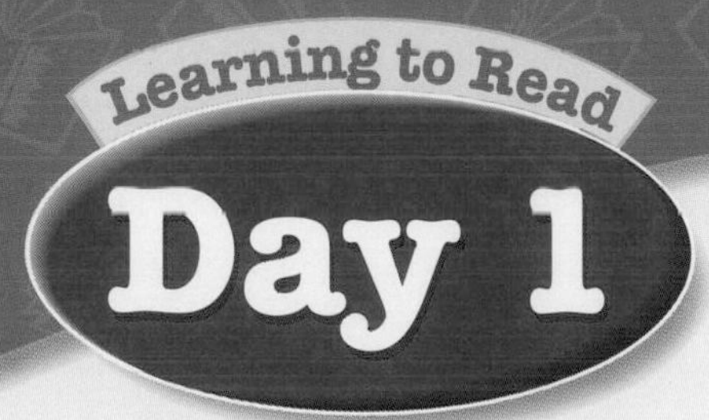

Teacher Read Aloud

Oral Language/Comprehension

Read Aloud

Purposes • oral language • listening strategy • comprehension skill

Selection Summary
In this retelling of Aesop's classic fable, Sun and Wind argue about who is stronger and have a contest to see who can make an unsuspecting traveler remove his cloak.

Key Concepts
Gentle persuasion can be stronger than force.

English Language Learners

Teach the adjective *strong*, and work on making comparisons. Comparatives may be problematic for some children since they vary in different languages. To prepare for the story, review weather vocabulary and the clothes children wear in each kind of weather.

Building Background

Tell children that they're going to hear a story called *The Sun and the Wind.* ***Which do you think is stronger, the sun or the wind? Why?***

Strategy: Summarize

Teacher Modeling Explain that *summarizing,* or thinking about the important parts of a story, is a good way to remember it and retell it.

Think Aloud

When I summarize as I read, I make a "thinking list" of the important things along the way: the characters and where the story takes place, and what happens in the beginning, the middle, and the end. Let's think about those parts of this story to help us summarize it in our own words later.

Comprehension Focus: Story Structure: Plot

Teacher Modeling Explain that in many stories, the characters have a problem they want to solve.

Think Aloud

When I read, I think about the problem the characters have at the beginning of the story and how they try to solve it. Those are two more important things to mention when I tell someone about the story.

Listening to the Story

As you read, change your voice to emphasize the gruffness of the wind and the steady patience of the sun. Note that the Read Aloud art is also available on the back of the Theme Poster.

Responding

Summarizing the Story Tell children you'll help them summarize the story:

- ***Who are the characters in this story?***
- ***What problem did Sun and Wind have? What did they do to solve it?***
- ***Who won the contest? How?***
- ***Do you think Sun and Wind will have another contest? Why do you think that?***
- ***What did you like best about the story?***

Practice Book pages 173–174 Children will complete the pages during small group time.

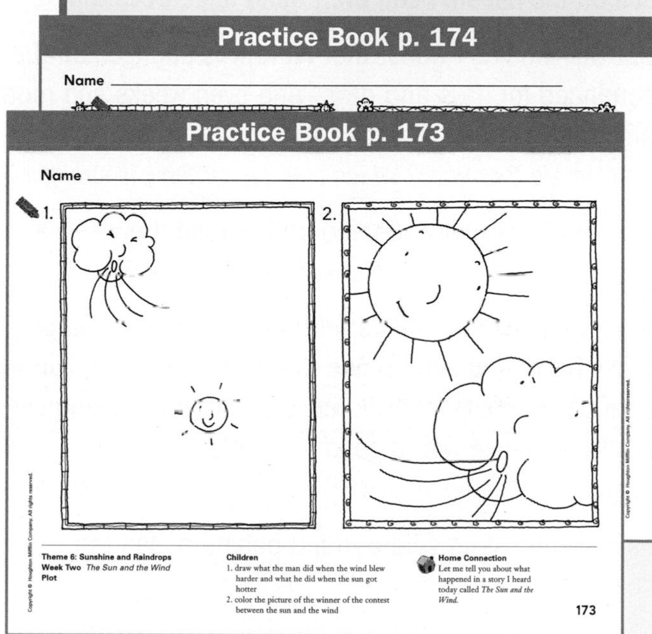

Practice Book p. 174

Name ______________________

Practice Book p. 173

Name ______________________

1. 2.

Theme 6: Sunshine and Raindrops
Week Two *The Sun and the Wind*
Plot

Children
1. draw what the man did when the wind blew harder and what he did when the sun got hotter
2. color the picture of the winner of the contest between the sun and the wind

Home Connection
Let me tell you about what happened in a story I heard today called *The Sun and the Wind.*

173

At Group Time

Dramatic Play Center

Have groups of three work together to act out the story. Provide a large paper sun and a "blowing" cloud for Sun and Wind to hold, and an overcoat or other large wrap for the Traveler.

Teacher's Note

Tell children that *The Sun and the Wind* is a fable, a story that teaches a lesson. Share the moral with children and discuss its meaning: "Gentle persuasion is often stronger than force." Children may enjoy hearing other fables.

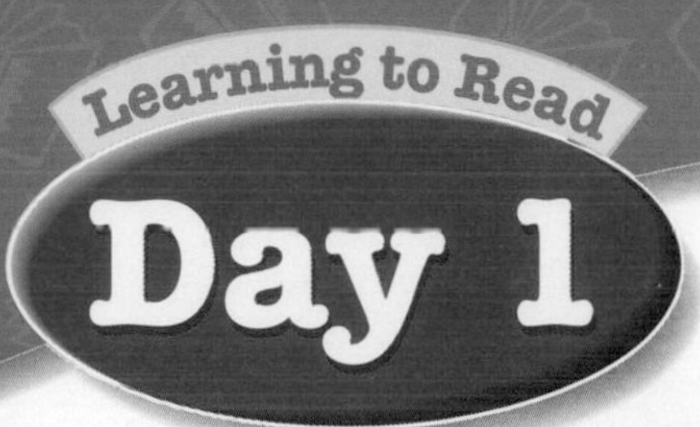

The Sun and the Wind

An Aesop's Fable

Long, long ago, when people thought such things could happen, Sun and Wind had an argument. Each one thought it was stronger than the other. So their argument went on and on, for a very long time.

"I'm stronger," said Sun, "because I can make plants and flowers and trees grow. I can even chase clouds away."

"Oh, that's nothing," bragged Wind. "I'm so strong I help huge ships sail on the ocean. I can even bend large trees with my breath."

But Sun wouldn't admit that Wind was stronger. So the argument continued for days and days—and even weeks and months—without any sign of stopping. **(Ask:** *Who are the characters in this story? What problem do they have? Which one do you think is stronger?***)**

One day a traveler appeared on the road. He was walking slowly and wearing a great, heavy cloak. And that gave Wind an idea.

"Ah, I think I know how to find out just who is stronger," Wind said. "Let's have a contest to find out which one of us can make that man take off his coat. That will prove which of us is stronger." Sun agreed that the contest was a good idea. **(Say:** *Oh, now the characters will try to solve their problem. How? Who do you think will win? Why?***)**

"You go first," Sun said and hid behind a cloud to watch what Wind could do.

Wind blew a mighty gust toward the traveler. *Whoooooosh.* The man ducked his head down a bit and held on tightly to his hat. But he didn't take off his heavy cloak. In fact, he pulled it even closer to him. So Wind filled its cheeks with cold, blustery air again and blew even harder. *Whoooooosh!* The back of the heavy cloak flapped straight out behind the man. He stopped, fastened up all his buttons, and turned up his collar—but he didn't take off his cloak. **(Ask:** *Is the problem solved yet? Why not?***)**

By now, Wind was almost out of breath. Sun came from behind the cloud and quietly said, "My turn." **(Ask:** *What do you think Sun will do?***)** Sun began to shine gently. The traveler was glad to feel the warmth—first on his head, and then on his back. Soon he took off his hat. After a moment, he loosened his collar. But Sun just burned hotter. Soon, the man unbuttoned his buttons. And finally, when the Sun was at its highest in the sky, the traveler mopped his forehead with a great, white handkerchief, fanned his face with his floppy hat, and—with a loud sigh—took off his great, heavy cloak.

At that, Wind finally had to admit that Sun had won the contest—at least *this* time! **(Ask:** *What did Sun and Wind decide about who was stronger? Do you think they'll argue again? Why? Retell the important parts of this story in your own words.***)**

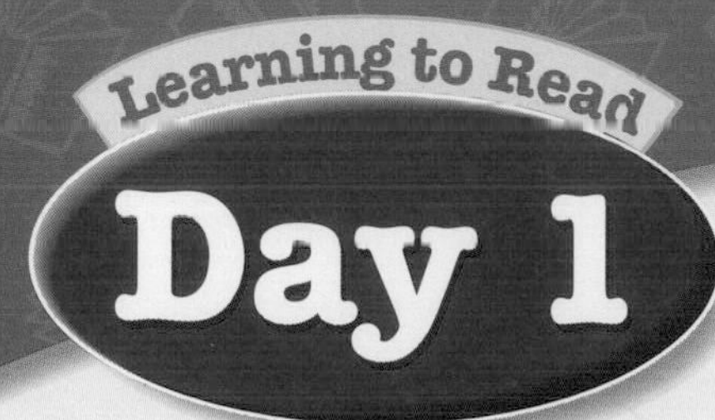

OBJECTIVES

Children

- identify pictures whose names begin with /k/

MATERIALS

- **Alphafriend Cards** *Fifi Fish, Keely Kangaroo, Tiggy Tiger*
- **Alphafriend Audiotape** Theme 6
- **Alphafolder** *Keely Kangaroo*
- **Picture Cards** for *f, k, t*
- **Phonics Center:** Theme 6, Week 2, Day 1

Home Connection

A **take-home version** of Keely Kangaroo's Song is on an **Alphafriends Blackline Master.** Children can share the song with their families.

English Language Learners

Display pictures of objects that begin with /k/. As you say the words, exaggerate the sound and have children put their hands in front of their mouths to feel the air exhaling.

Phonemic Awareness

Beginning Sound

Introducing the Alphafriend: Keely Kangaroo

Use the Alphafriend routine to introduce Keely Kangaroo.

1. **Alphafriend Riddle** Read these clues:
   - *This Alphafriend is an animal. Her sound is /k/. Say it with me: /k/.*
   - *This animal can hop and kick with her big feet and strong legs.*
   - *She keeps her baby in a pouch or a pocket.*

   When most hands are up, call on children until they guess *kangaroo.*

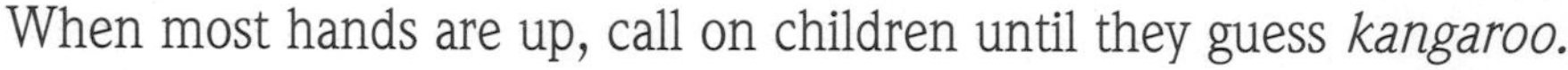

2. **Pocket Chart** Display Keely Kangaroo in the pocket chart. Say her name, exaggerating the /k/ sound slightly, and have children echo.
3. **Alphafriend Audiotape** Play Keely Kangaroo's song. Listen for words that start with /k/.
4. **Alphafolder** Have children look at the illustration and name the /k/ pictures.
5. **Summarize**
   - *What is our Alphafriend's name? What is her sound?*
   - *What words in our Alphafriend's song start with /k/?*
   - *Each time you look at Keely Kangaroo this week, remember the /k/ sound.*

Keely Kangaroo
(Tune: The Farmer in the Dell)

Keely Kangaroo
And Keely's kiddie, too,
Will fly a kite and kick
a ball
And play a big kazoo.

Listening for /k/

Compare and Review: /f/, /t/ Display Alphafriends *Fifi Fish* and *Tiggy Tiger* opposite *Keely Kangaroo.* Review each character's sound.

Tell children you'll name some pictures and they should signal "thumbs up" for each one that begins like Keely's name. Volunteers put those cards below Keely's picture. For "thumbs down" words, volunteers put the cards below the correct Alphafriends.

Pictures: *key, fork, king, ten, feet, kite, fox, tooth, kiss, toys*

Tell children they will sort more pictures today in the Phonics Center.

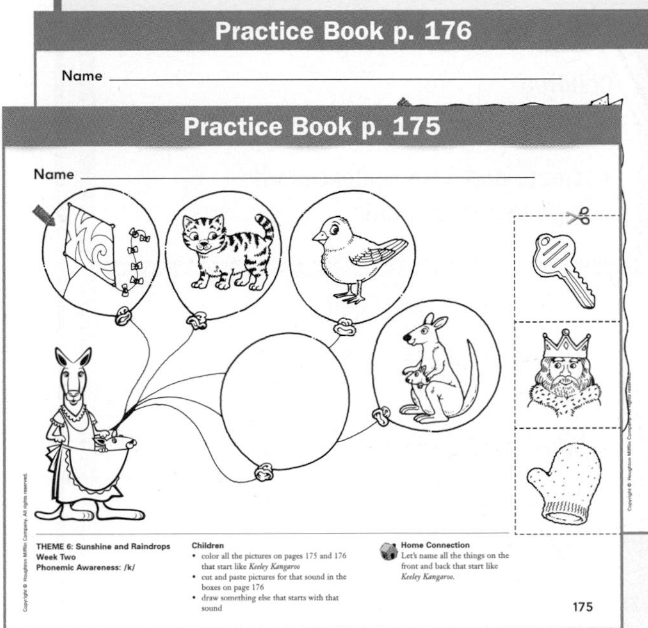

Practice Book p. 176

Name

Practice Book p. 175

Name

THEME 6: Sunshine and Raindrops
Week Two
Phonemic Awareness: /k/

Children
- color all the pictures on pages 175 and 176 that start like *Keeley Kangaroo*
- cut and paste pictures for that sound in the boxes on page 176
- draw something else that starts with that sound

Home Connection
Let's name all the things on the front and back that start like *Keeley Kangaroo.*

175

Apply

Practice Book pages 175–176 Children will complete the pages at small group time.

Use the Phonics Center materials for **Theme 6, Week 2, Day 1.**

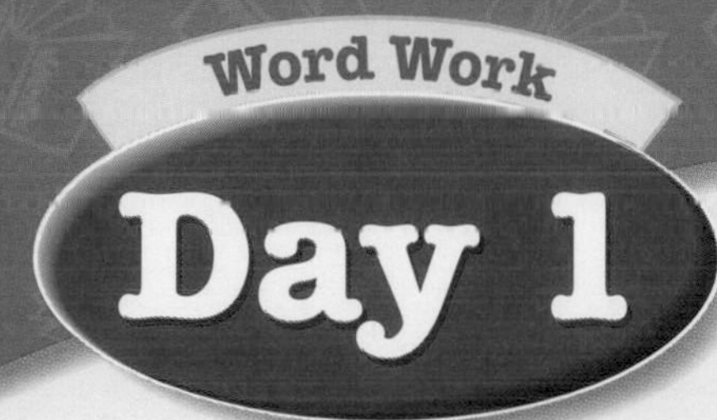

High-Frequency Word Practice

OBJECTIVES

Children

- read high-frequency words
- create and write sentences with high-frequency words

MATERIALS

- ***Higglety Pigglety: A Book of Rhymes,*** page 6
- **Word Cards** *and, I, is, like, My, to*
- **Picture Cards** *dig, dog, white*
- **Punctuation Card:** period

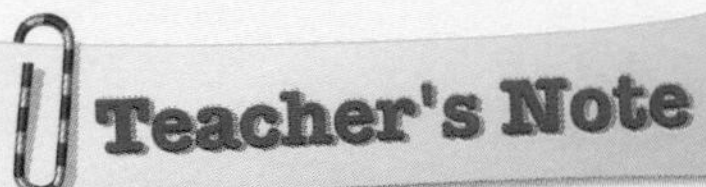

Prepare cards for *dig* and *tan* for the sentence building activity.

Matching Words

- Display cards for the high-frequency words *and, I, like, my, is,* and *to* in a pocket chart. Call on children to identify each word and to match it on the Word Wall.
- Remind children that these are words they often see in books. Read "Everybody Says" on page 6 of *Higglety Pigglety,* asking children to nod when they hear any of the words.

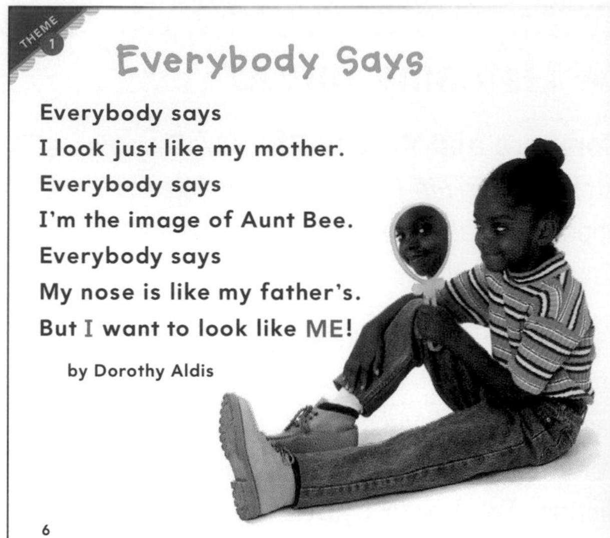

THEME 1

Everybody Says

Everybody says
I look just like my mother.
Everybody says
I'm the image of Aunt Bee.
Everybody says
My nose is like my father's.
But I want to look like ME!

by Dorothy Aldis

6

***Higglety Pigglety: A Book of Rhymes,* page 6**

- Distribute the cards. Reread the poem line for line, asking children to match their cards to the same ones in the poem. Children will match *I, like, my, is,* and *to.*

Writing Opportunity Add the word cards *dig* and *tan* to the pocket chart, along with the other cards listed in Materials, and have children build sentences. To start children off, use the ones shown. Then have each child write and illustrate a sentence that uses at least one of the words on the cards.

DAY 1

Oral Language

Using Weather Action Words

Listening and Speaking Remind children that *action* words are names for movements. Explain that today they will think about action words that help tell about the weather.

- Together, recall *The Sun and the Wind*. Have children think about what Sun and Wind do to try to make the man take off his coat. List their suggestions on chart paper.
- Brainstorm addtional action words for Sun and Wind. Then add *Rain* to the chart. Prompt children as needed to think of appropriate action words: ***What can rain do on a window? What can rain do on the streets?***
- As children suggest words, have them use the words in oral sentences. Explain that later in the week, they will use words like these to write a weather report.

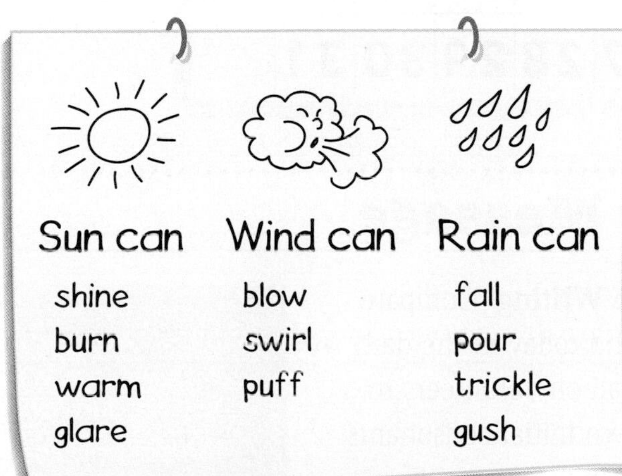

Sun can
shine
burn
warm
glare
Wind can
blow
swirl
puff
Rain can
fall
pour
trickle
gush

Put the chart in the Writing Center. Children can draw a picture of their favorite weather and use action words to write about it.

OBJECTIVES

Children

- use action words for types of weather

Portfolio Opportunity

Save children's writing samples to show their use of action words and the conventions of print.

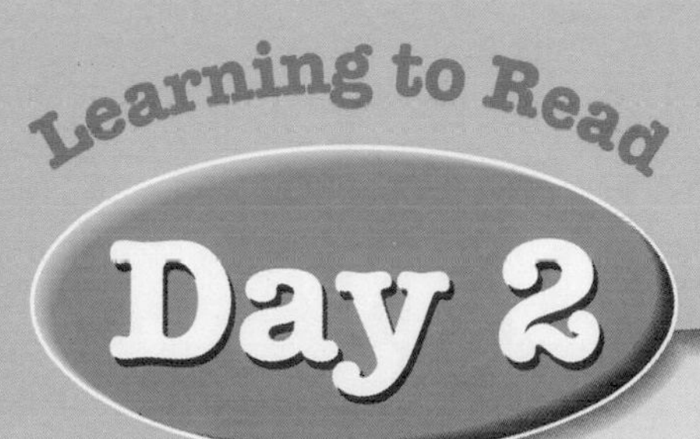

Day at a Glance

Learning to Read

Big Book:

All to Build a Snowman

- ✓ **Phonics: Initial Consonant *k*,** *page T74*
- ✓ **High-Frequency Word: *here*,** *page T76*

Word Work

High-Frequency Word Practice, *page T78*

Writing & Language

Vocabulary Expansion, *page T79*

Half-Day Kindergarten

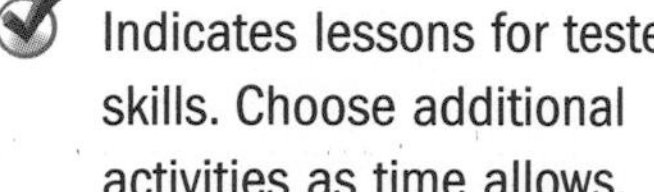

✓ Indicates lessons for tested skills. Choose additional activities as time allows.

Opening

Calendar

Sunday	Monday	Tuesday	Wednesday	Thursday	Friday	Saturday
			1	2	3	4
5	6	7	8	9	10	11
12	13	14	15	16	17	18
19	20	21	22	23	24	25
26	27	28	29	30	31	

After conducting the calendar routine, record the outside temperature. ***Is the number higher or lower than it was yesterday? Does that mean it is warmer or colder outside?***

Daily Message

Interactive Writing Compare yesterday and today in the daily message. Call on volunteers to supply known initial consonants and to spell high-frequency words.

Yesterday we read about the sun and the wind. Today we will read about snow.

Recall that the words on the Word Wall are in ABC order. ***I will say the alphabet, and you raise your hand when I come to a letter that begins a word on the wall. A... Yes, there are four words that begin with a. Who will point to them and read them?*** Continue with the other words.

Routines

Daily Phonemic Awareness
Blending and Segmenting Onset and Rime

Display the following Picture Cards in random order: fan, *fox, gate, goat, hat, hand, king, kiss, ten, top.* Then use the cheer from yesterday to name each picture.

Teacher:	*I'll say /g/. You say /oat/.*
	I'll say /g/. You say /oat/.
	/g/!
Children:	*/oat/!*
Teacher:	*/g/!*
Children:	*/oat/!*
Teacher:	*What's the word?*
Children:	Goat!

Have partners think of a word to segment and take turns leading the cheer.

Getting Ready to Learn

To help plan their day, tell children that they will

- listen to a Big Book: *All to Build a Snowman.*
- learn the new letters *K* and *k,* and sort words that begin with *k.*
- sort and categorize seasonal items in the Math Center.

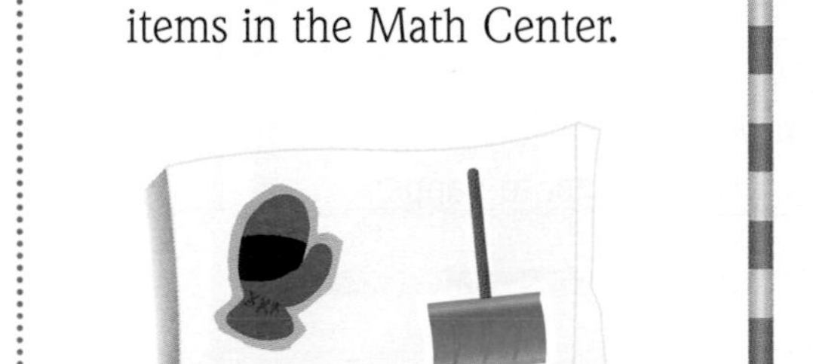

Reading
All to Build a Snowman
by Samuel Tang
Illustrated by Anja Rieger

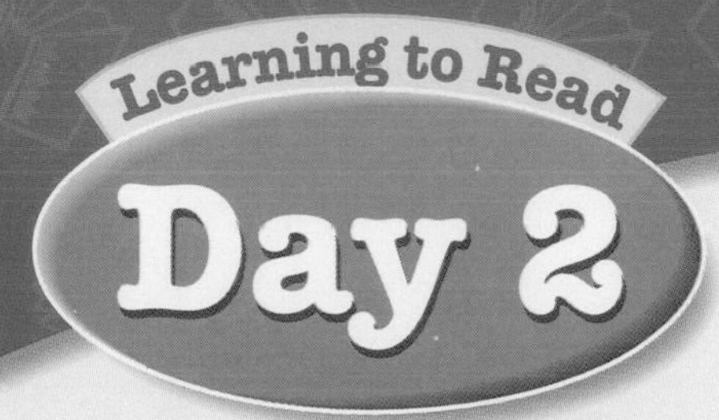

Sharing the Big Book

Oral Language/Comprehension

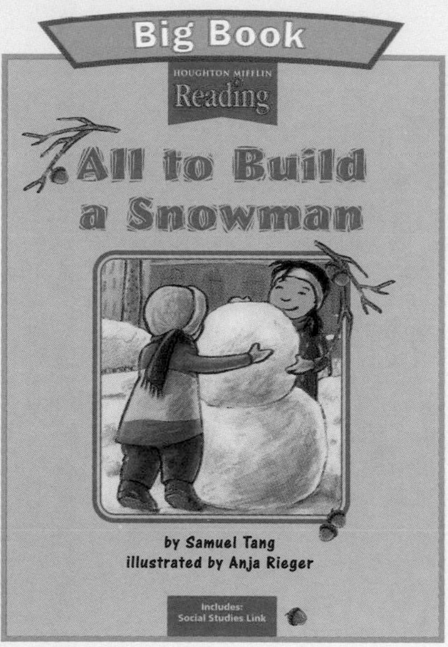

Purposes • concepts of print • story language • reading strategy • comprehension skill

Selection Summary

Kim and Tim and their dog Slim go to the park to build a snowman. A series of surprising mishaps provides them with just what they need—twigs, acorns, a pine cone, a hat, and a scarf—to finish their snowman in style.

Key Concepts

How to build a snowman
One event often causes another to happen

Building Background

Read aloud the title and the names of the author and illustrator. Ask children what they know about building snowmen. Encourage children who have built snowmen to tell how they added faces or decorations.

Strategy: Summarize

Teacher Modeling Read the first page of the story, and then model the Summarize Strategy:

Think Aloud

To summarize means to tell a story in your own words. Here's how I do it. To start, I think about the characters and what they do. So far, I know that Kim and Tim are important characters and they want to build a snowman. As we read, let's see what happens when they do.

Comprehension Focus: Story Structure: Plot

Teacher Modeling Remind children that characters in a story often have a problem they want to solve. How the characters solve the problem is called the *plot.*

Think Aloud

As we read, we'll see if Kim and Tim have a problem building the snowman. If they do, we'll remember to watch for how they solve the problems as we read. These are also important things to mention when we summarize the story later.

Sharing the Story

Read the selection, emphasizing the rhythm and rhyme. Track the print with a pointer or your finger as you read. Pause for children to examine the cause and effect events in the pictures.

Responding

Personal Response Help children name the important characters and events in the story. Then use these prompts to get their response to the selection:

- ***What did you like best about the story?***
- ***Do you think a story like this could really happen? Why or why not?***
- ***Would you like to build a snowman?***

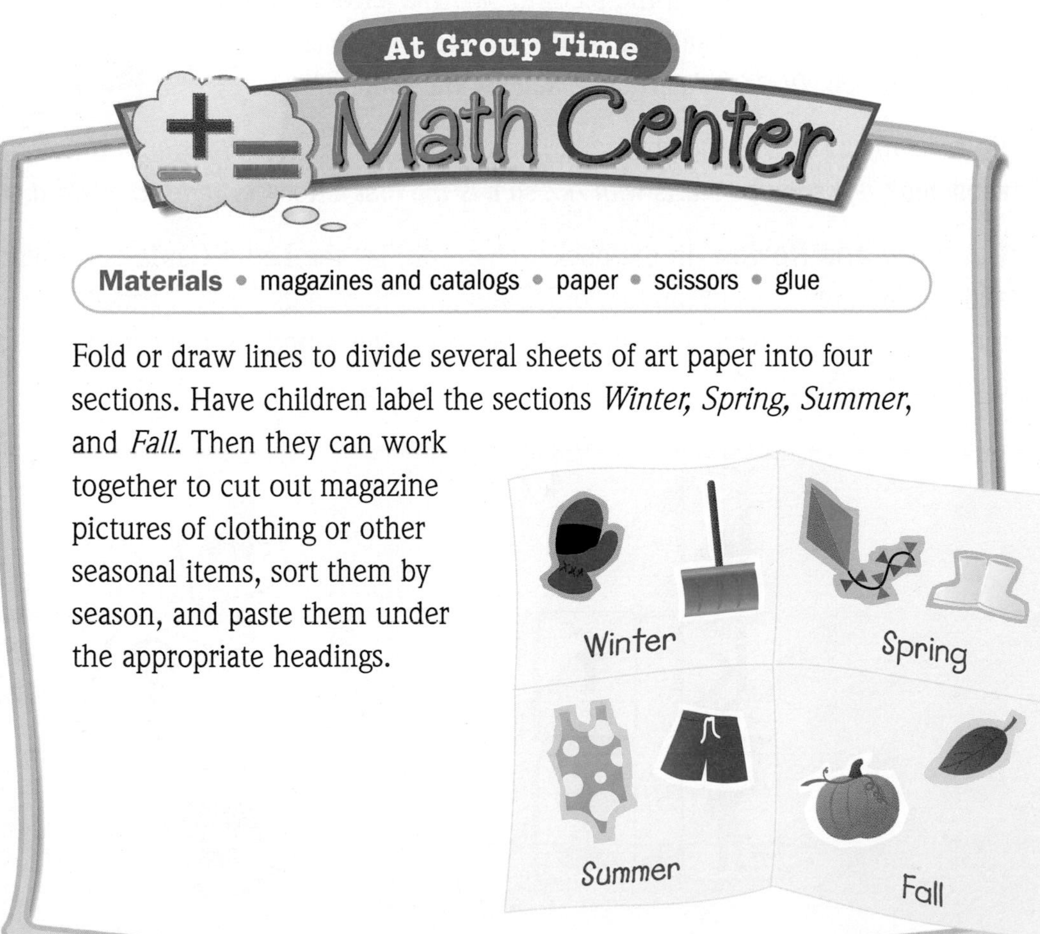

Materials • magazines and catalogs • paper • scissors • glue

Fold or draw lines to divide several sheets of art paper into four sections. Have children label the sections *Winter, Spring, Summer,* and *Fall.* Then they can work together to cut out magazine pictures of clothing or other seasonal items, sort them by season, and paste them under the appropriate headings.

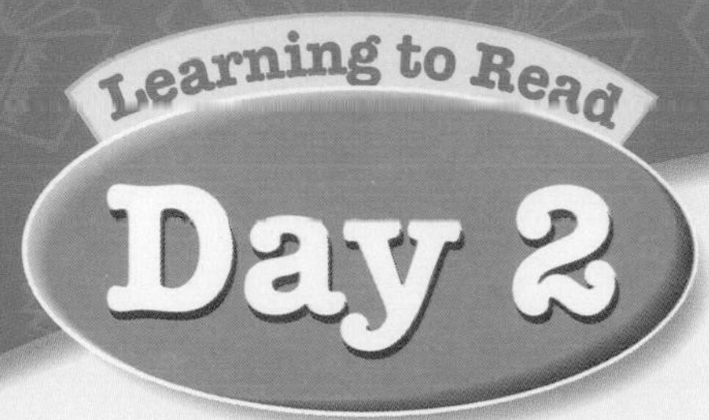

Phonics

Initial Consonant k

OBJECTIVES

Children

- identify words that begin with /k/
- identify pictures whose names start with the letter *k*
- form the letters *K, k*

MATERIALS

- **Alphafriend Card** *Keely Kangaroo*
- **Letter Cards** *f, k, t*
- **Picture Cards** for *f, k, t*
- **Blackline Master:** 176
- **Phonics Center:** Theme 6, Week 2, Day 2

Develop Phonemic Awareness

Beginning Sound Read or sing the lyrics of Keely Kangaroo's song, and have children echo it line-for-line. Have them listen for the /k/ words and blow a "kiss" for each one.

Keely Kangaroo
(Tune: The Farmer in the Dell)

Keely Kangaroo
And Keely's kiddie, too,
Will fly a kite and kick
a ball
And play a big kazoo.

Connect Sounds to Letters

Beginning Letter Display the *Keely Kangaroo* card, and have children name the letter on the picture. Say: ***The letter* k *stands for the sound /k/, as in* kangaroo. *When you see a* k, *remember* Keely Kangaroo. *That will help you remember the sound /k/.***

Write *kangaroo* on the board. Underline the *k*. ***What is the first letter in the word* kangaroo?** *(k)* **Kangaroo *starts with /k/, so* k *is the first letter I write for that word.***

Compare and Review In the pocket chart, display the Letter Cards as shown and the Picture Cards in random order. Review the sounds for *k, f,* and *t*. In turn, children can name a picture, say the beginning sound, and put the card below the right letter.

Tell children they will sort more pictures today in the Phonics Center.

Extra Support (Meeting Individual Needs)

To help children remember the sound for *k*, point out that Keely Kangaroo has a kiddie. Saying these words will help them remember /k/.

Handwriting

Writing *K, k* Tell children that now they'll learn to write the letters that stand for /k/: capital *K* and small *k*. Write each letter as you recite the handwriting rhyme. Chant each rhyme as children "write" the letter in the air.

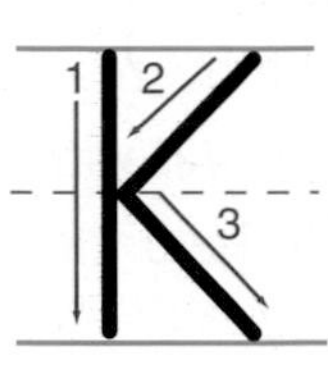

Handwriting Rhyme: K

Make one line,
a tall straight stick.
Add one arm in a wave
and one leg in a kick:
That's *K* big *K*, big *K*!

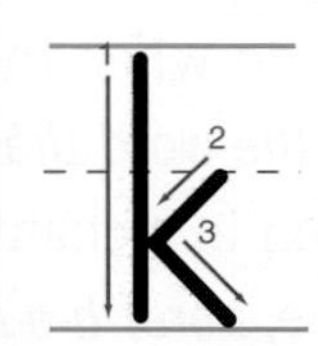

Handwriting Rhyme: k

Make one line,
a tall straight stick.
Now add a little kick.
That's a *k*, a small *k*,
a small *k*!

Apply

Practice Book page 177 Children will complete the page at small group time.

Blackline Master 167 This page provides additional handwriting practice for small group time.

Use the Phonics Center materials for **Theme 6, Week 2, Day 2.**

Practice Book p. 177

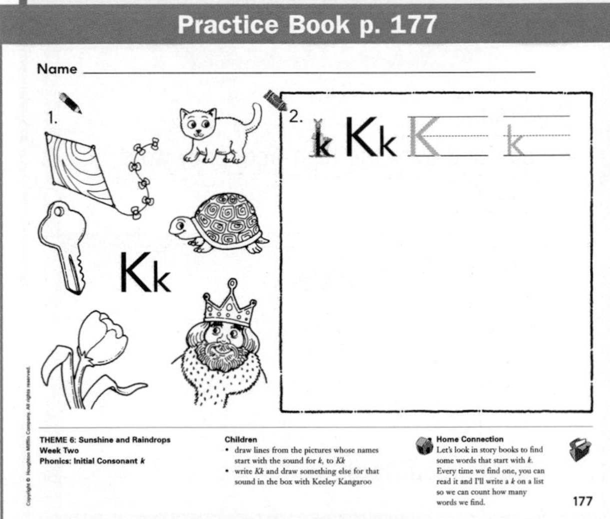

Name ______

1.

Kk

2. k Kk K k

THEME 6: Sunshine and Raindrops
Week Two
Phonics: Initial Consonant *k*

Children
- draw lines from the pictures whose names start with the sound for *k*, to *Kk*
- write *Kk* and draw something else for that sound in the box with Keeley Kangaroo

Home Connection
Let's look in story books to find some words that start with *k*. Every time we find one, you can read it and I'll write a *k* on a list so we can count how many words we find.

177

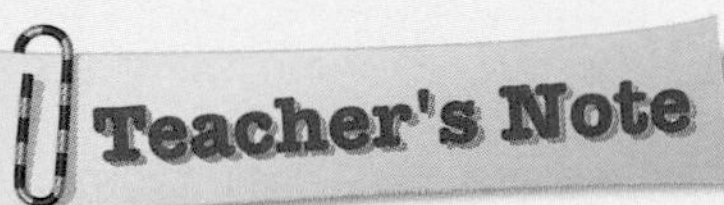

Handwriting practice for the continuous stroke style is available on **Blackline Master 193.**

Portfolio Opportunity

Save the **Practice Book** page to show children's grasp of the letter-sound association.

Save **Blackline Master 167** for a handwriting sample.

DAY 2

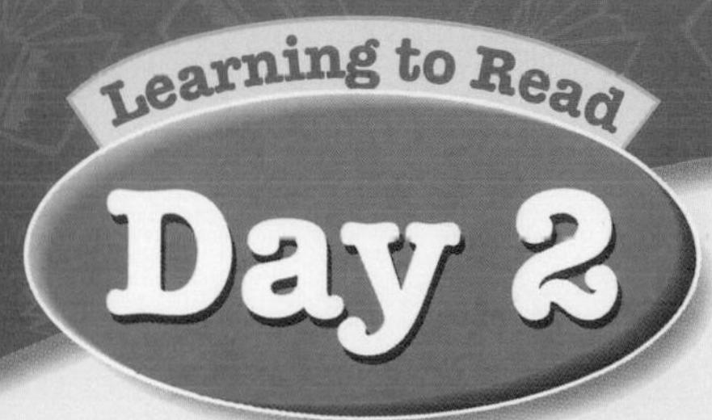

High-Frequency Word

New Word: here

OBJECTIVES

Children

- read and write the high-frequency word *here.*

MATERIALS

- **Word Cards** *a, and, here, Here, I, is, see*
- **Picture Cards** *cat, cow, dog, farm, goat, hen, horse, pig*
- **Punctuation Card:** period

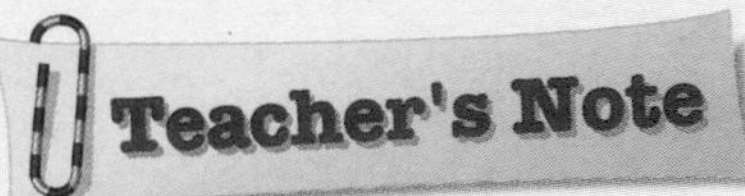

Prepare the word cards *at* and *can* for the sentence reading activity.

Teach

Tell children that today they will learn to read and write a word that they will often see in stories. Say *here* and use it in context.

Here is my nose. Bring the books over *here.* Ready or not, *here* I come.

Explain that *here* names a place nearby and is spelled differently than the word *hear* that tells what children do when they listen. Write *here* on the board. Say: ***This is the way we spell* here, *the word that names a place close by. Spell it with me,* h-e-r-e, here.** Lead children in a chant, clapping on each beat, to help them remember the spelling: ***h-e-r-e, here! h-e-r-e, here!***

Post *here* on the Word Wall, and remind children to look there when they need to remember how to write the word.

Practice

Reading Build the following sentences in the pocket chart. Children can take turns reading. Then place the pocket chart in the Phonics Center along with additional Picture Cards so that children can practice building and reading their own sentences.

Write the words for the song "Where Is Thumbkin?" on chart paper.

- Share the rhyme with children. Invite those children who know the song to sing it and perform the hand motions.
- Then read the words again, tracking the print with your hand. Have children point to the word *Here* when you come to it. Then ask volunteers to go back and frame the word with their hands while classmates spell it.

"Where is Thumbkin?"

Where is Thumbkin?
Where is Thumbkin?
Here I am.
Here I am.
How are you today, sir?
Very well, I thank you.
Run away, run away.

Apply

Practice Book page 178 Children will read and write *here* as they complete the Practice Book page. On Day 3, they will practice reading *here* in the **Phonics Library** story "Kit."

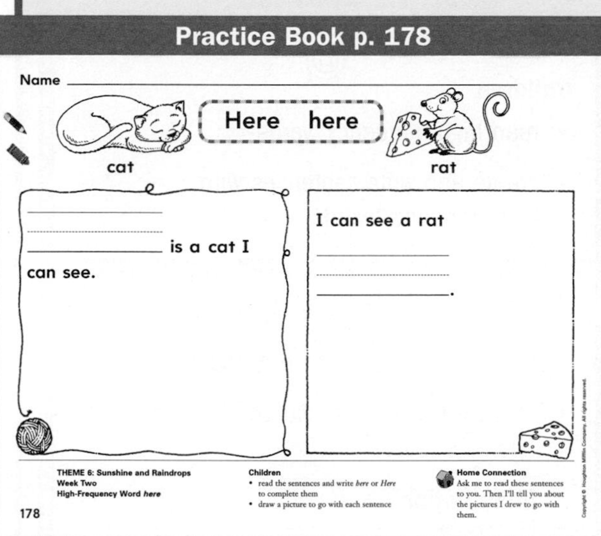

Practice Book p. 178

Name ______

Here here

cat

rat

______ is a cat I can see.

I can see a rat ______.

THEME 6: Sunshine and Raindrops
Week Two
High-Frequency Word *here*

178

Children
- read the sentences and write *here* or *Here* to complete them
- draw a picture to go with each sentence

Home Connection
Ask me to read these sentences to you. Then I'll tell you about the pictures I drew to go with them.

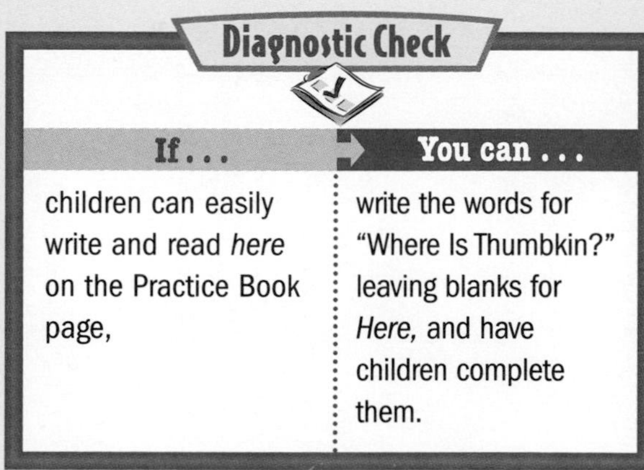

Diagnostic Check

If . . .	You can . . .
children can easily write and read *here* on the Practice Book page,	write the words for "Where Is Thumbkin?" leaving blanks for *Here,* and have children complete them.

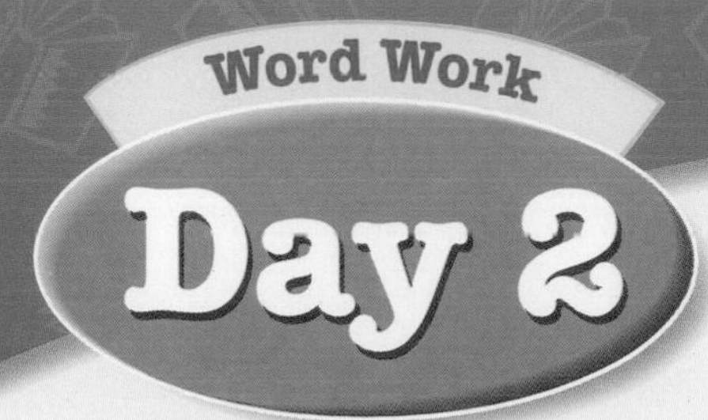

High-Frequency Word Practice

Building Sentences

Tell children that you want to build a riddle with word cards. Explain that the riddle tells about a place where people can go.

- Display the word cards in random order. Put the Word Card *I* in the pocket chart, and read it.
- ***I want the next word to be* can. *Who can find that word? That's right! This word is* can. *Now who can read my sentence so far?***
- Continue building *I can go here to see a* _____. Children choose an animal picture card for the blank.
- Read the completed riddle with children. Then call on volunteers to name the place where they could see the pictured animal. Examples: *I can see a lion at a zoo; I can see a horse at a farm.*

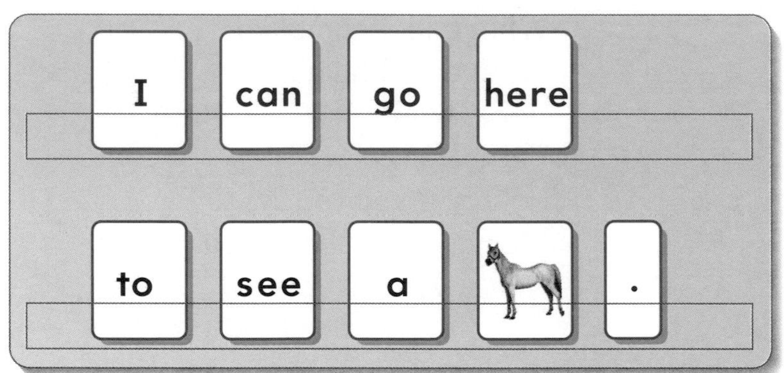

Writing Opportunity Have children think of their own riddle and illustrate the answer. They can lable their pictures using the words in the pocket chart.

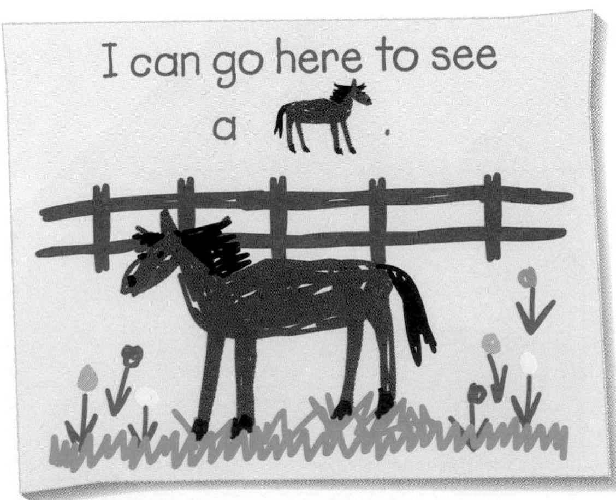

OBJECTIVES

Children

- read high-frequency words
- create and write sentences with high-frequency words

MATERIALS

- **Word Cards** *a, go, here, I, see, to*
- **Picture Cards** *goat, horse, lion, pig, seal, tiger, yak, zebra*
- **Punctuation Card:** period

For this activity, you will need to prepare the word card *can.*

Vocabulary Expansion

Using Weather Action Words

Viewing and Speaking Display and review the chart children developed during yesterday's vocabulary skill lesson. (See page T69.)

- Then brainstorm other types of weather or weather-related words. Add them to the chart.
- Now have children think of appropriate action words for each type of weather. As needed, use prompts: ***How does light, fluffy snow come down? How do hard, icy clusters of snowflakes come down?***

Put the chart in the Writing Center. Partners can take turns choosing one type of weather, describing it with appropriate action words, and asking the other child to guess the weather. Together they can write about their choices.

OBJECTIVES

Children

- use action words for types of weather

Portfolio Opportunity

Save children's writing samples as an indication of their expanding vocabulary skills.

Meeting Individual Needs — English Language Learners

Help children understand nuances in meaning among the action words, especially for weather that does not occur in your area. As you talk about things snow can do, for example, have English speaking-children act out what you describe. Share also photos that help to depict different action: a blizzard, snowdrifting, heavy snow hanging on trees, and so on.

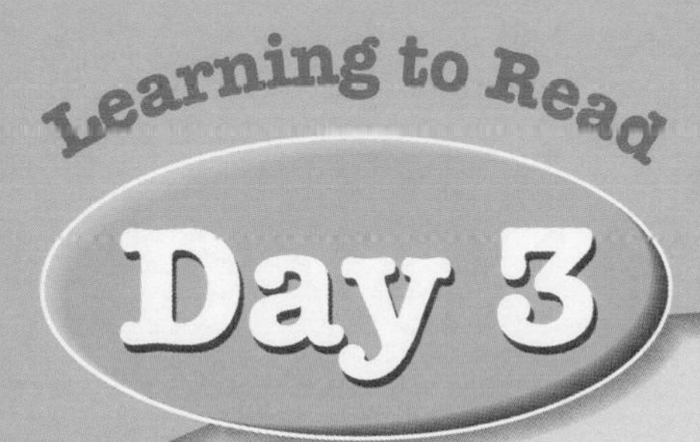

Opening

Calendar

Sunday	Monday	Tuesday	Wednesday	Thursday	Friday	Saturday
			1	2	3	4
5	6	7	8	9	10	11
12	13	14	15	16	17	18
19	20	21	22	23	24	25
26	27	28	29	30	31	

After recording the day's temperature, tell children that the temperature is usually part of a weather report. Explain that a *weather report* tells what the weather is like. Ask children why people listen to a weather report. ***Why would people want to know the temperature?***

Daily Message

Interactive Writing Compare yesterday and today in the daily message. Call on volunteers to supply known initial consonants and to spell high-frequency words.

Yesterday was cold
and windy.
Today is sunny.
Today we will write
a weather report.

Have children take turns finding Word Wall words with a pointer as you call them out.

Day at a Glance

Learning to Read

Big Book:

All to Build a Snowman

 **Phonics: Blending *k* *–it*, *page T88***

Word Work

Building Words, *page T90*

Writing & Language

Shared Writing, *page T91*

 **Half-Day Kindergarten**

 Indicates lessons for tested skills. Choose additional activities as time allows.

Routines

Daily Phonemic Awareness
Blending and Segmenting Onset and Rime

- Read "Rainy Day" on page 13.
- Play a guessing game. ***I'll say some words. You put them together to make words from the poem: /d/ /ay/*** (*day*); ***/w/ /et/*** (*wet*); ***/r/ /oad/*** (*road*).
- Continue with other one-syllable words or names of children.
- ***Now I'll say a word and you take it apart:* sun. *Say the beginning sound and then the rest of the word.*** (/s/ /un/); **me** (/m/ /ē/); **like** (/l/ /ike/).
- Continue with other one-syllable words or names of children.

Rainy Day

I do not like a rainy day.
The road is wet, the sky is gray.
They dress me up, from head to toes,
In lots and lots of rubber clothes.
I wish the sun would come and stay.
I do not like a rainy day.

by William Wise

13

***Higglety Pigglety: A Book of Rhymes,* page 13.**

Getting Ready to Learn

To help plan their day, tell children that they will

- reread and talk about the Big Book: *All to Build a Snowman.*

- read a story called "Kit."

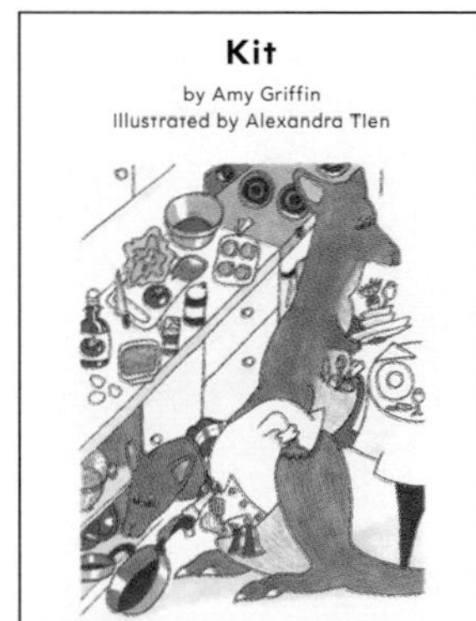

- follow directions to build a snowman in the Math Center.

DAY 3

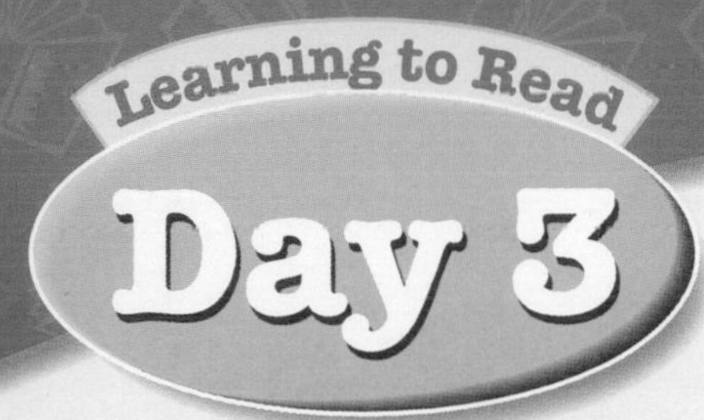
Learning to Read
Day 3

Sharing the Big Book

OBJECTIVES

Children

- recognize story plot
- recognize the purpose of quotation marks
- tell what a period and an exclamation point signify

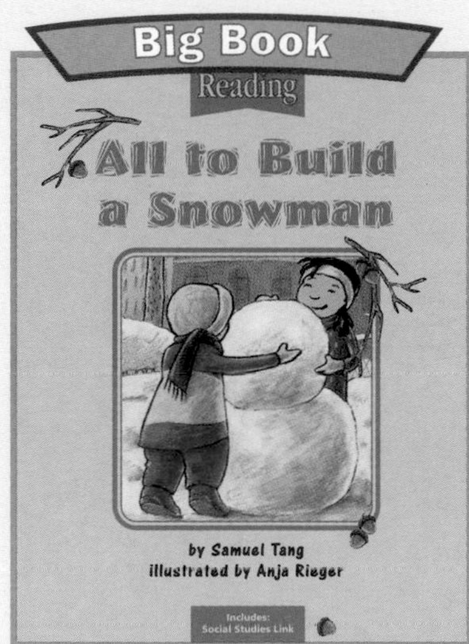
Big Book
Reading
All to Build a Snowman
by Samuel Tang
illustrated by Anja Rieger

Reading for Understanding Reread the story, emphasizing the rhyme and rhythm. Pause for Supporting Comprehension points.

MEETING INDIVIDUAL NEEDS

Extra Support

Provide support in understanding the cause and effect relationships that ultimately provide the snowman's features. Reread pages 6–15, pausing after each for children to discuss the picture.

Kim and Tim and their dog Slim
went out to build a snowman.
1

page 1

They pushed and packed,
and rolled and stacked,
2
all to build a snowman.
3

pages 2–3

A lady sat near
and said, "Look here."
4
"What fun to build a snowman!"
5

pages 4–5

Then wind and snow
startled a crow,
6
making some branches
fall far below.
7
pages 6–7

That made some acorns
drop down and thump.
8
That made the kitten
meow and jump.
9
pages 8–9

That made the dog
bark and chase.
10
That made Dad
get caught in the race.
11
pages 10–11

Supporting Comprehension

pages 4–5

Strategy: Summarize

Teacher-Student Modeling Remind children that to retell a story, good readers think about the characters and what they do.

- ***Who are the characters in the story? What has happened in the story so far?***

pages 6–7

Cause and Effect

- ***Why was the crow startled?*** (The wind blew snow onto it.) ***What did this cause the crow to do?*** (knock some branches from the tree)

pages 8–9

Drawing Conclusions

- ***What was the squirrel doing when the crow knocked the branches down? What happened to one of the acorns the squirrel had gathered?***

pages 9–11

Comprehension Focus: Story Structure: Plot

Teacher-Student Modeling Remind children that stories often have a problem the characters must solve.

- ***What problem do the characters have?*** (Slim, the dog, is chasing the kitten.) ***Do you think the lady will get her kitten back? How will the characters solve the problem?***

DAY 3

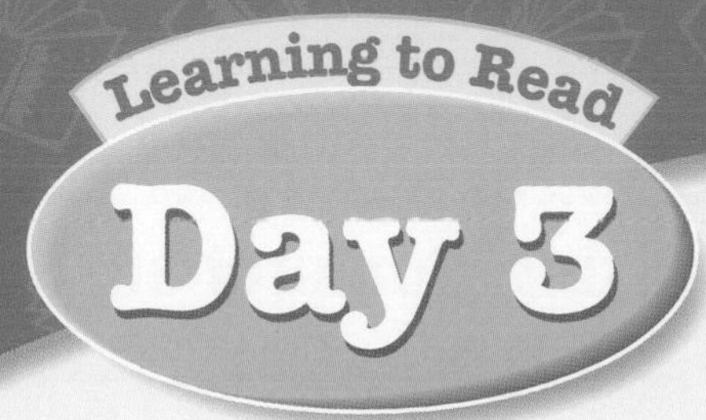

Supporting Comprehension

pages 14–15

Making Predictions

- *What do you think will happen next? How will the kitten get down?*

pages 16–17

Comprehension Focus: Story Structure: Plot

Student Modeling *How did the lady get her kitten back? Where do you think Slim is?*

pages 16–17

Making Judgments

- *How does the lady feel about having her kitten back? Do you think she is angry with Slim? Why or why not?*

Revisiting the Text

pages 13–15

Concepts of Print

Quotation Marks, End Punctuation

- Reread pages 13–15, pointing out the quotation marks. Explain that quotation marks show the exact words a character says.
- Ask if children recognize the end marks. *Exclamation points show words that should be said with excitement. Who will say the words the way the lady might say them?*

That made the lady begin to cry —

pages 12–13

"Oh my!
Oh my!
Oh my!
Oh my!"
14
"My kitten is on the snowman!"
15

pages 14–15

The kitten, at last, was safe and sound.
16
17

pages 16–17

pages 18–19

pages 20–21

Supporting Comprehension

pages 18–20

Noting Details

- *What did Kim and Tim find to help them build their snowman? Where did all these things come from?*

pages 20–21

Strategy: Summarize

Student Modeling *Why did Kim and Tim go to the park? Who can tell all the things that happened to make the kitten meow and jump? What happened first? What happened next?*

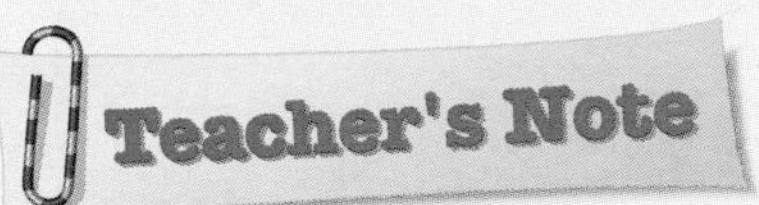

Teacher's Note

Language Patterns This story contains a strong rhyme scheme. On a rereading, have children supply the rhyming words.

DAY 3

Challenge

Children may recognize that the names *Kim, Tim,* and *Slim* rhyme; they all have the same ending sounds and spellings. Ask what word children can build if they put the letter *h* in front of the letters *-im.*

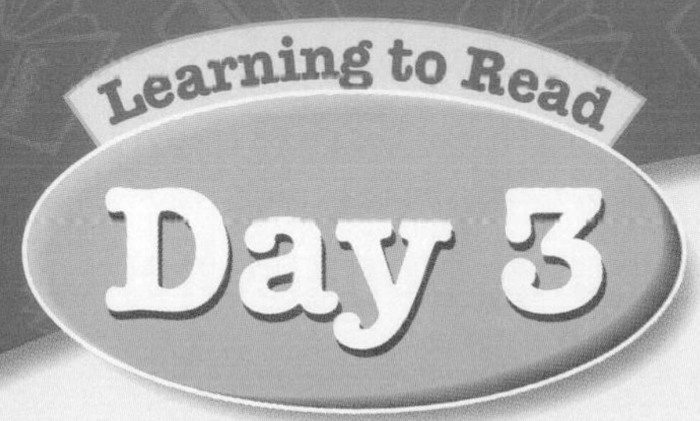

Practice Book p. 179

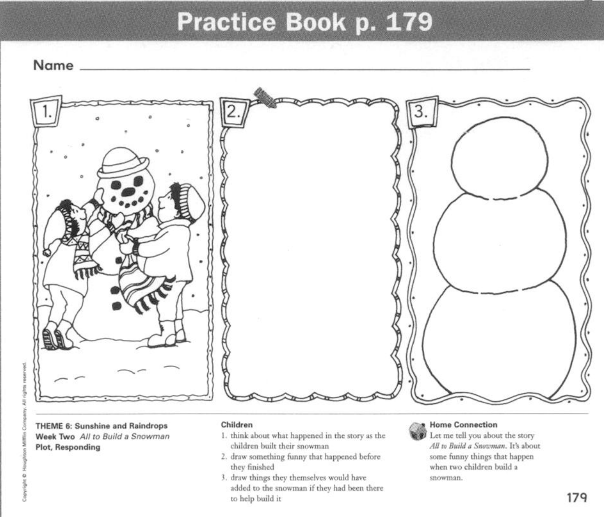

Name ______

1. 2. 3.

THEME 6: Sunshine and Raindrops
Week Two *All to Build a Snowman*
Plot, Responding

Children
1. think about what happened in the story as the children built their snowman
2. draw something funny that happened before they finished
3. draw things they themselves would have added to the snowman if they had been there to help build it

Home Connection
Let me tell you about the story *All to Build a Snowman*. It's about some funny things that happen when two children build a snowman.

179

Vocabulary

startle to surprise

make an unexpectedly loud noise to demonstrate the meaning of *startle.* Have children use the word in oral sentences.

Diagnostic Check

If . . .	You can . . .
children need more practice in identifying the plot of a story,	help them identify the problem and solution in known stories or books in the class library.

Responding to the Story

Retelling Use these prompts to help children summarize the story:

- ***Who went to the park to build a snowman? Who else was at the park?*** (Kim, Tim, Slim, and Dad; a lady with her kitten)
- ***What startled the crow? What happened after that?***
- ***What did Kim and Tim find to help them build their snowman? Could they have finished the snowman without these things? Why do you say that?***
- ***Do you think the acorns will stay on the snowman for long? Why or why not?***
- ***What part of the story was your favorite?***

Literature Circle Have small groups discuss whether or not a story like this could happen in real life.

Practice Book page 179 Children will complete the page at small group time.

At Group Time

Art Center

Materials • black construction paper • white chalk and assorted other colors

Display page 21 of *All to Build a Snowman.* Ask children what time of day it is when Kim and Tim leave the park. Then have children draw a winter night scene using chalk on black construction paper.

At Group Time

Math Center

Materials • white paper circles in three sizes (12 inch, 8 inch, 4 inch) • buttons • ribbon or strips of fabric

Share *Snowballs* by Lois Ehlert to inspire children. Place materials in the Math Center for children to use in creating their own snow people. When children share their snow people, have them identify the shapes they used as circles and explain how they knew in what order to put the snowballs.

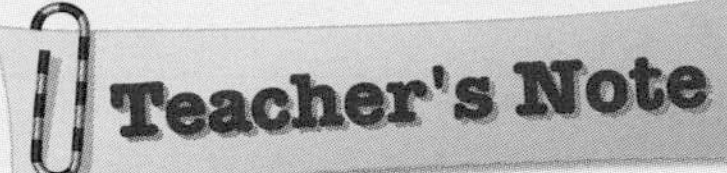

Teacher's Note

Look for *Snowballs* by Lois Ehlert at your school library.

DAY 3

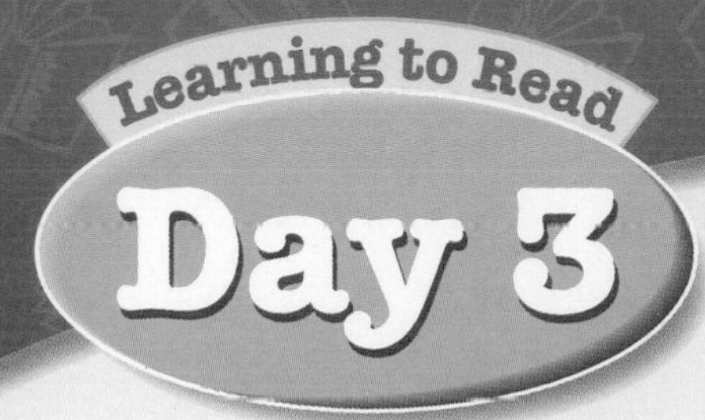

Blending k -it

Objectives

Children

- identify words with initial consonant *k*, /k/
- blend and read words with *b, f, h, k, l, p, s,* and *-it*

Materials

- **Alphafriend Cards** *Iggy Iguana, Keely Kangaroo*
- **Letter Cards** *b, f, h, i, k, l, p, s, t*
- **Alphafriend Audiotape** Theme 6

Practice Book p. 180

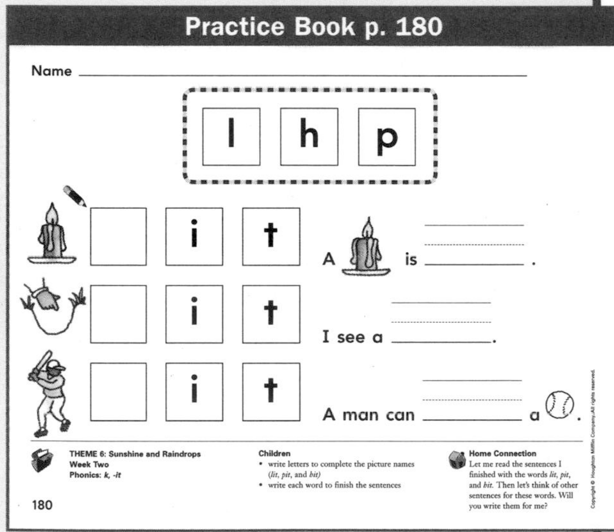
Name

l h p

i t A is .

i t I see a .

i t A man can a .

THEME 6: Sunshine and Raindrops
Week Two
Phonics: k, -it

Children
• write letters to complete the picture names (*lit, pit,* and *hit*)
• write each word to finish the sentences

Home Connection
Let me read the sentences I finished with the words *lit, pit,* and *hit*. Then let's think of other sentences for these words. Will you write them for me?

180

Meeting Individual Needs — Extra Support

Place the Picture Cards for *k* and assorted other Picture Cards on a desk or table top. Have children sort the cards into "*k*, /k/" and "not *k*, /k/" piles.

Connect Sounds to Letters

Review Consonant *k* Play Keely Kangaroo's song, and have children clap for each /k/ word. Write *K* and *k* on the board, and list words from the song.

Blending *-it* Tell children that they'll build a word with *k*, but first they'll need a vowel ("helper letter"). Display Alphafriend *Iggy Iguana.*

Who remembers this character's name? Yes, this is Iggy Iguana. Say* Iggy Iguana *with me. Iggy's letter is the vowel* i*, and the sound* i *usually stands for is /ĭ/. Hold up the Letter Card *i.* ***You say /ĭ/. Listen for the /ĭ/ sound in these words: /ĭ/* inch, */ĭ/* is, */ĭ/* it.**

Hold up the Letter Cards *i* and *t.* Remind children that they know the sound for *t.* Model blending the sounds as you hold the cards apart and then together: **/ĭ/ /t/, it. *I've made the word* it. *The sound for* i *is first, and the sound for* t *is last.*** Have volunteers move the cards as classmates blend.

Have volunteers find the word *it* on the Word Wall.

Blending *-it* Words Build *it* in a pocket chart. Then put *k* in front of *-it,* and model blending /k/ /it/, *kit.* Have children blend the sounds while you point. Model blending *-it* with familiar consonants to make *bit, fit, hit, kit, lit, pit,* and *sit.*

Apply

Practice Book page 180 Children complete the page at small group time.

Phonics in Action

Applying Phonics Skills and High-Frequency Words

Phonics/Decoding Strategy

Teacher-Student Modeling Discuss using the Strategy to read words in the **Phonics Library** story, "Kit."

Think Aloud

The title begins with capital K. *The sound for* K *is /k/. I know the sounds for* i, t: */ĭ/ /t/,* -it. *Let's blend: /k/ /it/,* Kit. *Is Kit a real word? Does it make sense here? Who is Kit?*

Do a picture walk through the first few pages of the story. Ask children what they think Kit the kangaroo will do.

Coached Reading

Have children read each page silently before reading with you. Prompts:

pages 10-11 Have volunteers model how they blended *Kit* and *fit.* ***In this story, Kit is putting on a chef's hat. What do you think Kit will cook?***

pages 12-13 Together, blend *lit* and *sit.* ***Why do you think Kit lit the stove? Why will the kangaroos sit at the table?***

pages 14–15 ***What did the kangaroos do to their hamburgers?*** (They bit the hamburgers.) Have volunteers read the sentences on page 14, modeling how they blended the *-it* words. ***Did the kangaroos enjoy their meal? How do you know? What did they say about it?***

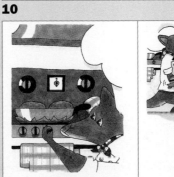

Phonics Library

Purposes

- apply phonics skills
- apply high-frequency words

9

A hat can fit Kit.

10

A pan can fit.

11

Kit lit it.

12

Kit can sit here.
I can sit.

13

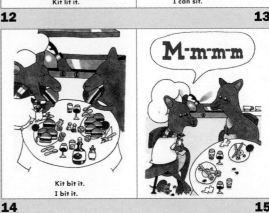

Kit bit it.
I bit it.

14

15

DAY 3

Home Connection

Children can color the pictures in the take-home version of "Kit." After rereading on Day 4, they can take it home to read to family members.

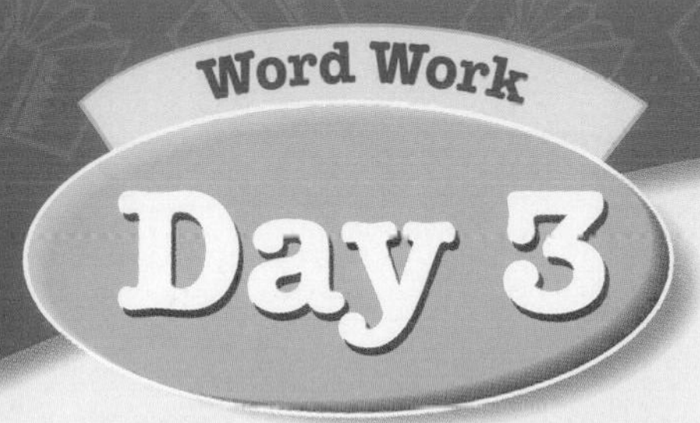

OBJECTIVES

Children

- blend initial consonants with *–it* to read words

MATERIALS

- **Letter Cards** *b, f, h, i, k, l, p, s, t*

Building Words

Word Family: *–it*

Review with children that they know all the sounds and letters to build the word *it.* Have children help you build *it,* using the Letter Cards. ***First you stretch out the sounds: /ĭ/ /t/. How many sounds do you hear? The first sound is /ĭ/. I'll put up* i *to spell that. The next sound is /t/. What letter should I choose for /t/? Now blend /ĭ/ /t/,* it. *What letter should I add to build* kit*? Blend /k/ /it/,* kit.**

Replace *k* with *b* and say: ***What happens if I change /k/ to /b/?*** Continue making and blending *-it* words by substituting *f, h, l, p,* and *s.*

List the words on a chart and post it in the Writing Center. If you already have an *-it* family chart, add the word *kit* to it.

Have small groups work together to build *-it* words. Children can use block letters or other manipulatives in your collection.

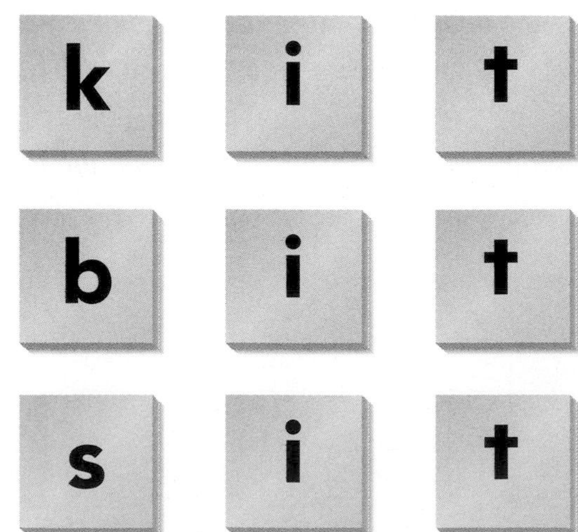

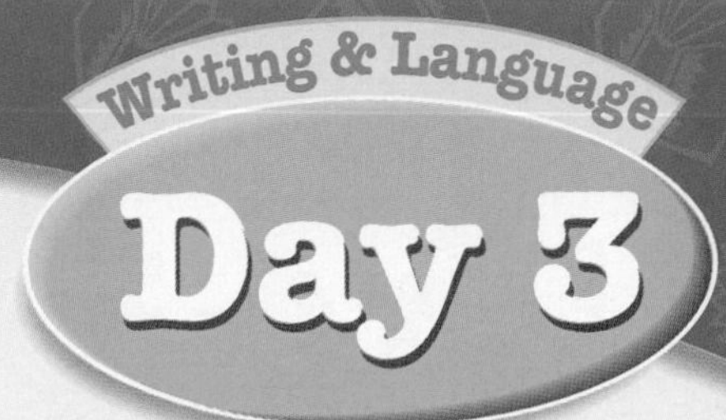

Shared Writing

Weather Observations

Viewing and Speaking Tell children that weather forecasters and scientists observe the weather and record information about it. Today children will do the same thing. They will look outside to observe the weather, and then they'll tell their classmates what they observe.

- If possible, go outside with children so they can make their observations. If the weather is inclement, children can observe from a window.
- Write the sentence stem *I see* ______ on chart paper to help children record their observations. Continue with the sentence stem *It feels* ______.
- Write the sentence stem *Today it is* ______ *and* ______. Call on volunteers to suggest words to complete the sentence.
- Incorporate children's suggestions into a shared writing experience. Encourage children to use interesting describing words.

I see____.	It feels____.
rain	rainy
clouds	wet
gray sky	cool

Today it is____and____.
It is cloudy and gray.
It is rainy and cool.

OBJECTIVES

Children

- make observations about the weather
- help to record the information

DAY 3

Learning to Read

Day 4

Opening

Day at a Glance

Learning to Read

Big Book:

What Can We Do?

 **Phonics: Reviewing /k/; Blending *–it* Words,** *page T96*

Word Work

Building Words, *page T98*

Writing & Language

Interactive Writing, *page T99*

 **Half-Day Kindergarten**

 Indicates lessons for tested skills. Choose additional activities as time allows.

Calendar

Sunday	Monday	Tuesday	Wednesday	Thursday	Friday	Saturday
			1	2	3	4
5	6	7	8	9	10	11
12	13	14	15	16	17	18
19	20	21	22	23	24	25
26	27	28	29	30	31	

When recording the temperature and reporting the weather, have children tell whether or not today is suitable for building snowmen and why. Discuss what activities *are* suitable for today's weather.

Daily Message

Modeled Writing Focus on today's weather in the daily message.

Today is a sunny winter day.
We'll write a weather report about it.

Choose a volunteer to point to the new word that was added to the Word Wall this week. *(here)* ***Here is in the* h *column because it begins with an* h. *Who can read the word in the column before* h, *the word that starts with* g?** Continue reading the remaining words.

Routines

Daily Phonemic Awareness
Blending and Segmenting Onset and Rime

Play "Pat, Pat, Clap."

- Remind children that in "Pat, Pat, Clap," they pat for each sound you say and then clap to say the word.
- Pat and clap with children as you say: */k/ /it/,* **kit;** */v/ /an/,* **van.**
- Continue with other words from the list.
- ***Now I'll say a word. You "pat, pat" the beginning and ending sounds, then "clap" to say the word again. Listen:*** **sun.** (/s/ /un/, *sun*)
- Continue with other words from the list.

"Pat, Pat, Clap"

mat	pig	hen
bug	hat	sit
fan	mop	get
lap	jet	run

Getting Ready to Learn

To help plan their day, tell children that they will

- read the Social Studies Link: *What Can We Do?*

- build words with *k* in the Phonics Center.

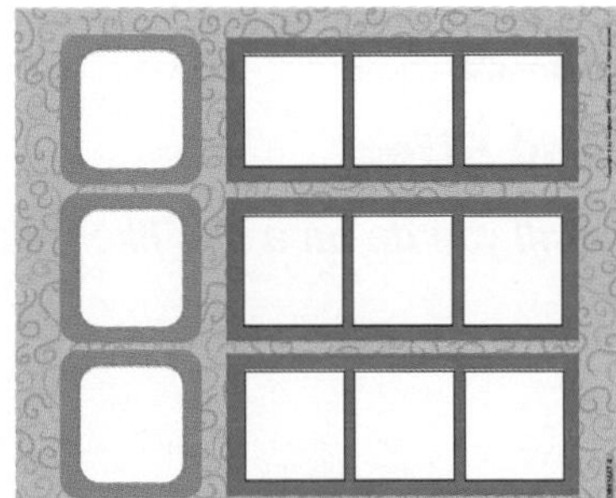

- reread a book called "Kit."

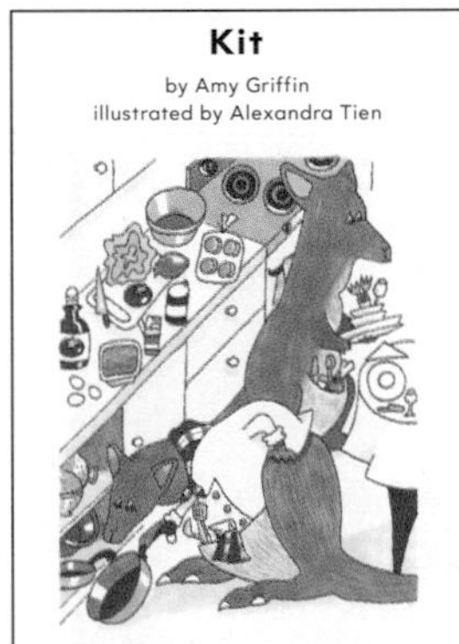

DAY 4

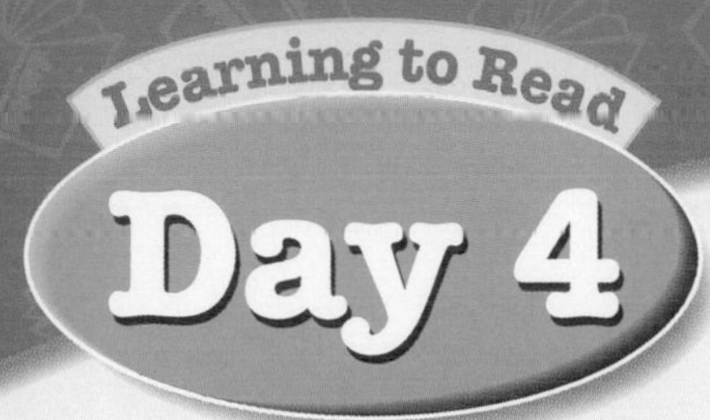

Sharing the Big Book

Social Studies Link

OBJECTIVES

Children

- identify end punctuation in sentences

Big Book

pages 23–29

Oral Language

sandcastle: We've read about castles in fairy tales. This is a *sand*castle. Tell us about a sandcastle.

English Language Learners

Display a variety of pictures of children's activities in different types of weather. Use the pictures to introduce vacabulary that will help children to understand the selection and to participate in class discussions.

Building Background

Suppose you woke up on a windy, rainy day. What would you do? Play outside? Read a good book? What else? Read the title and discuss a few pictures. Explain that different parts of the country have different kinds of weather and that this book shows how children play in each kind.

Reading for Understanding Pause for discussion as you share the selection.

pages 24–25

Strategy: Summarize

Student Modeling ***Remember we learned that to summarize means to tell something in your own words. I'll read the title. Who can summarize what the picture shows?***

page 24

Drawing Conclusions

- *Why is a sunny day a good day to build a sandcastle?*

page 26

Making Judgments

- *How would you answer the question on this page? What do you know about snow that will help you answer?*

pages 28–29

Cause and Effect

- *What will you do on a day like today? Why?*

What can we do on a sunny day?
We can build a sandcastle.
24

What can we do on a windy day?
We can fly a kite.
25

pages 24–25

What can we do on a snowy day?
We can build a snowman.
26

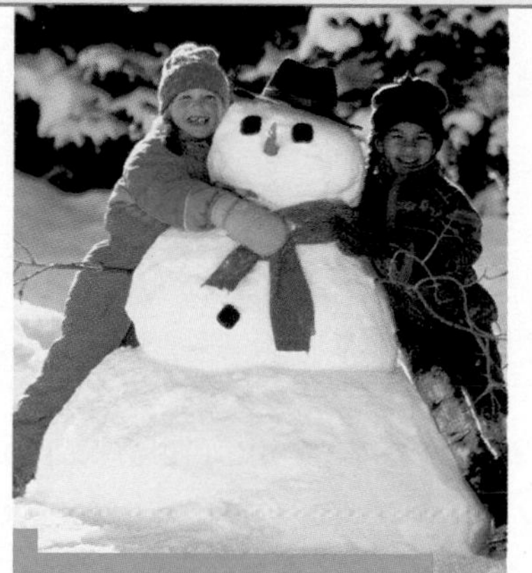

What can we do on a snowy day?
We can build a snowman.
26

pages 26–27

What is the weather like today?
28

What will you do?
How will you play?
29

pages 28–29

Revisiting the Text

page 26

Concepts of Print

End Punctuation

- ***Which sentence is a question? How do you know?*** (the first; question mark at end of sentence) ***Why does the second sentence end with a period?*** (It is a telling sentence; telling sentences end with periods.)

Responding

Retelling Help children summarize the selection by using the photographs. After the summary, choose children to select the type of weather they like best and tell why.

Challenge

For children who are ready for a challenge, prepare cards for the words and end marks in one or two sentences from the selection. One child builds a sentence and then challenges a partner to read it and find it in the book.

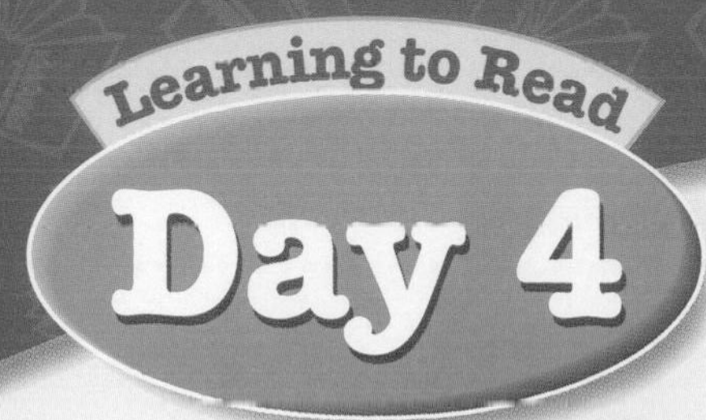

OBJECTIVES

Children

- identify initial *k* for words that begin with /k/
- blend initial consonants with *-it*

MATERIALS

- ***From Apples to Zebras: A Book of ABC's,*** page 12
- **Alphafriend Card** *Iggy Iguana*
- **Letter Cards** *b, f, h, i, k, l, s, t*
- **Word Cards** *here, I*
- **Phonics Center:** Theme 6, Week 2, Day 4

Teacher's Note

During writing, children may ask how to spell words from the *-it* family. Help children find *it* on the Word Wall and add the appropriate initial consonant(s).

Home Connection

Challenge children to look at home for items whose names begin with the consonant *k.* Children can draw pictures to show what they have found.

Phonics

Blending -it Words

Connect Sounds to Letters

Review Consonant *k* Using self-stick notes, cover the words on page 12 of *From Apples to Zebras: A Book of ABC's.* Then display the page. Ask what letter children expect to see first in each word and why. Uncover the words so children can check their predictions.

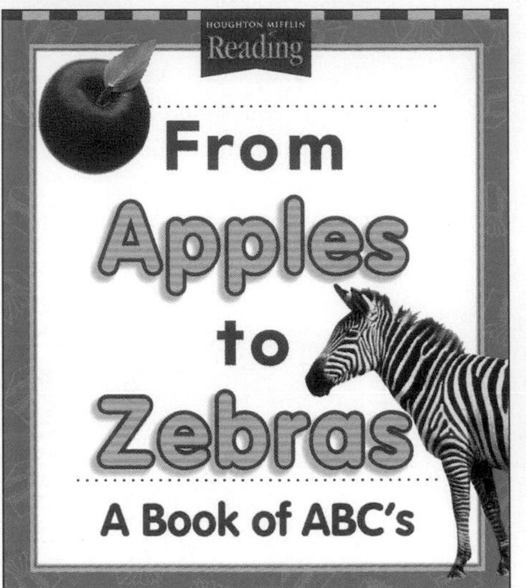

Reviewing *-it* Remind children that to build some words with *k,* they also need a vowel ("helper letter") because every word has at least one of those. Ask which Alphafriend stands for the vowel sound /ĭ/. (Iggy Iguana) Display Iggy and have children think of other words that start with /ĭ/. *(into, inchworm, itch)*

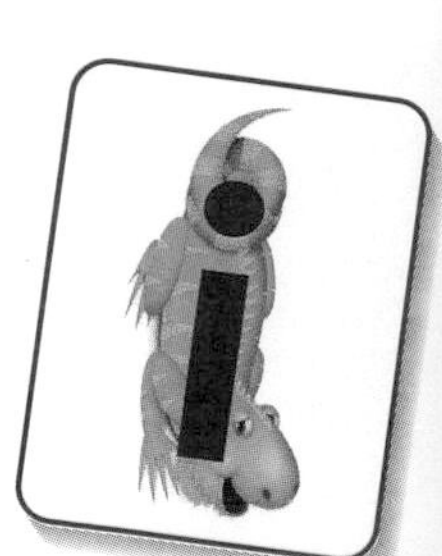

Hold up Letter Cards *i* and *t.* ***Watch and listen as I build a word from the Word Wall: /ĭ/ /t/,*** **it,** ***/ĭ/ /t/,*** **it.**

Blending *-it* Words Put Letter Card *k* in front of *-it.* ***Now let's blend my new word: /k/ /it/,*** **kit.** Continue, having volunteers build and blend *bit, fit, hit, lit,* and *sit.*

Apply

Begin a sentence with the first three cards shown. For *fit,* ask what letter you need to spell each sound.

Repeat the activity with *I can sit here.* Then have volunteers read the sentences and blend the *-it* words.

Tell children they will build more sentences today in the Phonics Center.

Practice Book page 181 Children will complete this page at small group time.

Phonics Library In groups today, children will also read *-it* words as they reread the **Phonics Library** story "Kit." See suggestions, page T89.

Use the Phonics Center materials for **Theme 6, Week 2, Day 4**.

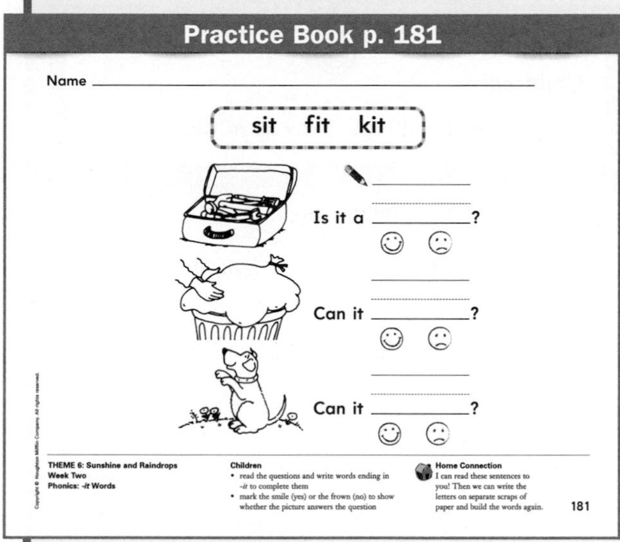

Practice Book p. 181

Name ____________________

sit fit kit

Is it a ________?

Can it ________?

Can it ________?

THEME 6: Sunshine and Raindrops
Week Two
Phonics: *-it* Words

Children
- read the questions and write words ending in *-it* to complete them
- mark the smile (yes) or the frown (no) to show whether the picture answers the question

Home Connection
I can read these sentences to you! Then we can write the letters on separate scraps of paper and build the words again.

181

Portfolio Opportunity

Save children's Practice Book pages and other writing samples for *-it* words in their portfolios.

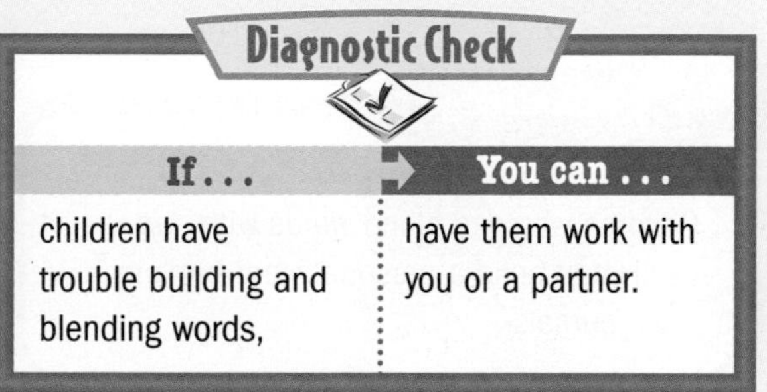

Diagnostic Check

If . . .	You can . . .
children have trouble building and blending words,	have them work with you or a partner.

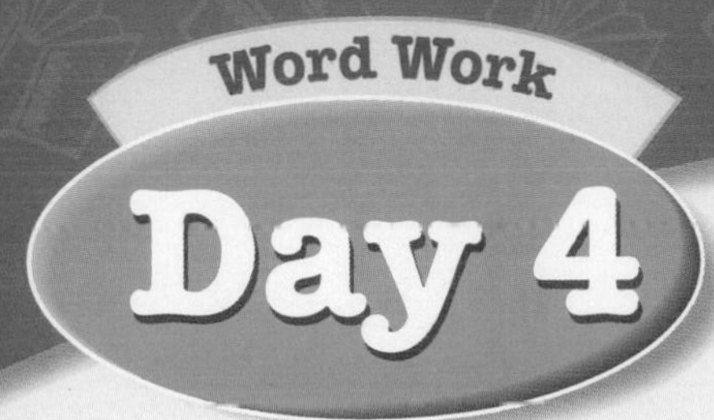

Building Words

Word Families: –it, –an, –at

Demonstrate how to build *it* in the pocket chart, stretching out the sounds. ***I want to make the word* kit. *Which letter should I put in front of* it?** Replace *k* with known consonants to build *bit, fit, hit, lit, pit,* and *sit.*

Next, use letter cards to build *an.* ***First, let's stretch out the sounds: /ă/ /n/. How many sounds do you hear? The first sound is /ă/. I'll put up an a to spell that. The last sound is /n/. What letter should I choose for that?*** Blend /ă/ and /n/ to read *an.*

Continue building words with initial consonants:

- Ask which letter you should add to build *can*. Model how to read *can* by blending /k/ with /an/.
- Replace *c* with *f*. ***What happens if I change /k/ to /f/?*** Continue making and blending *-an* words by substituting *m, N, p, r, t,* and *v*.
- Repeat, this time making *at* and then blending new words by adding initial consonants *b, c, f, h, m, p, r,* and *s*.

an	at
can	bat
fan	cat
man	fat
Nan	hat
pan	mat
ran	pat
tan	rat
van	sat

Have children write *-it, -an,* and *-at* words on white boards or paper. They can read their lists of words to partners.

OBJECTIVES

Children

- make and read *–it, –an, –at* words

MATERIALS

- **Letter Cards** *a, b, c, f, h, i, k, l, m, N, n, p, r, s, t, v*

Challenge

Children who can blend words with *–an* easily can build a personal word bank in their journals.

Writing & Language
Day 4

Interactive Writing

A Weather Report

Viewing and Speaking Remind children that they have been observing the weather and using interesting words to talk and write about the weather.

- Display the chart of weather action words from earlier in the week and the chart of weather observations from yesterday's shared writing. (See pages T69, T79, and T91.) Review the charts with children.
- Remind children that a *weather report* tells what the weather is like. Suggest that children help you write a weather report for today. On chart paper, write the title "Today's Weather Report."
- ***First, let's write a sentence that tells the main idea about today's weather.*** Write the sentence stem *Today it is* ______ *and* ______. Call on volunteers to suggest words to complete the sentence.
- ***Now let's add some details. What do you notice about the weather today? Let's use good action words and describing words. Let's check the thermometer and add the temperature, too.***
- Incorporate children's suggestions into an interactive writing experience. Call on volunteers to write letters, known words, and end punctuation marks.

Today's Weather Report

Today it is rainy and cool.
The rain is pouring down.
Gray clouds cover the sky.
A chilly wind blows. Brrr!
The temperature is 40°.

At Group Time
Writing Center
It is rainy and grey.
It is cold and wet.

Put the weather report in the Writing Center. Children "read" it on their own or with a partner. Children can copy and illustrate one of the sentences. You may wish to bind the pages together to make a class book.

OBJECTIVES

Children

- contribute weather words to a weather report
- write letters, words, or end punctuation marks for an interactive writing activity

Portfolio Opportunity

Save children's work as samples of their ability to write to task.

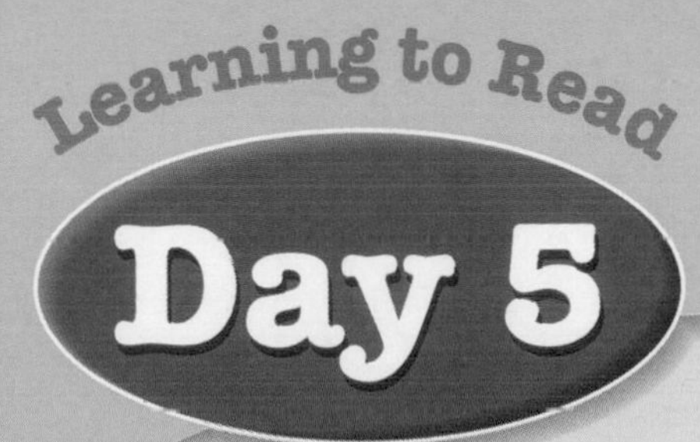

Day at a Glance

Learning to Read

Revisiting the Literature:

The Sun and the Wind, All to Build a Snowman, What Can We Do?, "Kit"

 **Phonics Review: Initial Consonants; *-at, -an, -it,* words; *page T104***

Word Work

Building Words, ***page T106***

Writing & Language

Independent Writing, ***page T107***

Half-Day Kindergarten

 Indicates lessons for tested skills. Choose additional activities as time allows.

Opening

Calendar

Sunday	Monday	Tuesday	Wednesday	Thursday	Friday	Saturday
			1	2	3	4
5	6	7	8	9	10	11
12	13	14	15	16	17	18
19	20	21	22	23	24	25
26	27	28	29	30	31	

Review the temperatures recorded this week. ***Which day of the week had the highest (or lowest) temperature? How many days had the same temperature?***

Daily Message

Modeled Writing After writing the message, allow each child to circle a letter they can name or box a word they can read. Children will enjoy seeing how much of the message they "know."

Today is Friday.
It is time to look at all the books we read.

Have children chant the spelling of each word on the Word Wall today: **h-e-r-e *spells* here; i-s *spells* is.**

Routines

Daily Phonemic Awareness
Blending and Segmenting Onset and Rime

Read "First Snow." Then use the blending cheer for words from the poem.

Teacher: *I'll say /f/. You say /all/.*
I'll say /f/. You say /all/.
/f/!
Children: */all/!*
Teacher: */f/!*
Children: */all/!*
Teacher: *What's the word?*
Children: Fall!

Have partners confer on new words to segment and take turns leading the cheer. *(tall, big, mud, Sam, fat, ten)*

THEME 6
First Snow
Snow makes whiteness where it falls.
The bushes look like popcorn-balls.
And places where I always play,
Look like somewhere else today.
by Marie Louise Allen
26

***Higglety Pigglety: A Book of Rhymes*, page 26**

Getting Ready to Learn

To help plan their day, tell children that they will

- reread and talk about the books they've read this week.

What Can We Do?

- take home a story they can read, "Kit."

Kit
by Amy Griffin
illustrated by Alexandra Tien

- report on the weather or an outdoor activity in their journals.

Aaron's
Journal

DAY 5

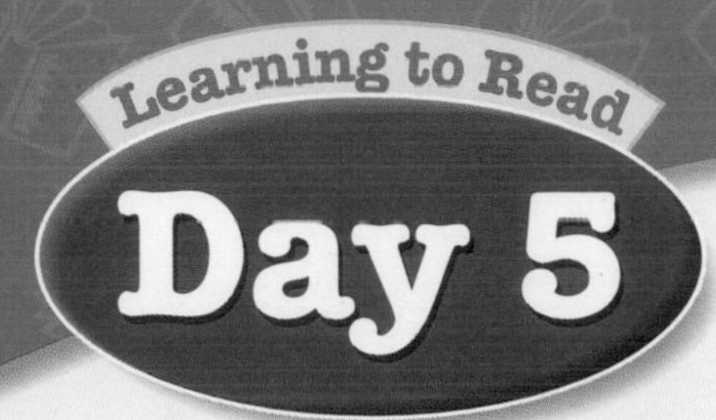

Revisiting the Literature

Literature Discussion

Tell children that today they will compare the stories and books you shared all week. First, help children recall the selections:

- Have volunteers tell about the contest in *The Sun and the Wind.*
- Page through *All to Build a Snowman* and have children take turns telling the chain of events.
- Review an episode or two from *What Can We Do?* and invite children to tell why the activities are good ones for specific kinds of days.
- Together, read the first line in the **Phonics Library** story "Kit." Ask volunteers to model how they blended the words *fit* and *Kit.*

Ask children to vote for their favorite book of the week, and then read aloud the winner.

Comprehension Focus: Story Structure: Plot

Comparing Books Remind children that some selections tell stories and others give information. Ask which of this week's selections gave information. Then talk about the *stories,* or made-up selections about characters who have a problem and try to solve it.

Have children identify the problem in *The Sun and the Wind* and tell how it was solved. Repeat with *All to Build a Snowman.* Then browse through both selections and help children summarize what happened at the beginning, middle, and end.

www.eduplace.com

Log on to **Education Place** for more activities relating to Sunshine and Raindrops.

www.bookadventure.org

This Internet reading-incentive program provides thousands of titles for children to read.

Building Fluency

Rereading Familiar Texts

Phonics Library: "Kit" Remind children that they've learned the new word *here,* and that they've learned to read words with *k* or *-it.* As they reread the Phonics Library stories, have them look for *-it* words.

Review Feature several familiar **Phonics Library** titles in the Book Corner. Have children demonstrate their growing skills by choosing one to reread aloud, alternating pages with a partner. From time to time ask children to point out words or pages that they can read more easily now than the first time.

Oral Reading Beginning readers often concentrate so heavily on the decoding that they miss the meaning at first. Helping them to preview a story and build background will lead to better comprehension and more fluent reading. Walk through the illustrations in "Kit" together. Help children understand that Kit is the cook and the other kangaroo is telling the story. Model what the storyteller says, and then have children try it.

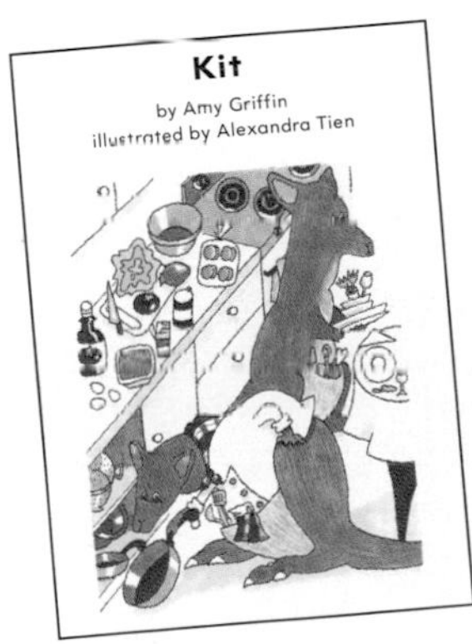

Pat and Nan
by Elizabeth Kiley
illustrated by Penny Carter

Blackline Master 36 Children can complete the page and take it home to share their reading progress.

My Reading Log
I can read
My new words
is here

Leveled Books

The materials listed below provide reading practice for children at different levels.

Little Big Books

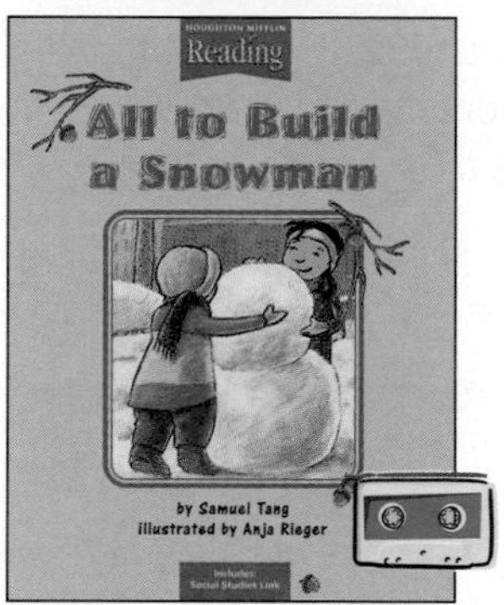

Little Readers for Guided Reading

Houghton Mifflin Classroom Bookshelf

DAY 5

Home Connection

Remind children to share the **take-home version** of "Kit" with their families.

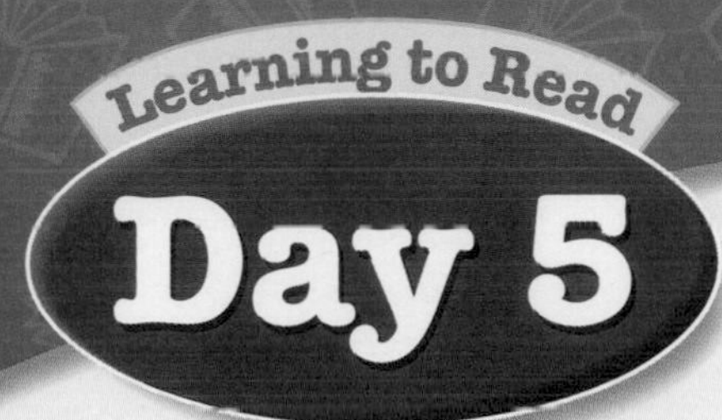

OBJECTIVES

Children

- build and read words with initial consonants and short *a* + *t*, short *a* + *n*, short *i* + *t*
- make sentences with high-frequency words

MATERIALS

- **Word Cards** *a, and, go, here, I, is, Is, it, like, my, see, to*
- **Picture Cards** choose for sentence building
- **Punctuation Cards:** period, question mark

Teacher's Note

As children become more comfortable with the phonics review activity during the year, vary it by having the word builders write words from different families (for example, *-an, -at, -it* words). Keep a list on chart paper, and then cut the words out for children to sort by family.

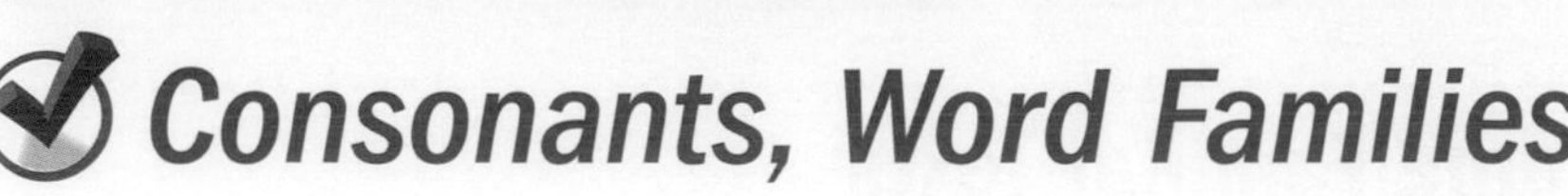

Phonics Review

Consonants, Word Families

Review

Explain to children that they will now have a chance to be word builders and word readers. Have a group of word builders stand with you at the chalkboard.

- ***Let's build the word*** at. ***First, count the sounds... What sound is first? What letter spells /ă/? Yes, everyone write*** **a.** Continue with the final sound.
- Now write *p* in front of your letters and have the word builders do the same. Ask the rest of the class (word readers) what new word was made.
- Have a new group of children exchange places with the word builders. Ask them to erase the *p,* write *m,* and ask the word readers to say the new word.
- Continue until everyone builds a word by replacing one letter. Examples: *bat, cat, sat, hat, rat, fat; an, pan, man, can, fan, ran, tan, van; it, sit, fit, hit, bit, kit, lit, pit.*

High-Frequency Words Review

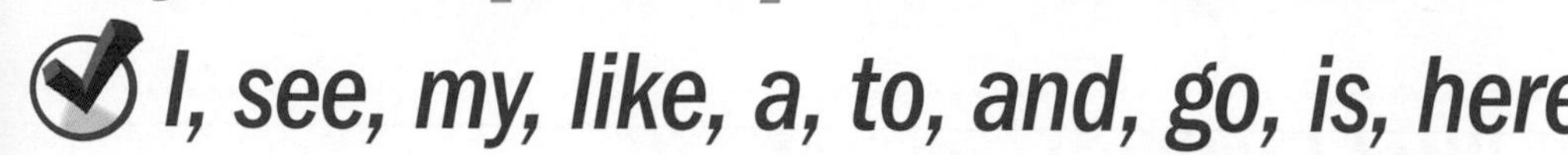

I, see, my, like, a, to, and, go, is, here

Review

Prepare cards for *can* and *It.* Then give each small group the Word Cards, Picture Cards, and Punctuation Card needed to make a sentence. Each child holds one card. Children stand and arrange themselves to make a sentence for others to read.

Apply

Practice Book page 182 Children can complete this page independently and read it to you during small group time.

Phonics Library Have children take turns reading aloud to the class. Each child might read one page of "Kit" or a favorite **Phonics Library** selection from a previous week. Remind readers to share the pictures!

Questions for discussion:

- *Do you hear any rhyming words in either story? What letters are the same in those words?*
- *Find a word that starts with the same sound as Keely Kangaroo's name. What is the letter? What is the sound?*
- *This week we added the word* here *to the Word Wall. Find the word* here *in "Kit."*

Practice Book p. 182

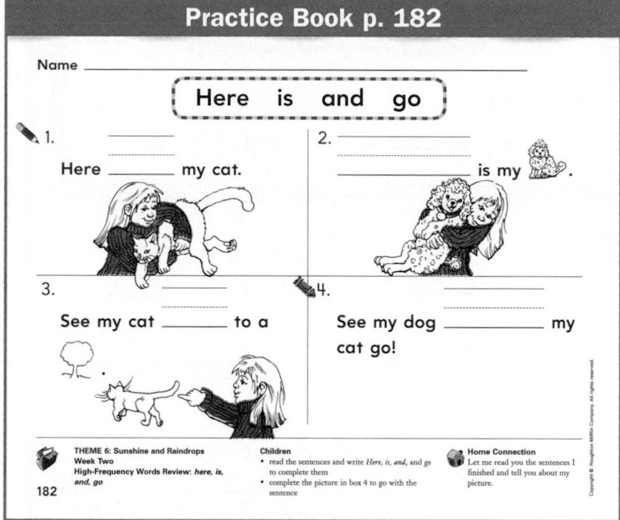

Name ______

Here is and go

1. Here ______ my cat.
2. ______ is my [dog].
3. See my cat ______ to a [tree].
4. See my dog ______ my cat go!

182

THEME 6: Sunshine and Raindrops
Week Two
High-Frequency Words Review: *here, is, and, go*

Children
- read the sentences and write *Here, is, and,* and *go* to complete them
- complete the picture in box 4 to go with the sentence

Home Connection
Let me read you the sentences I finished and tell you about my picture.

Portfolio Opportunity

Save the Practice Book page to show children's recognition of high-frequency words.

Diagnostic Check

If . . .	You can . . .
children easily remember the consonant sounds,	have them begin their own ABC books with drawings for each consonant they have learned.
children pause at high-frequency words in **Phonics Library** selections,	have partners read words on the Word Wall together.

DAY 5

OBJECTIVES

Children

- build and read *–at, –an,* and *–it* words

MATERIALS

- **Letter Cards** *a, b, c, f, h, i, k, l, m, n, p, r, s, t, v*

Building Words

Word Families: *–an, –at, –it*

Prompt children to think about the sounds in *an* and tell you what letters you need to spell the word.

Along the bottom of the pocket chart, line up the letters *m, f, r, t, c, v,* and *p.* ***Now I want to make the word* fan. *Who can tell me which letter I should take from here to make* fan?** Have a volunteer take the letter *f* and place it in front of *an.*

Continue building *-an* words, using initial consonants *m, f, r, t, c,* and *p.* On chart paper, keep a list of all the *-an* words you make, and reread the list together. Ask children what they notice about the words. (They rhyme; they all have the letters *a, n.*)

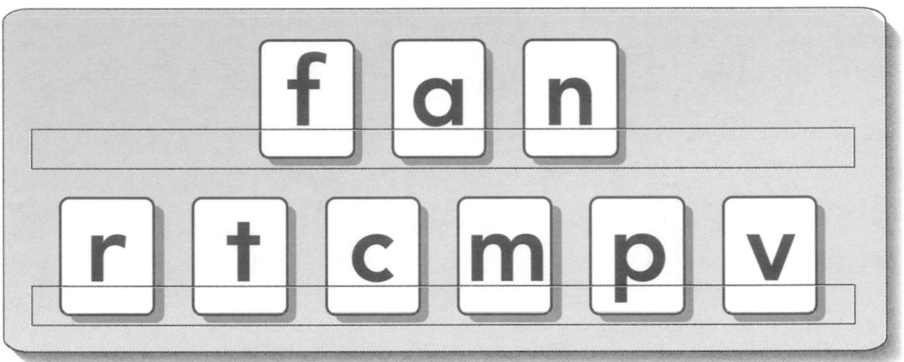

Continue the activity with *-at* words and *-it* words. Examples: *at, cat, fat, mat, Nat, pat, rat, vat; it, bit, fit, hit, kit, lit, pit, sit.*

Have small groups work together to build *-an, -at,* and *-it* words with magnetic letters or alphabet blocks. Children can use their new words to create and illustrate rhyming phrases for the Word Bank section of their journals.

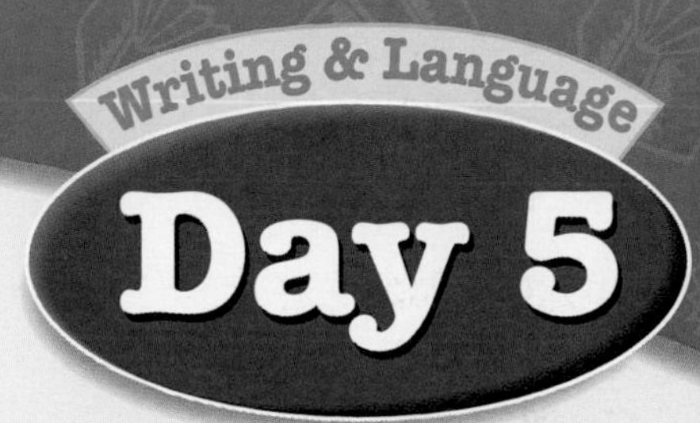

Independent Writing

Journals Reread the charts from this week's shared and interactive writing. Point out all the weather action words children added to their charts and used in their weather report. Tell children that today they'll have a chance to report on the weather in their journals.

- Pass out the journals.
- ***What new weather words did you learn this week? What did you learn about building a snowman? What did you learn about the activities people do in different kinds of weather? Maybe you will write a report about today's weather; if so, what should you write first so that later you'll remember what day the report is about?***
- Remind children that they can use the Word Wall and the posted weather words as they write. Also remind them to use what they know about letter sounds to help them spell words.
- If time permits, allow children to share what they've written with the class.

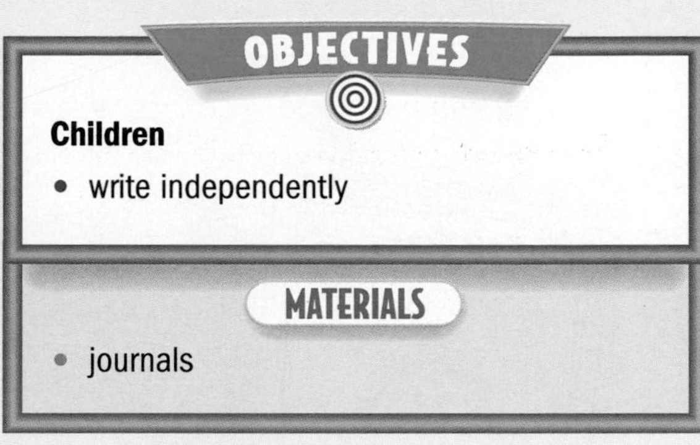

OBJECTIVES

Children

- write independently

MATERIALS

- journals

Portfolio Opportunity

Put bookmarks in journal entries you would like to share with parents. Occasionally have children choose their best efforts or favorite works for sharing as well.

DAY 5

Literature for Week 3

Different texts for different purposes

Teacher Read Alouds:

- Chicken Soup with Rice
- The Sun and the Wind
- The Woodcutter's Cap

Purposes

- oral language
- listening strategy
- comprehension skill

Big Books:

Higglety Pigglety: A Book of Rhymes

Purposes

- oral language development
- phonemic awareness

From Apples to Zebras: A Book of ABC's

Purposes

- alphabet recognition
- letters and sounds

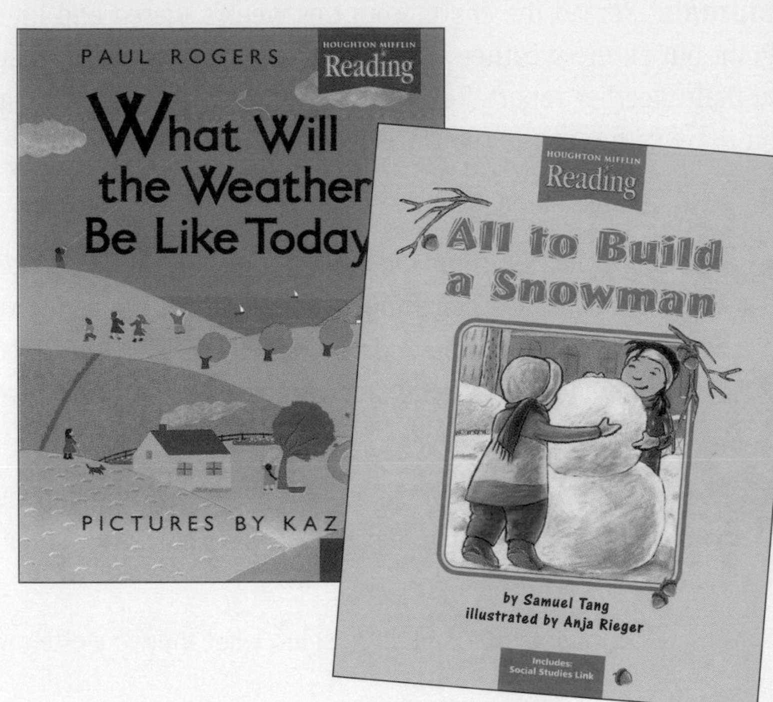

Big Book: Main Selections

Purposes

- concepts of print
- reading strategy
- story language
- comprehension skill

Also available in Little Big Book and audiotape

Also available in Little Big Book and audiotape

Science Link
Checking the Weather

Social Studies Link
What Can We Do?

Also in the Big Books:
- Science Link
- Social Studies Link

Purposes

- reading strategies
- comprehension skills
- concepts of print

Also available in Take-Home version

Purpose

- applying phonics skills and high-frequency words

Leveled Books

On My Way Paperback

Here, Kit!
by ***A. J. Cooper***
page T153

Little Readers for Guided Reading
Collection K

Houghton Mifflin Classroom Bookshelf
Level K

www.eduplace.com
Log on to *Education Place* for more activities relating to *Sunshine and Raindrops*

www.bookadventure.org
This free Internet reading incentive program provides thousands of titles for students to read.

Week 3

Suggested Daily Routines

Instructional Goals	Day 1	Day 2
Learning to Read ✓ *Phonemic Awareness:* Blending and Segmenting Onset and Rime *Strategy Focus:* Evaluate, Predict/Infer ✓ *Comprehension Skill:* Fantasy/ Realism, Story Structure: Plot ✓ *Phonics Skills* *Phonemic Awareness:* Beginning Sound /qu/ Initial Consonant *Q, q* *Compare and Review:* Initial Consonants: *h, l* ✓ *High-Frequency Words: is, here* ✓ *Concepts of Print:* Capitalize First Word in Sentence; End Punctuation	**Opening Routines,** *T114–T115* Word Wall • **Phonemic Awareness:** Blending and Segmenting Onset and Rime **Teacher Read Aloud** *The Woodcutter's Cap, T116–T119* • **Strategy:** Evaluate • **Comprehension:** Realism/Fantasy Phonics **Instruction** • Phonemic Awareness, Beginning Sound /qu/, *T120–T121;* ***Practice Book,*** *185–186*	**Opening Routines,** *T124–T125* Word Wall • **Phonemic Awareness:** Blending and Segmenting Onset and Rime **Sharing the Big Book** *What Will the Weather Be Like Today?, T126–T127* • **Strategy:** Evaluate • **Comprehension:** Fantasy/Realism Phonics **Instruction, Practice** • Initial Consonant *q, T128–T129* • ***Practice Book,*** *187* **High-Frequency Word** • Review Words: *is, here, T130–T131* • ***Practice Book,*** *188*
Word Work *High-Frequency Word Practice:* Word Families: *-it, -an, -at*	**High-Frequency Word Practice** • Words: *here, I, is, T122*	**High-Frequency Word Practice** • Building Sentences, *T132*
Writing & Language *Vocabulary Skill:* Action Words *Writing Skill:* Writing a Story	**Oral Language** • Action Words, *T123* • Listening and Speaking, *T123*	**Vocabulary Expansion** • Action Words, *T133* • Viewing and Speaking, *T133*

✓ = tested skills

Leveled Books

Have children read in appropriate levels daily.

Phonics Library
On My Way Practice Readers
Little Big Books
Houghton Mifflin Classroom Bookshelf

Managing Small Groups — Day 1

Teacher-Led Group
- Reread familiar **Phonics Library** selections

Independent Groups
- Finish ***Practice Book,*** *183–186*
- ***Phonics Center:*** Theme 6, Week 3, Day 1
- Book, Dramatic Play, Writing, other Centers

Managing Small Groups — Day 2

Teacher-Led Group
- Begin ***Practice Book,*** *187–188* and handwriting **Blackline Masters 173 or 199.**

Independent Groups
- Finish ***Practice Book,*** *187–188* and handwriting **Blackline Masters 173 or 199.**
- ***Phonics Center:*** Theme 6, Week 3, Day 2
- Book, Writing, other Centers

Lesson Planner CD-ROM: Customize your planning for *Sunshine and Raindrops* with the Lesson Planner.

Day 3

Opening Routines, *T134–T135*

Word Wall

- **Phonemic Awareness:** Blending and Segmenting Onset and Rime

Sharing the Big Book

All to Build a Snowman, T136–T137

- **Strategy:** Evaluate
- **Comprehension:** Story Structure: Plot, *T136; **Practice Book,** 189*
- **Concepts of Print:** Quotation Marks, End Punctuation, *T137*

Phonics

Practice, Application

- Review Consonant *qu, T138–T139*

Instruction

- Blending *-it, T138–T139; **Practice Book,** 190*
- **Phonics Library:** "Fan," *T139*

Building Words

- Word Family: *-it, T140*

Shared Writing

- Writing a Story, *T141*
- Listening and Speaking, *T141*

Managing Small Groups

- Read **Phonics Library** selection "Fan"
- Write letters *I, i;* begin **Blackline Masters 165 or 191.**
- Begin ***Practice Book,*** *189–190*

Independent Groups

- Finish **Blackline Masters 165 or 191** and ***Practice Book,*** *189–190*
- Art, other Centers

Day 4

Opening Routines, *T142–T143*

Word Wall

- **Phonemic Awareness:** Blending and Segmenting Onset and Rime

Sharing the Big Book

Science Link: "Checking the Weather," *T144*

Social Studies Link: "What Can We Do?," *T145*

- **Strategy:** Predict/Infer
- **Comprehension:** Noting Details, Drawing Conclusions
- **Concepts of Print:** Capital at Beginning of Sentence, End Punctuation

Phonics

Practice

- Review Initial Consonant *qu, T146–T147; **Practice Book,** 191*

Building Words

- Word Families: *-it, -an, -at, T148*

Interactive Writing

- Writing a Story, *T149*
- Listening and Speaking, *T149*

Managing Small Groups

Teacher-Led Group

- Reread Phonics Library selection "Fan"
- Begin ***Practice Book,*** *191*

Independent Groups

- Finish ***Practice Book,*** *191*
- ***Phonics Center:*** Theme 6, Week 3, Day 4
- Writing, Science, other Centers

Day 5

Opening Routines, *T150–T151*

Word Wall

- **Phonemic Awareness:** Blending and Segmenting Onset and Rime

Revisiting the Literature

Comprehension: Story Structure: Plot, Fantasy/Realism, *T152*

Building Fluency

- **On My Way Practice Reader:** "Here's Kit!," *T153*

Phonics

Review

- Consonants, Word Families, *T154*

High-Frequency Word Review

- Word: *I, see, my, like, a, to, and, go, is, here, T155; **Practice Book,** 192*

Building Words

- Word Families: *-at, -an, -it, T156*

Independent Writing

- Journals: Independent Writing, *T157*

Managing Small Groups

Teacher-Led Group

- Reread familiar **Phonics Library** selections
- Begin ***Practice Book,*** *192,* **Blackline Master 36.**

Independent Groups

- Reread **Phonics Library** selections
- Finish ***Practice Book,*** *192,* **Blackline Master 36.**
- Centers

Week 3

Setting up the Centers

Teacher's Note

Management Tip In each Center provide a variety of materials and activities so that children of all ability levels can participate successfully. You may identify some children who can guide their partners as pairs work together in the Centers.

The Mitten: A Ukrainian Folktale *by Jan Brett*

Mushroom in the Rain *by Mirra Ginsburg*

On the Same Day in March *by Marilyn Singer*

This Place Is Dry *by Vicki Cobb*

Splash
splatter
slosh
splish-splash
Run
dash
dart
fly
hurry
Go
rush
hustle

Phonics Center

Materials • Phonics Center materials for Theme 6, Week 3

Children make words with the letters *h, l, qu,* and the word family *-it* this week. They also build sentences with Word and Picture Cards. See pages T121, T129, and T147 for this week's Phonics Center activities.

Book Center

Materials • books of traditional stories about weather, different climates around the world

Share and then place copies of stories about weather in the Book Center. Add nonfiction books about places whose climate is different from local weather. See the Teacher's Note on page T117 and page T127 for this week's Book Center suggestions.

Writing Center

Materials • crayons • markers • lined and unlined writing paper

Children illustrate action words telling what they would do in a certain type of weather. Later they illustrate more action words and record them in their journals. Finally they reread the class story in the Writing Center. See pages T123, T133, and T149 for this week's Writing Center activities.

Dramatic Play Center

Materials • story props: knit cap and toy animals or a blanket

Children recreate *The Woodcutter's Cap* using a knit cap and toy animals, or they re-enact the story by using a blanket and playing the roles themselves as you retell the story. See page T117 for this week's Dramatic Play Center activity.

Art Center

Materials • black construction paper • white crayon • glue • assorted natural items (acorns, bits of pine boughs, feathers, leaves, twigs)

Children draw a snowman, gluing on items to add special features, then they use the picture to retell *All to Build a Snowman.* See page T137 for this week's Art Center activity.

Science Center

Materials • newspaper weather maps • paper • crayons or markers

Children compare the symbols on newspaper weather maps to those they use on their daily calendar routine. See page T145 for this week's Science Center activity.

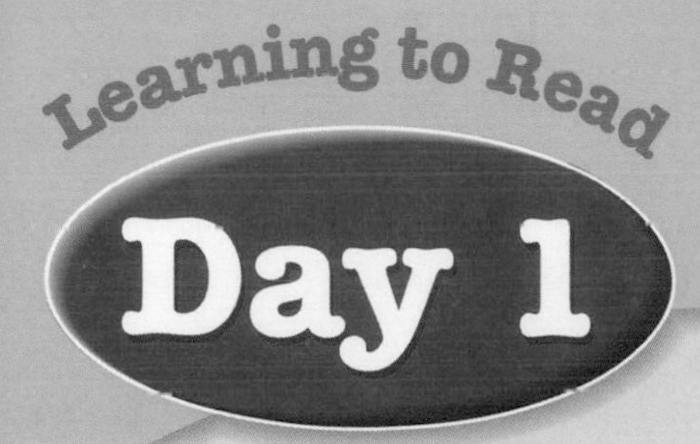

Day at a Glance

Learning to Read

Teacher Read Aloud

The Woodcutter's Cap

✓ **Learning About / kw /,** *page 120*

Word Work

✓ **High-Frequency Word Practice** *page 122*

Writing & Language

Oral Language, *page 123*

Half-Day Kindergarten

✓ Indicates lessons for tested skills. Choose additional activities as time allows.

Opening

Calendar

Sunday	Monday	Tuesday	Wednesday	Thursday	Friday	Saturday
			1	2	3	4
5	6	7	8	9	10	11
12	13	14	15	16	17	18
19	20	21	22	23	24	25
26	27	28	29	30	31	

Review the weather words and symbols you've added to the calendar. Continue to monitor the daily temperature. This week, use describing language to discuss temperature. Introduce children to words like *mild, chilly, cool, frosty, frigid.*

Daily Message

Interactive Writing As you write, model how to write letters whose sounds you hear. Children can begin to contribute known consonant sounds and word families. Show children how to write the symbol for "degree."

Today is Monday.
It is sunny and mild.
Our thermometer
tells us it is 50°.

Recall that the words on the Word Wall are in ABC order. Sing the Alphabet Song to review. ***Now find the letter* g *with your eyes. Who can read the word that starts with* g?** (go) Repeat with the other letters and words.

Routines

Daily Phonemic Awareness

Blending and Segmenting Onset and Rime

- Read "The Itsy Bitsy Spider" on page 27 of *Higglety Pigglety.* Then extend the literacy experience. Say the word parts. Children repeat and blend.
- ***Where did the spider go? Listen: / ŭ / / p /*** *(up)* ***the water spout. What washed the spider out? / r / / ain /.*** *(rain)* ***Poor Spider! She got all / w / / et /.*** *(wet)* ***But soon, out came the / s / / un /.*** *(sun)* ***It dried up all the / r / / ain /.*** *(rain)* ***Where did Spider go at the end? / u / / p /*** *(up)* ***the spout again. Then she spun a beautiful, spidery / w / / eb /.*** *(web)*
- Have partners work together to take apart orally and put together these words: *sun, wet, web, run, sit, can, not.*

THEME 6

First Snow

Snow makes whiteness where it falls.
The bushes look like popcorn-balls.
And places where I always play,
Look like somewhere else today.

by Marie Louise Allen

26

***Higglety Pigglety: A Book of Rhymes*, page 26**

Getting Ready to Learn

To help plan their day, tell children that they will

- listen to a story called *The Woodcutter's Cap.*

- meet a new Alphafriend.

- act out a story in the Dramatic Play Center.

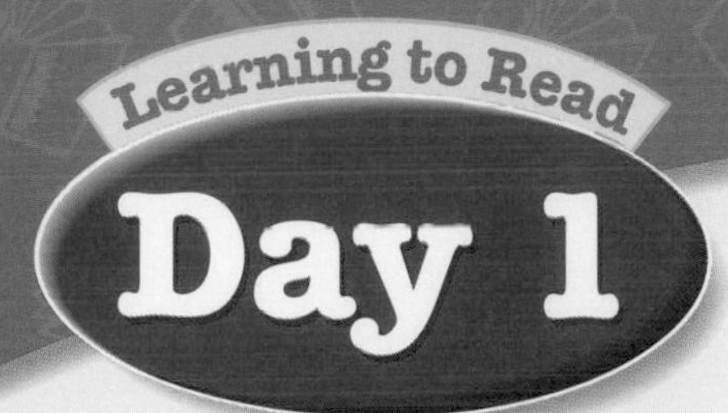

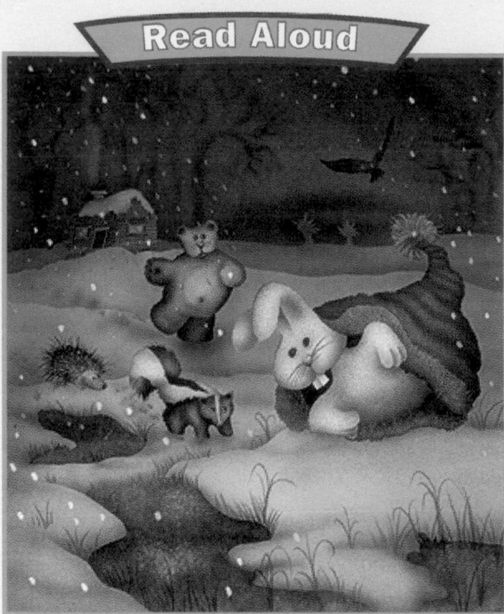

Purposes • oral language • listening strategy • comprehension skill

Selection Summary

A woodcutter's cap becomes a cozy den for a series of woodland creatures: a rabbit, a skunk, a porcupine, an eagle, a wolf, and a bear! It's only when a tiny bee tries to make its way into the cap that all the animals scatter.

Key Concepts

There is always room for one more

English Language Learners

Use pictures to introduce the story animals: *rabbit, skunk, porcupine, eagle, bear, wolf, bee.* Help children describe the animals, noting special features important to the story for example, the skunk's smell and the porcupine's quills.

Teacher Read Aloud

Oral Language/Comprehension

Building Background

Introduce this very old story called *The Woodcutter's Cap.* To explain the meaning of *woodcutter,* take the word apart. Children know what *cut* means; a *cutter* is someone who cuts. A *woodcutter* cuts wood for a living. In this story, the woodcutter's winter cap is blown away by the wind. Ask what kind of cap the story might be about.

Strategy: Evaluate

Teacher Modeling Tell children that good readers think about how a story makes them feel. Remind children to think about what they liked best about the story as you read.

Think Aloud

As I read a story, I think about what I like most about it, and sometimes what I don't like. I want to know how well the author told the story. You think about that, too, and we'll talk about it later.

Comprehension Focus: Realism/Fantasy

Student Modeling Children know that some stories are about real things and others are make-believe. Show the illustration on T119. ***Look at the picture. What do you see? Would a real rabbit hide in a cap? What about other animals? Do you think this story will be about real animals or make-believe animals? How did you decide?***

Listening to the Story

As you read the story, use your voice to show the tension as each new animal crawls into the cap. Note that the Read Aloud art is also available on the back of the Theme Poster.

Responding

Retelling Help children summarize parts of the story.

- ***Was the woodcutter's cap a good place to keep warm? Why?***
- ***Why didn't Rabbit tell Skunk that there wasn't enough room? As each animal moved in, what happened to the cap?***
- ***How did the animals feel about Bee's arrival? How do you know?***
- ***Before reading, we thought that this would be a make-believe story. Were we right? Why?***
- ***What did you like best about the story?***

Practice Book pages 183–184 Children will complete the pages at small group time.

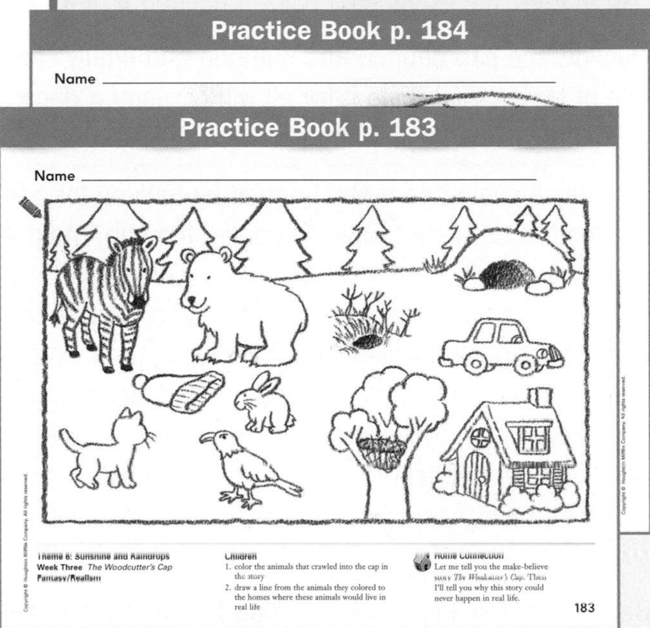
Practice Book p. 184

Name

Practice Book p. 183

Name

Theme 6: Sunshine and Raindrops
Week Three *The Woodcutter's Cap*
Fantasy/Realism

Children
1. color the animals that crawled into the cap in the story
2. draw a line from the animals they colored to the homes where these animals would live in real life

Home Connection
Let me tell you the make-believe story *The Woodcutter's Cap*. Then I'll tell you why this story could never happen in real life.

183

For a fun reinactment, use a soft blanket to simulate the cap and have children take the part of the animals. As you narrate, they act out the story, crawling into their make-believe "cap" until Bee arrives and the woolly cap pops!

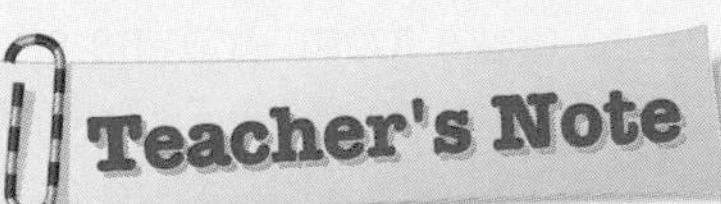

Children who enjoyed this story will also enjoy listening to *The Mitten: A Ukrainian Folktale* by Jan Brett and *Mushroom in the Rain* by Mirra Ginsburg.

Oral Language

Figurative Language Share similes such as "snow... like a thick, white, blanket" and "quills... sharp as needles." Discuss how words can paint pictures for readers.

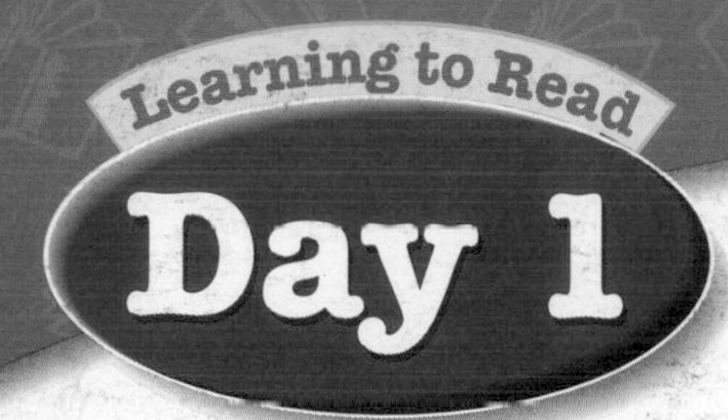

The Woodcutter's Cap

A Traditional Russian Tale

Once upon a time, a woodcutter lived alone in the deep, deep woods. Each winter, he hung his warm, woolly cap on a peg outside his door. One day, a gust of wind whisked the cap out into the woods.

"No matter," the woodcutter said. "I needed a new cap anyway."

Outside, the cap flapped and fluttered and finally came to rest in a pile of leaves. And there it lay all winter. Soon a deep snow covered everything like a thick, white blanket.

One day a snowshoe rabbit hopped by, looking for a warm spot. "Perfect!" said Rabbit when she spied the cap. (**Ask:** *We know that rabbits hop. But do they talk? What does this tell us about the story?*) So Rabbit moved into the warm and cozy cap. Just when she was ready to fall asleep, Skunk wandered by, looking for a warm spot, too. Now Rabbit didn't really want to share the cap, especially with Skunk, but she knew all too well what skunks do when they get angry, so she said nothing. She just rolled over. And the snow kept falling. (**Ask:** *Do you think Rabbit was right not to say anything to Skunk? Why? What would a real skunk do?*)

Before nightfall, Porcupine waddled by. Spying the cap, he wiggled inside. Rabbit and Skunk, hoping not to get too near, said nothing. They just rolled over to make room. And the snow kept falling. (**Ask:** *Why didn't Rabbit and Skunk want to get too near Porcupine?*)

Next, Eagle's sharp eyes spied the cap and decided to make it a warm nest, so he moved in, too. Rabbit, Skunk, and Porcupine were NOT happy, but Eagle's long talons made them say nothing. They just squeezed together to make room. And the snow kept falling. (**Ask:** *What do you think will happen next?*)

Late at night, Wolf came by. By now, the cap was stretched tight as a drum. But seeing Wolf's big teeth, Rabbit, Skunk, Porcupine, and Eagle let him in. And the snow kept falling.

When the cap was as full as can be, a great, grumbly, rumbly noise was heard in the forest. It was Bear! Grumpy, lumpy Bear wanted to get inside the cap, too! (**Say:** *Oh no! It's a bear! What do you think the animals will do now? What would you do?*)

This time, Rabbit, Skunk, Porcupine, Eagle, and Wolf were so frightened they kept their eyes shut and didn't even peek! Bear was so big he had to back in. And with nowhere to go, the animals squeezed tighter, held their breaths, and settled down for a long winter's nap. (**Say:** *Would these animals be together in real life? What do you think?*)

All winter, the animals slept like sardines in a can. But one day, they heard "Buzzzz! Buzzzz! Bzzzz!" Closer and closer the noise came. (**Ask:** *What is it? What's coming? What will the animals do? Let's see if you're right.*)

"Bee!" said Bear.

"Bee!" said Wolf.

"Bee!" said Skunk.

"Let's go!" said Porcupine.

"Now!" said Eagle.

Out of the cap scrambled the animals, quick as a wink! The cap flew up in the air and blew right back to the woodcutter's door.

"Well, well, well," said the woodcutter. "It's my old cap. It spent the winter outside all right."

As he picked the cap up, a single feather fluttered out. "What on earth...?" He smiled. "Well, I'd say that this old cap kept someone warm this winter." And he was right, wasn't he? (**Ask:** *Did the woodcutter mind that the animals used his cap? What do you think? What did you like best about the story? Would you tell a friend to listen to it? What would you say?*)

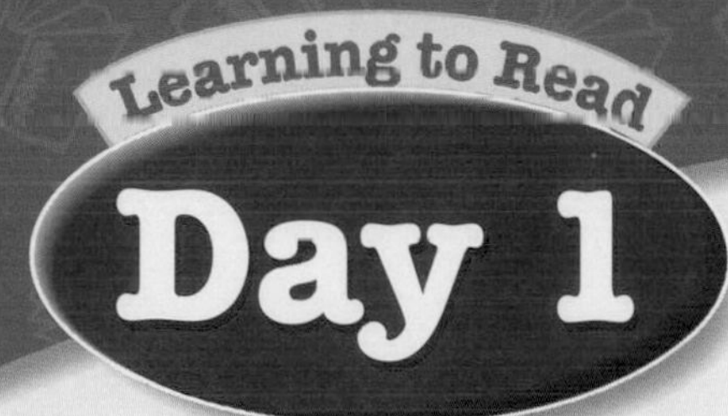

OBJECTIVES

Children

- identify pictures whose names begin with /kw/

MATERIALS

- **Alphafriend Cards** *Hattie Horse, Larry Lion, Queenie Queen*
- **Alphafriend Audiotape 00**
- **Alphafolder 00**
- **Picture Cards** *q, h, l*
- **Phonics Center:** Theme 6, Week 3, Day 1

Phonemic Awareness

Introducing the Alphafriend: Queenie Queen

Use the Alphafriend routine to introduce Queenie Queen.

1. **Alphafriend Riddle** Read these clues:
   - ***This Alphafriend is** not **an animal. Her sound is /kw/. Say it with me: /kw/.***
   - ***This Alphafriend lives in a castle and she wears a crown.***
   - ***She may be married to the king, and her children are the princess and the prince.***

   When most hands are up, call on children until they guess *queen.*

2. **Pocket Chart Display** Queenie Queen in a pocket chart. Say her name, emphasizing the /kw/ sound, and have children echo.

3.  **Alphafriend Audiotape** Play Queenie Queen's song. Listen for words that start with /kw/.

4. **Alphafolder** Have children look at the illustration and name the /kw/ pictures.

5. **Summarize**
   - ***What is our new Alphafriend's name? What is her sound?***
   - ***What words in our Alphafriend's song start with /kw/?***
   - ***Each time you look at Queenie Queen this week, remember the /kw/ sound.***

Queenie Queen's Song
(Tune: "On Top of Old Smokey")

Queenie has qualified to run in the race.
She'll run very quickly to keep up the pace.
Queenie is quite fit. She'll stretch for a while.
Queenie will not quit. She'll run every mile.

Home Connection

A take-home version of Queenie Queen's Song is an **Alphafriend Blackline Master.** Children can take this song home to share with their families.

Listening for / kw /

Compare and Review: /h/, /l/
Display Alphafriends *Hattie Horse* and *Larry Lion* opposite *Queenie Queen.* Review each character's sound.

Hold up the Picture Cards one at a time. Children signal "thumbs up" for pictures that start with Queenie Queen's sound, / kw /. When Queenie's pictures are in place, repeat with / h / and / l /.

Pictures: *quilt, hand, leaf, quarter, lock, hose, queen, hat, leash*

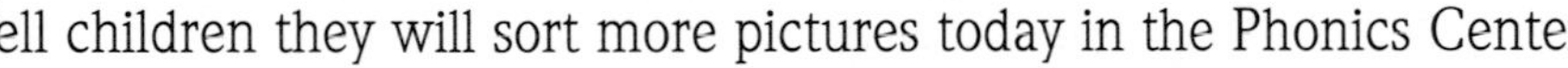

Tell children they will sort more pictures today in the Phonics Center.

Apply

Practice Book pages 185–186 Children will complete the pages at small group time.

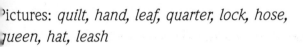

Use the Phonics Center materials for **Theme 6, Week 3, Day 1**.

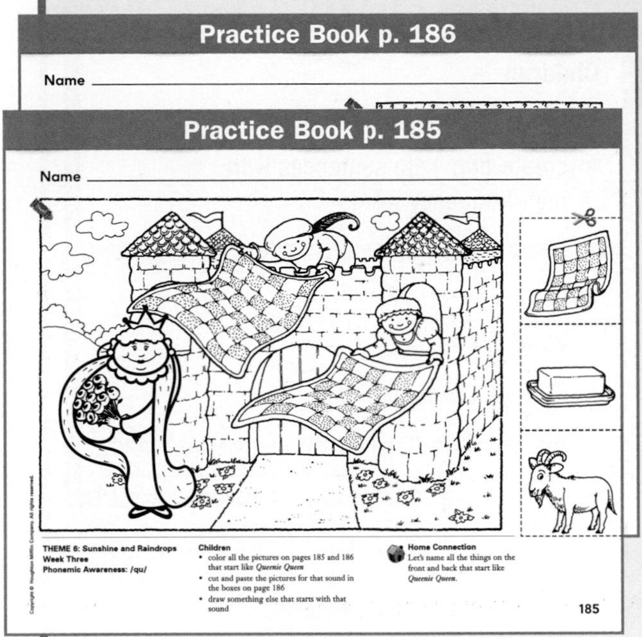
Practice Book p. 186

Name

Practice Book p. 185

Name

THEME 6: Sunshine and Raindrops
Week Three
Phonemic Awareness: /qu/

Children
- color all the pictures on pages 185 and 186 that start like *Queenie Queen*
- cut and paste the pictures for that sound in the boxes on page 186
- draw something else that starts with that sound

Home Connection
Let's name all the things on the front and back that start like *Queenie Queen.*

185

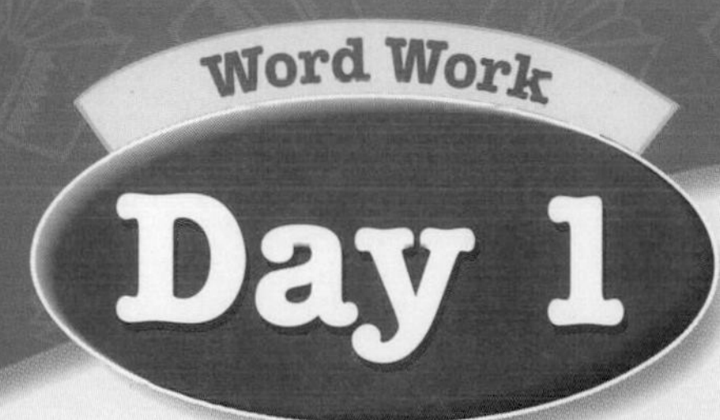

OBJECTIVES

Children

- read high-frequency words
- create and write sentences with high-frequency words

MATERIALS

- **Word Cards** *here, I, is*
- **Picture Cards** *cat, dog*
- **Punctuation Cards:** period, question mark

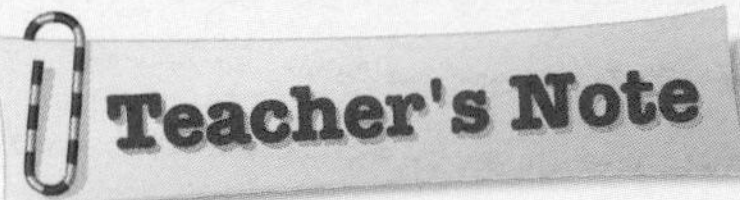

Write the fingerplay "Where Is Thumbkin?" on chart paper. Leave blanks for high-frequency words *here, I,* and *is*.

High-Frequency Word Practice

Matching Words

- Display Word Cards *I, here, is,* in a pocket chart. Call on children to read each word and to find it on the Word Wall.
- Recite "Where Is Thumbkin?" together. When the rhyme is familiar, have children stand up when they say the word *is.* At a second reciting, ask them to stand for *here,* and then for *I*.
- ***Now let's find the words in print.*** (Display the rhyme on the chart.) ***I'll point while we recite. When you see the word*** is, ***raise your hand.*** Repeat with *here* and *I*.

"Where is Thumbkin?"

Where is Thumbkin?
Where is Thumbkin?
Here I am.
Here I am.
How are you today, sir?
Very well, I thank you.
Run away, run away.

Have children write their names on sticky notes, changing *sir* to *ma'am* when appropriate. (Take this opportunity to teach the meanings of the formal words *sir* and *madam.*) Children read the new poem, with special attention to the high-frequency words *is, here,* and *I* as shown.

Writing Opportunity Children can work with you to "read" their new poem.

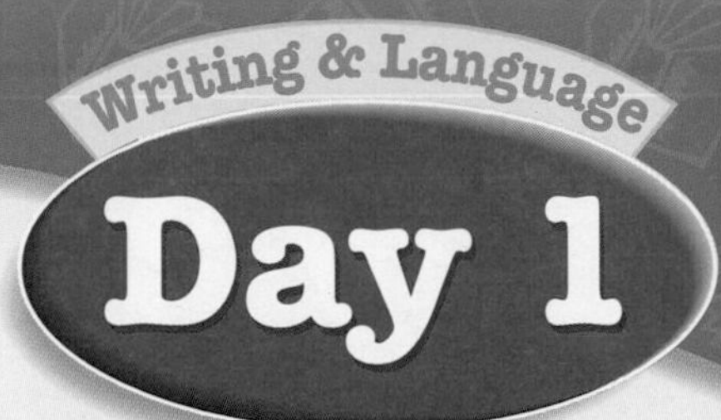

DAY 1

Oral Language

Action Words

Listening and Speaking Children have learned many weather words. Include action words by talking about things to do in all kinds of weather.

- ***If today were hot and sunny, what would you do?*** **Swim.** ***That's a good action word. What else? Tanner would*** **splash** ***in a pool. What's the action word? Right,*** **splash.** ***These are good action words. Let's write them down before we forget them. I'll write your names next to your ideas.***
- List the words on the chart, underlining the action word and adding children's names. Repeat for other kinds of weather, such as *Cold and Snowy* and *Cloudy and Windy.* Read the completed chart together. Add ideas as children think of them.

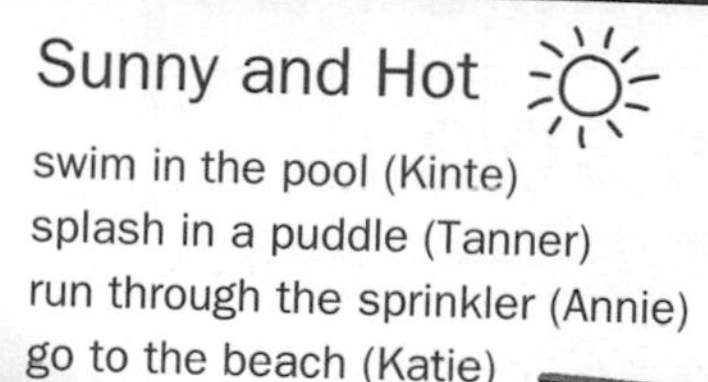

Sunny and Hot
swim in the pool (Kinte)
splash in a puddle (Tanner)
run through the sprinkler (Annie)
go to the beach (Katie)

Cold and Snowy
build a snowman (William, Seth, Toby)
sled down the hill (Frankie)
make snow angels (Mark, Ryan)

Cloudy and Windy
fly a kite (Jimmy, Gwen)
walk to the library (Don, Maddie)
bake cookies with Mom (Paul)

At Group Time

Writing Center

Post the chart in the Writing Center. Children find their own names and illustrate their idea. They can work with a partner if they would like. Later, have them share their drawings with the group.

OBJECTIVES

Children
- use action words orally

Portfolio Opportunity

Saving selected labeled illustrations allows you to assess children's ability to draw and write independently.

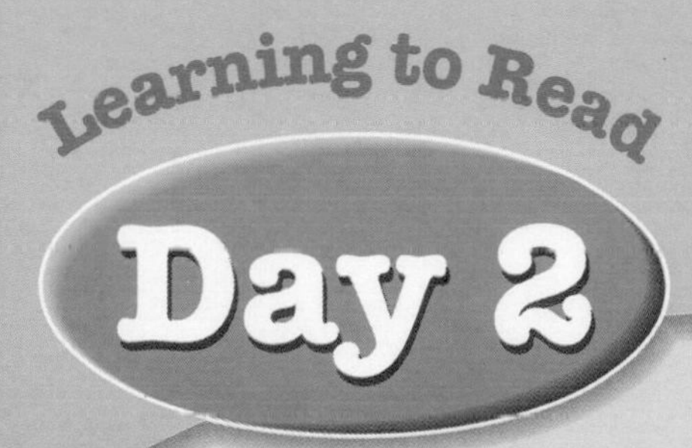

Day at a Glance

Learning to Read

Big Book:

What Will the Weather Be Like Today?

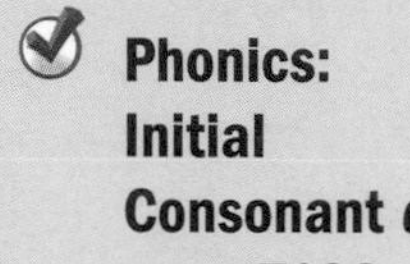
Phonics: Initial Consonant *q*, *page T128*

Word Work

High-Frequency Word Practice, *page T132*

Writing & Language

Vocabulary Expansion, *page T133*

Half-Day Kindergarten

Indicates lessons for tested skills. Choose additional activities as time allows.

Opening

Calendar

Sunday	Monday	Tuesday	Wednesday	Thursday	Friday	Saturday
			1	2	3	4
5	6	7	8	9	10	11
12	13	14	15	16	17	18
19	20	21	22	23	24	25
26	27	28	29	30	31	

Continue to focus on oral language development using action words to describe the weather. For example, you might describe the flag *dancing* in the wind; the rain *pounding* on the windows; or the clouds *rolling* in the sky.

Daily Message

Modeled Writing Call attention to action words in your daily message.

Teddy carried three bottles of bubbles to school. We'll blow bubbles outside today.

Review Word Wall words with children. While waiting for the bus line, or to go to the cafeteria, point to the words and have children recite them quickly.

Routines

Daily Phonemic Awareness

Blending and Segmenting Onset and Rime

- ***I'll say some sounds. You put them together to name an animal:*** / k /... / at / *(cat)*; / h / / en / *(hen)*.
- ***Here are some more. Listen carefully.*** (goat, fox, deer, pig, cow)
- ***Now we'll change places. I'll name an animal and you say the sounds in the animal's name. Listen:*** **dog.** (/ d / / og /); **cat** / k / / at / (/).
- Continue with more animal names. *(fox, pig, cow, goose, yak)*
- Now read "Hey, Diddle, Diddle." Children listen for animal names. Call on children to segment the names for others to blend.

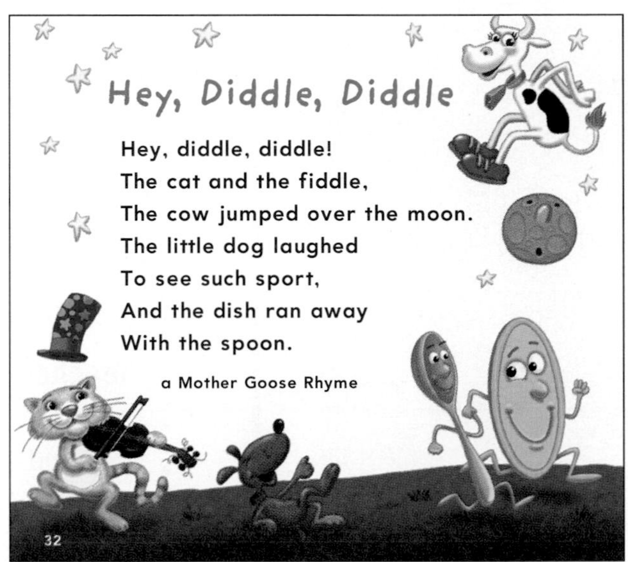

Hey, Diddle, Diddle
Hey, diddle, diddle!
The cat and the fiddle,
The cow jumped over the moon.
The little dog laughed
To see such sport,
And the dish ran away
With the spoon.
a Mother Goose Rhyme
32

***Higglety Pigglety: A Book of Rhymes,* page 32**

Getting Ready to Learn

To help plan their day, tell children that they will

- listen to a Big Book: *What Will the Weather Be Like Today?*

- learn the new letters *Q* and *q,* and sort words that begin with / kw /.

- think about and write action words and weather words.

DAY 2

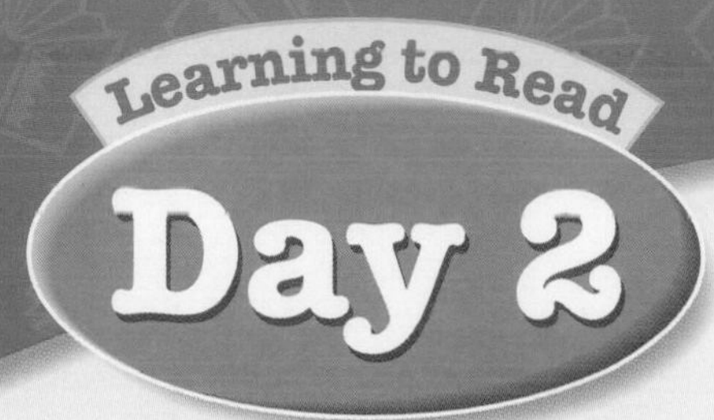

Sharing the Big Book

Oral Language/Comprehension

Building Background

Reading for Understanding Remind children they've heard the book before. Choose a few scenes and call on children to recall, for example, the weather each animal (the white cockatoo, the frog in the bog, the fish in the sea) likes. Then invite children to listen to the story again, chiming in when they can.

Strategy: Evaluate

Teacher-Student Modeling Ask children to recall what they liked best about the book and why. Then have them choose a favorite illustration and tell why they liked it. Encourage all children to participate. Remind them that it is important for readers to tell each other what they like about a book.

Sharing the Story

Reread the story, pausing for these discussion points:

pages 6–7

Noting Details

- *How can you tell this is a windy day?*

pages 14–15

Fantasy/Realism

- *Lizards and frogs are real animals. But how do you know that these lizards and frogs are make-believe?*

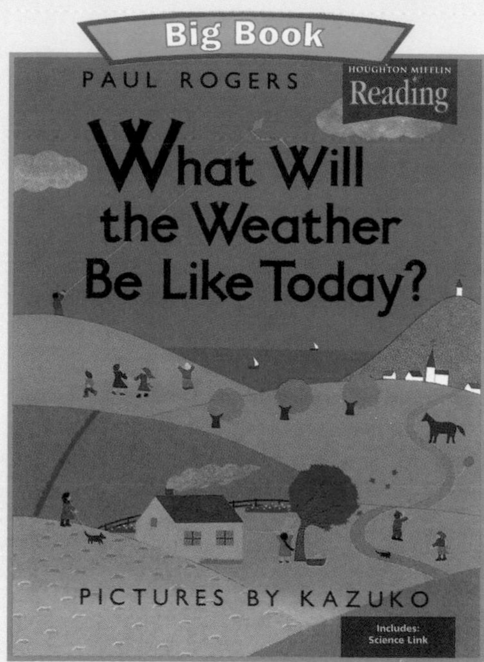

Purposes • concept of print • story language • reading strategy • comprehension skill

Extra Support

Before rereading, take a picture walk through the book. Invite comments and of from children. Point out various environments and the people and animals shown in each one.

pages 16–17

Capitalize First Word in Sentence; End Punctuation

- Track the print on page 16. Point to capital *T* in *The*. ***Why does this word begin with a capital? Who can show me the end of the sentence? How do you know?***
- Repeat with several other pages as needed.

page 18

Drawing Conclusions

- ***The book says that bees work whatever the weather. How can they do that? What do they do all day?*** (They make honey inside their hives.)

Responding

Literature Circle Browse through the Big Book together. Discuss each weather condition (windy, warm, frosty, snow, stormy). If children know these weather conditions, encourage them to describe what each one feels like and how it looks. ***Is the weather like the pictures in the book? How?***

Place weather-related books in the Book Corner. Encourage children to browse through the books and choose a climate or environment different from their own. They can choose one and talk about how it compares to local weather or climate.

English Language Learners

While children have heard the story before, remember that some of the structures in the text may prove challenging for English language learners. Simplify or paraphrase where needed.

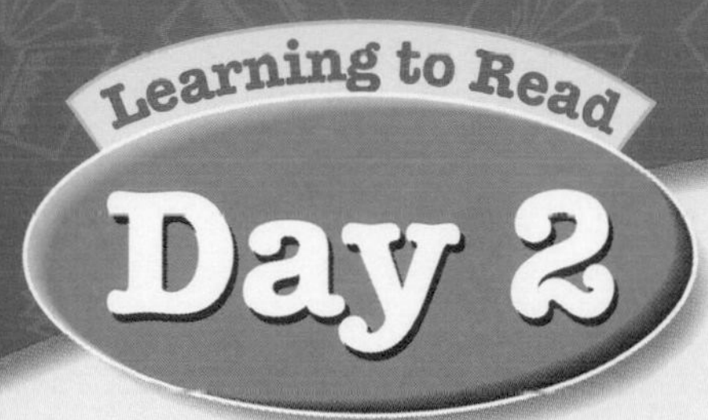

Phonics

Initial Consonant q

OBJECTIVES

Children

- identify words that begin with / kw /
- identify pictures whose names start with the letters *qu*
- form the letters *Q, q*

MATERIALS

- **Alphafriend Card** *Queenie Queen*
- **Letter Cards** *h, l, q*
- **Picture Cards** *hat, hen, horse, leaf, lemon, lion, quarter, queen, quilt*
- **Blackline Master 173** *h, l, q*
- **Phonics Center:** Theme 6, Week 3, Day 2

Develop Phonemic Awareness

Beginning Sound Play the Audiotape for Queenie Queen's song, and have children chime in when they can. Have them listen for the / kw / words and give a "thumbs up" for each one.

Queenie Queen's Song
(Tune: "On Top of Old Smokey")

Queenie has qualified to run in the race.
She'll run very quickly to keep up the pace.
Queenie is quite fit. She'll stretch for a while.
Queenie will not quit. She'll run every mile.

Connect Sounds to Letters

Beginning Letter Show *Queenie Queen,* and have children name her letters. ***Look! We need two letters to stand for / kw /, as in* queen. *Say it with me / kw /. The letters* qu *stand for / kw /. When you see* qu, *remember* Queenie Queen. *That will help you remember the sound / kw /.***

Write *queen* on the board. Underline *qu.* ***What are the first two letters in the word queen?*** *(qu)* **Queen *starts with / kw /, so I'll* write qu *first. If I wanted to write* quit, *what would I write first? How about* question? quilt? Quentin?**

Compare and Review: *h, l* In a pocket chart, place the Letter and Picture Cards randomly. Review the sounds for *qu, h,* and *l.* In turn, children name a picture, say the beginning sound, and put the card below the correct letter.

Tell children they will sort more pictures today in the Phonics Center.

MEETING INDIVIDUAL NEEDS — Extra Support

To help children remember the shape of the letter *q*, have them look at Alphafriend Queenie Queen's dress. It is shaped like the "tail" on the letter *q*.

Handwriting

Writing *Q, q* Teach the letters that stand for /kw/: capital *Q* and small *q*. Write each letter as you recite the handwriting rhyme. Children follow your letter strokes as they air-write the letter.

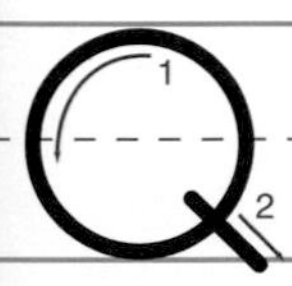

Handwriting Rhyme: Q

Capital *Q* starts like O.
Nice and fat and round.
But add a little stand up
stick just so it won't fall
down.

Handwriting Rhyme: q

Start small *q* with a circle,
Make it very stout.
Then don't forget to add
a tail,and curl it down
and out.

Apply

Practice Book page 187 Children complete the page at small group time.

Blackline Master 173 This page provides additional handwriting practice.

Use the Phonics Center materials for **Theme 6, Week 3, Day 2**.

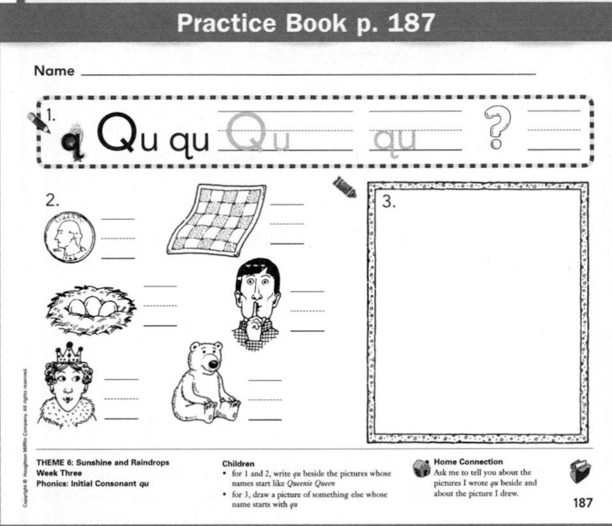

Practice Book p. 187

Name ______

1. q Qu qu Qu qu ?

2.

3.

THEME 6: Sunshine and Raindrops
Week Three
Phonics: Initial Consonant *qu*

Children
- for 1 and 2, write *qu* beside the pictures whose names start like *Queenie Queen*
- for 3, draw a picture of something else whose name starts with *qu*

Home Connection
Ask me to tell you about the pictures I wrote *qu* beside and about the picture I drew.

187

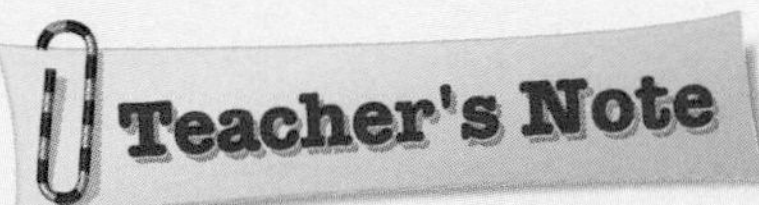

Handwriting practice for the continuous stroke style is available on **Blackline Master 199.**

Portfolio Opportunity

As children demonstrate the ability to form letters consistently and correctly, save selected pages to share with parents at conference time.

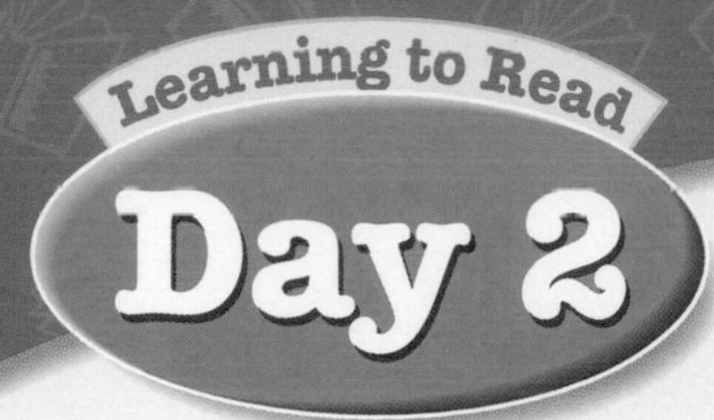

OBJECTIVES

Children

- read and write the high-frequency words *is, here*

MATERIALS

- **Word Cards** *go, here, I, Is, is, it, My, my*
- **Picture Cards** *bike, dog;* others for sentence building
- **Punctuation Cards:** period, question mark

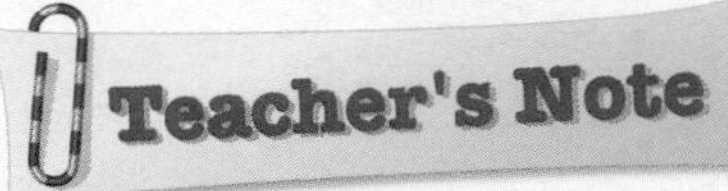

For this activity, you will also need to make a word card for *can.*

High-Frequency Words

Review Words: is, here

Teach

- *Today we'll practice reading and writing two words you already know. The first word is:* is. *Who will use* is *in a sentence? This is an important word because we use it all the time when we speak. Watch me write* is. *I'll point and you spell:* i-s, is. *Let's chant:* i-s is; i-s, is. *This will help you remember how to spell* is.
- *Our second word is* here. *Who will use* here *in a sentence?* Continue the routine of using the word in a sentence, writing, clapping, and chanting the spelling of *here.*

Word Wall Have children find the words *is* and *here* on the Word Wall. Remind them to use the Word Wall to spell words correctly.

Practice

Reading Build these sentences in a pocket chart. Children take turns reading them aloud. Add additional Picture Cards to the chart for children to build and read their own sentences.

- Use high-frequency words in classroom environmental print. Repeated exposure to the words encourages children to recognize them automatically. Show capital and lower-case forms.
- Ask children to "read around the room" to find target words in classroom signs, posters, book titles, and other classroom print.

Apply

Practicc Book page 188 Children will read and write *is* and *here* as they complete the Practice Book page. They will practice reading *is* and *here* in the **Phonics Library** story "Fan."

Practice Book p. 188

Name ______

Is here

1. ______ ______ my cat here?

2. Is my cat ______?

3. ______ ______ my cat here?

4. Here is my cat!

THEME 6: Sunshine and Raindrops
Week Three
High-Frequency Words Review *is, here*

Children
- read the questions and write *Is* and *here* to complete them
- read the last sentence and draw the cat in the place where the child found it

Home Connection
I finished the lines in this short story. Let me read it to you and tell you about the place the cat was hiding.

188

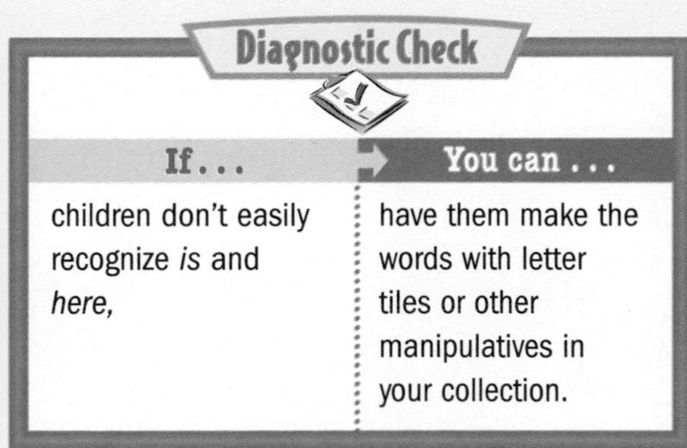

Diagnostic Check

If . . .	You can . . .
children don't easily recognize *is* and *here*,	have them make the words with letter tiles or other manipulatives in your collection.

High-Frequency Word Practice

OBJECTIVES

Children

- read high-frequency words
- create and write sentences with high-frequency words

MATERIALS

- **Word Cards** *a, here, Here, I, is, see*
- **Picture Cards** *farm, pig;* other assorted animal picture cards
- **Punctuation Card:** period

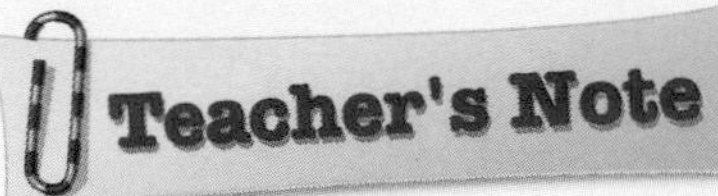

For this activity, you will also need word cards for *can* and *Can.*

Building Sentences

Tell children that you want to build some sentences.

- Display the Word Cards in random order. Put the Word Card *Here* in a pocket chart, and read it.
- ***I want the next word to be* is. *Who can find that word? That's right! This word is* is. *Now who can read my sentence so far?***
- Continue building the sentences *Here is a* (Picture Card: *farm*). *Can I see a* ____ *here?* Children choose a picture card for the blank.
- Read the sentences with children. Then call on volunteers to build a sentence to answer the question.

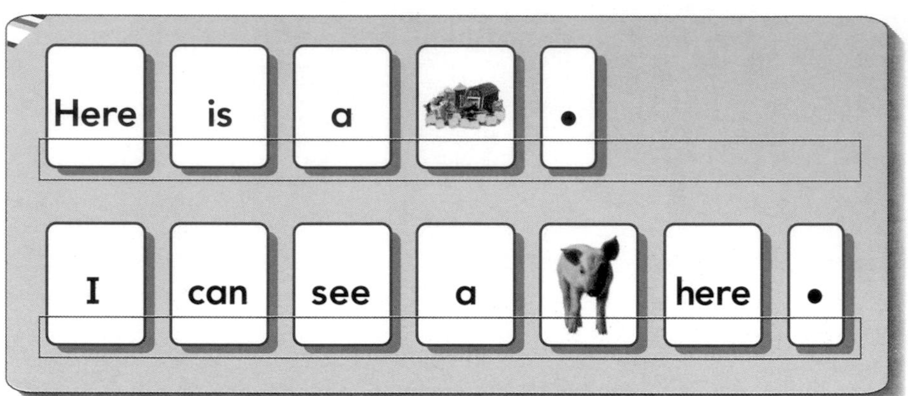

Writing Opportunity Have each child draw a picture of something found on a farm. Children then write sentences to tell about their pictures using the high-frequency words *here* and *is.* Children can use a rebus to complete the sentence or use temporary phonics spellings for words of which they are unsure.

Oral Language

Vocabulary Expansion

Viewing and Speaking Display the weather and action word chart (T123), and reread children's suggestions. Today, focus on expanding children's oral vocabulary. A good way to generate new vocabulary is to pantomime actions and have children describe what they view. Then use prompts like these:

- *Let's look back at what we wrote yesterday. Tanner said she would* **splash** *in the pool.* **Splash** *is a good action word. What other word could we use? Good,* **dive** *and* **float** *are wonderful action words! Who will use one in a sentence? Here's one:* **splish-splash!** *You say it. That's a sound and an action!*
- *Annie wanted to* **run** *through the sprinkler. How else can we describe running? She could* **dash, dart,** *or* **fly.** *These are good words to help us describe a run through the sprinkler.*
- *What other words tell how people move quickly? Do you* **hurry?** *Do you* **rush?** *Do you* **hustle?** *Let's write these words. I'll write while you think. Tomorrow we'll write a story together. Maybe we can use some of these words in our story.*

At Group Time
Writing Center

Put the chart in the Writing Center. Children can illustrate and label one of the action words. Ask them to think of more words to add to the chart. If children think of one, tell them to record it in their journals, writing the letters they hear in the word, and checking with you later to add to the chart.

OBJECTIVES

Children

- name action words

Portfolio Opportunity

Save children's writing samples as an indication of their understanding of action words.

DAY 2

English Language Learners

English language learners will need support to understand the nuances in meaning among synonymous words. Use pictures, dramatization, and realia to develop meaning. Help children to focus on words that are most common and have the widest application.

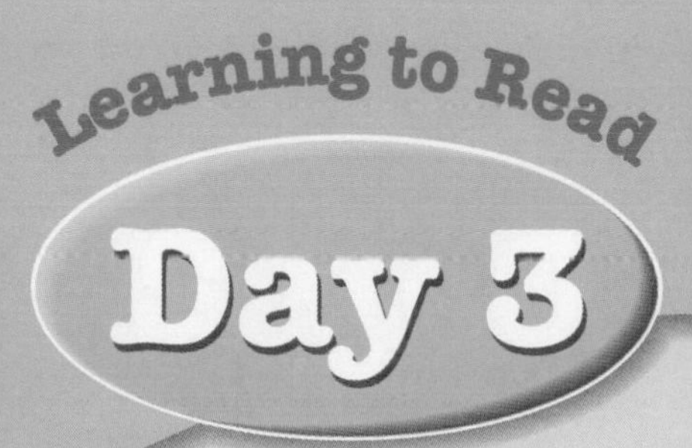

Day at a Glance

Learning to Read

Big Book:

All to Build a Snowman

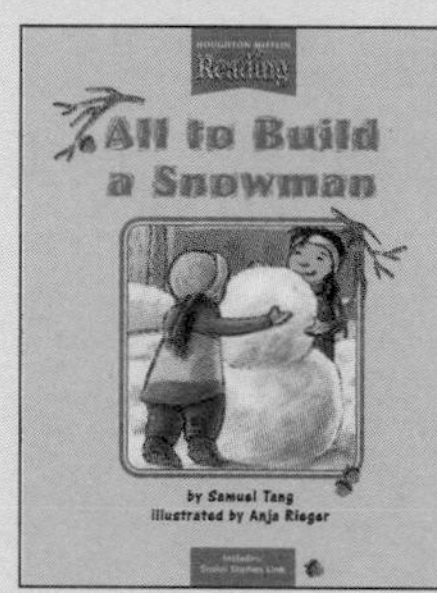

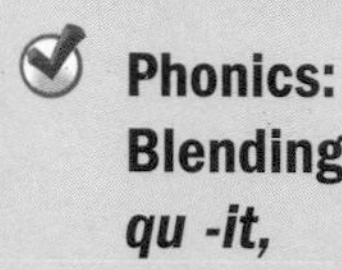
Phonics: Blending *qu -it*, *page T138*

Word Work

Building Words, *page 140*

Writing & Language

Shared Writing, *page T141*

Half-Day Kindergarten

✓ Indicates lessons for tested skills. Choose additional activities as time allows.

Opening

Calendar

Sunday	Monday	Tuesday	Wednesday	Thursday	Friday	Saturday
			1	2	3	4
5	6	7	8	9	10	11
12	13	14	15	16	17	18
19	20	21	22	23	24	25
26	27	28	29	30	31	

Continue expanding weather vocabulary during your calendar routine. Look at the sky together. Help children describe what they see. Use words such as *cloudy, murky, clear, gray, blue-gray, brilliant, colorful, vivid.* Encourage children to use these words in their conversations.

Daily Message

Modeled Writing Incorporate expanded vocabulary in the daily message. Call specific attention to how this vocabulary helps the writing seem lively.

Today the sky is murky and gray. We hope the sun comes out because we re going to fly kites on the playground.

Ask children to find the new words *is* and *here* on the Word Wall. Then review all the words as children chant: ***i-s spells is; h-e-r-e spells here.***

Routines

Daily Phonemic Awareness
Blending and Segmenting Onset and Rime

- Recite "Sing a Song of Sixpence" several times until children can join in. Then expand the literature experience.
- ***This is an old rhyme. Your parents may know it, too. I'll say some words parts. You tell me the word. Listen carefully:***
- Recite the rhyme, choosing a word from each line for children to blend, for example: "Sing a /s/ /ong/ *(song)* of sixpence."
- Repeat the rhyme again, this time pausing at a word for children to segment into beginning and end sounds.

Sing a Song of Sixpence
ÍSing a song of sixpence,
A pocket full of rye,
Four and twenty blackbirds
Baked in a pie.
When the pie was opened,
The birds began to sing.
Wasn't that a dainty dish
To set before the King?
a Mother Goose Rhyme
11

***Higglety Pigglety: A Book of Rhymes,* page 11**

DAY 3

Getting Ready to Learn

To help plan their day, tell children that they will

- reread and discuss the Big Book: *All to Build a Snowman.*

- read a **Phonics Library** story called "Fan."

- make a winter-scene collage.

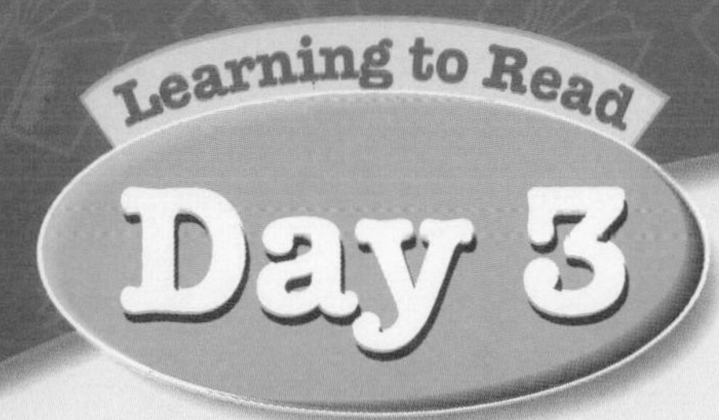

Sharing the Big Book

Oral Language/Comprehension

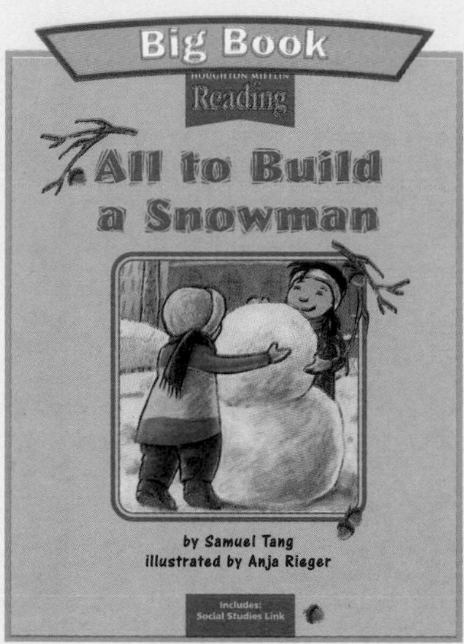

Big Book
Reading
All to Build a Snowman
by Samuel Tang
illustrated by Anja Rieger

Purposes • concept of print • story language • reading strategy • comprehension skill

Building Background

Reading for Understanding Browse through *All to Build a Snowman,* reminding children of the story. For each episode, have children retell what is happening. As you talk, use descriptive weather words: *frosty, chilly, snowy, bright, sunny,* and *wintery.*

Strategy: Evaluate

Student Modeling ***Think about the first time you heard this story. How did you like it? Would you read it again and again if you could? Remember, it's fine to like one book better than another. But it's important to say why you like it.***

Comprehension Focus: Story Structure: Plot

Student Modeling ***The characters in the Big Book, the children who made the snowman, had a problem. Who remembers what the problem was?*** (Things fell from a tree and scared the cat; the cat ran and Slim began to chase it.)

Sharing the Story

Reread the story, pausing for these discussion points:

pages 6–9

Cause and Effect

- ***What made the kitten meow and jump?*** (An acorn fell on it.) ***What made the acorns drop down and thump?*** (Some branches fell on a squirrel who was carrying the acorns.) ***What startled a crow making some branches fall far below?*** (The wind blew snow onto the crow.)

Ask questions to help children practice cause and effect and forms of verbs. Ask: *What made the pigeons flutter and fly?* Model: *The cat made the pigeons flutter and fly.* For more proficient speakers, ask: *Why did the pigeons flutter and fly?* Model: *The pigeons fluttered and flew because the cat chased them.*

pages 4–5

Concepts of Print: Quotation Marks, End Punctuation

- Point out the quotation marks on page 4. ***These words tell the exact words someone says.*** Point to the end mark. Ask what a period means.
- ***Now look at page 5. Listen as I read. What does the lady say? Point to the quotation marks that show what she says.***

pages 10–15

Story Structure: Plot

- ***What happens to the lady's cat? That's a problem, isn't it? Do you think the cat has a problem, too? What is it?*** (Yes; it is stranded on top of the snowman.)

age 18–20

loting Details

- ***How is the snowman dressed now? Where did his clothing come from?***

Responding

iterature Circle This story contains a series of actions and reactions. Have hildren discuss each one and how it, in turn, caused something else to happen. o children think the author wrote a good story? Why or why not?

ractice Book Page 189 Children complete the page at small group time.

Materials • Black construction paper • white crayon • glue • assorted natural items: acorns, bits of pine boughs, feathers, leaves, twigs

Children draw snowmen with white crayon on black or dark construction paper, dressing them appropriately. Children glue a few items to the drawing. They use the picture to retell the story.

Practice Book p. 189

Name

1. 2.

THEME 6: Sunshine and Raindrops
Week Three *All to Build a Snowman*
Plot, Responding

Children
1. color the pictures that show something that happened in the story
2. draw two more things that they remember happened in the story

Home Connection
We heard a story today called *All to Build a Snowman.* Ask me to tell it to you. I can point to the pictures as I tell that part.

189

Extra Support

Some children may never have built a snowman. Discuss how to build one, including the materials needed. Children pantomime "rolling" a snowball to make a tall snowman.

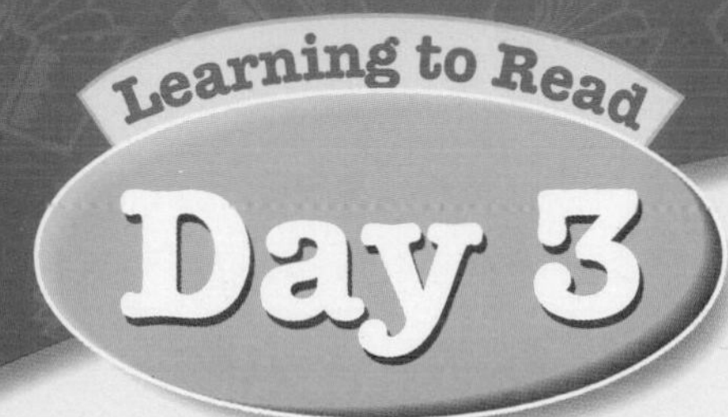

Phonics

Blending qu -it

OBJECTIVES

Children

- identify words with initial consonant *qu*, / kw /
- blend and read words with *b, f, h, k, l, p, qu, s* and *-it*

MATERIALS

- **Alphafriends** *Iggy Iguana, Queenie Queen*
- **Letter Cards** *b, f, h, i, k, l, p, q, s, t, u*
- **Alphafriend Audiotape** Theme 6

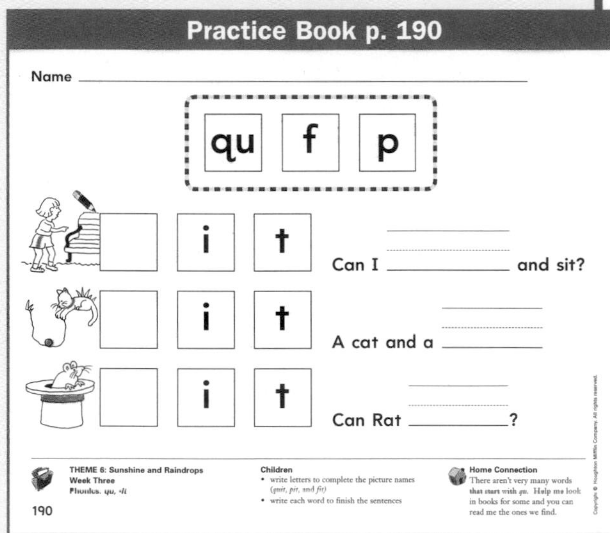

Practice Book p. 190

Name ______________________

qu f p

[ ] i t Can I ________ and sit?

[ ] i t A cat and a ________

[ ] i t Can Rat ________?

THEME 6: Sunshine and Raindrops
Week Three
Phonics: *qu, -it*

190

Children
- write letters to complete the picture names (*quit, pit,* and *fit*)
- write each word to finish the sentences

Home Connection
There aren't very many words that start with *qu*. Help me look in books for some and you can read me the ones we find.

Connect Sounds to Letters

Review *qu* Play Queenie Queen's song. Children sing along as they can. Write *qu* on the board. As you sing / kw / words, point to the letters.

Blending *-it* Tell children they'll build a word with *qu*. Remind them they'll need a vowel. Point to Alphafriend Iggy Iguana.

- *You remember Iggy. Say it:* Iggy Iguana. *Iggy's letter is the vowel* i, *and this is his sound: / ĭ /. You say it with me. / ĭ /. The letter* i *stands for Iggy's sound. Say this after me: / ĭ /* if, */ ĭ /* is, */ ĭ /* itch.
- Remind children that they know the sound for t, / t /. Display Letter Cards *i* and *t*. */ ĭ / / t /,* it. *Look! I've made the word* it. *Who will come up and show us how to make* it *again? Who can use* it *in a sentence? This is an important word. We use* it *when we speak and when we read.*

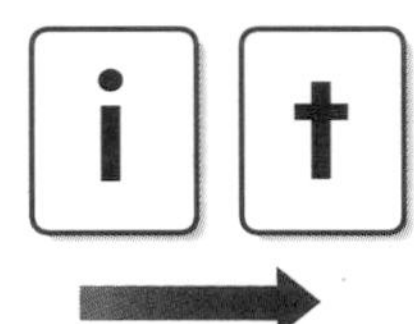

Choose a child to point to *it* on the Word Wall.

Blending *-it* Words Explain that knowing *it* will help children read other words. Put *qu* in place, point, and blend / kw / / it /, *quit.* Remind children that two letters, *qu,* stand for / kw /. Have children read *quit* as you point.

Now help children blend and read words with *-it* and other familiar consonants: *bit, fit, hit, kit, lit, pit,* and *sit.*

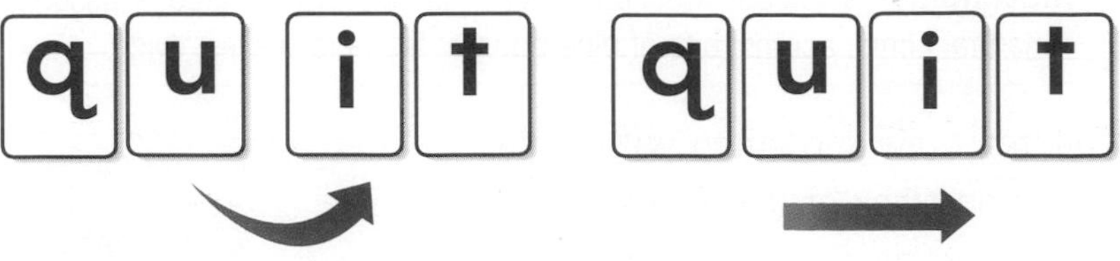

Extra Support

Read "Quack! Quack! Quack!" *Higglety Pigglety: A Book of Rhymes,* page 29. Children echo the words and listen for the / kw / sound.

Apply

Practice Book page 190 Children complete the page at small group time.

Phonics in Action

Houghton Mifflin Reading
Phonics Library
Sunshine and Raindrops

Applying Phonics Skills and High-Frequency Words

Phonics/Decoding Strategy

Teacher/Student Modeling Discuss using the Phonics/Decoding strategy to read **Phonics Library** the story. ***Here's a story you can read on your own. Let's talk about what happens when you come to a word that you might not know right away.***

Think Aloud

I see this word in the title: "Fan." I can blend /f/ /an/, to make fan. Point to Fan and read it with me. I think Fan *is an ant because I see an ant on the cover.* Fan *must be her name. Here's what we did: we looked at the letters, said the sounds for each one, and checked to make sure that it made sense. Let's find out more about Fan the ant.*

n a brief picture walk, have children point to Fan the ant, and then identify he rebus pictures *apple, orange, cookie.*

Coached Reading

Iave children "whisper read" before pausing. Prompts:

age 17 *Where is Fan in the picture?* (at a picnic table) *What do you think an ant will do at a picnic?*

age 19 *What did Fan eat first? Who can read the -it family word? Now let's all read the page together.*

age 21 *Fan is having dessert. What did she have? What -it family word did you read?* (bit)

age 23 *Poor Fan! She is full. Let's read the last page together. How does the sentence end? What does the exclamation mark mean? How should we read it?*

Phonics Library

Purposes

- apply phonics skills
- apply high-frequency words

17

Here is Fan.

18

Fan bit an [apple].

19

Fan bit an [orange].

20

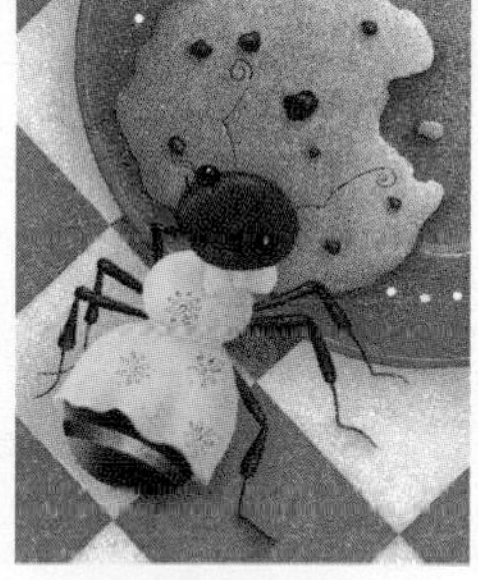

Fan bit a [cookie].

21

Fan sat.

22

Fan quit!

23

Home Connection

Children can color the pictures in the take-home version of "Fan." After rereading on Day 4, they take it home to read to family members.

DAY 3

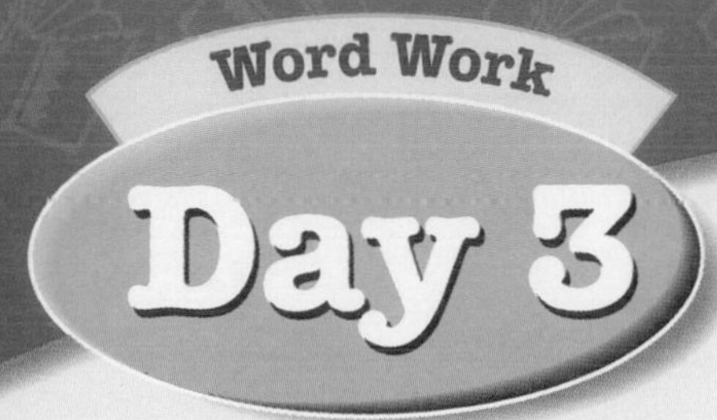

Building Words

Word Family: *-it*

Remind children that they know how to write the word *it.* Choose a child to model with Letter Cards.

- ***Now what letters do I need to make* quit*? Listen /kw/. What letters stand for this sound? Be careful! This is tricky! (Display* q *and* u.*) Look! We have made* quit*. Let's read it:* quit*. Who will use* quit *in a sentence?***
- ***Now what happens if I change /kw/ to /b/? Right, I'd write* bit*. Let's make more words.*** (Continue with *f, h, k, l, p, s.*)

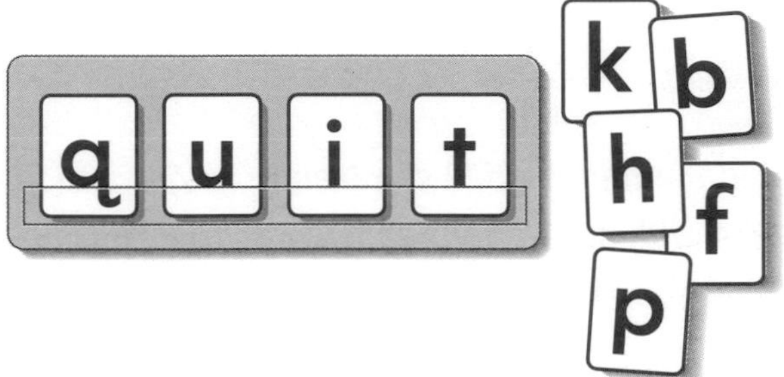

List the words on a chart and post it in the Writing Center. If you already have an *-it* family chart, add the word *quit* to it.

Have small groups work together to make *-it* words. Children can use magnetic letters or other manipulatives in your collection.

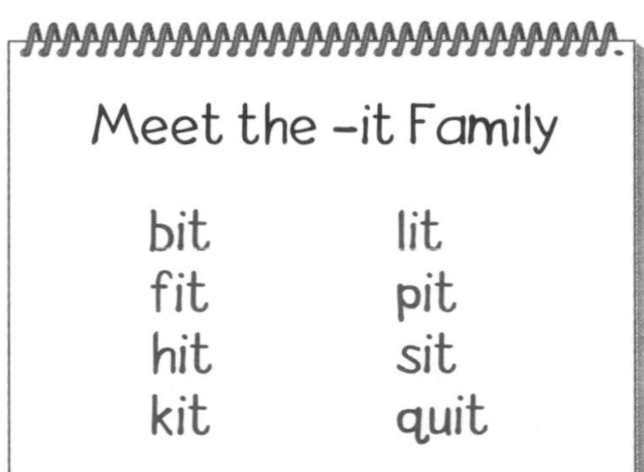

Meet the -it Family
bit
fit
hit
kit
lit
pit
sit
quit

OBJECTIVES

Children

- blend initial consonants with *-it* to read words

MATERIALS

- **Letter Cards** *b, f, h, i, k, l, p, q, s, t, u*

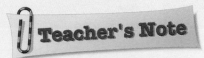

Teacher's Note

Explain that in English, the letters *qu* are buddies. They always go together to make a word. Teach this little rhyme:

"Q"and "u" have been buddies for so long.
"Q" needs "u" when they walk along.

Shared Writing

Writing a Story

Listening and Speaking Revisit the word lists children made to describe weather and action words. Then tell children that they'll write a story today. They'll choose action words to make the writing lively. Use a chart like the one shown here to remind children of the *who, what,* and *where* of a story. Use these prompts.

- ***What shall we write about? We'll say that in the first sentence so that everyone will know what our story is about.***
- ***I like Salvadore's word,*** windy. ***It tells just what kind of day it is. What word shall we use to describe the sky? Sarah says*** cloudy. ***I'll write that. What mark shall we put at the end of this sentence?***
- ***How shall we end our story?***
- ***Now we have to think of a title. What shall we call it? Remember that a good title tells what the story is about.***
- ***Let's read our story. Tomorrow we'll read it again. Maybe we'll want to add something. Perhaps we'll have an idea to make our story even more exciting.***

OBJECTIVES

Children

- participate in shared writing

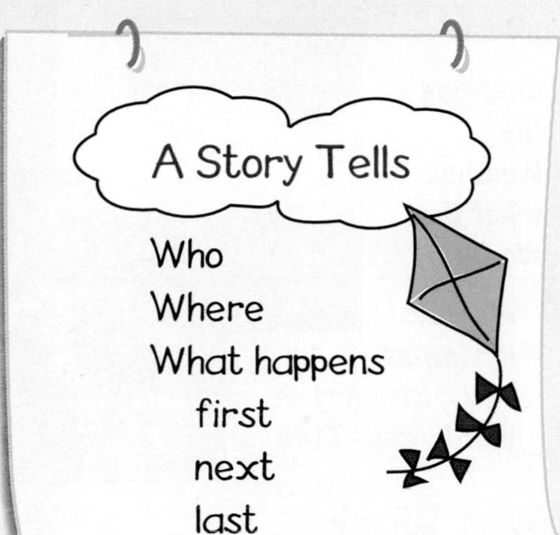

A Story Tells
Who
Where
What happens
first
next
last

DAY 3

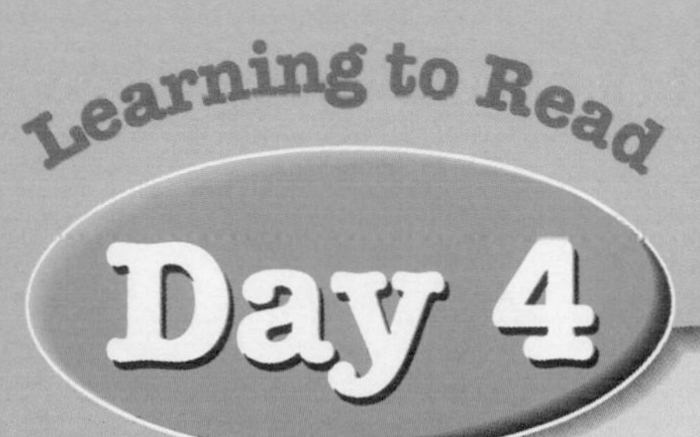

Day at a Glance

Learning to Read

Big Book:

Checking the Weather, What Can We Do?

✓ **Phonics:** ***Reviewing /kw/; Blending -it, Words, page T146***

Word Work

Building Words, ***page T148***

Writing & Language

Interactive Writing, ***page T149***

Half-Day Kindergarten

✓ Indicates lessons for tested skills. Choose additional activities as time allows.

Opening

Calendar

Sunday	Monday	Tuesday	Wednesday	Thursday	Friday	Saturday
			1	2	3	4
5	6	7	8	9	10	11
12	13	14	15	16	17	18
19	20	21	22	23	24	25
26	27	28	29	30	31	

When recording weather during your calendar routine, have children talk about activities and clothing suitable for today's weather. Use lots of describing words in your discussion.

Daily Message

Modeled Writing Use words that begin with *qu* in today's message. Point them out. Define the words if necessary.

Today we will learn what to do during a fire drill. Keisha's dad works for the fire department. He can answer all our questions.

Distribute word cards for the words that are posted on the Word Wall. Children match the word cards to the words on the Word Wall. As each match is made, have children chant the spelling: **i-s *spells* is.**

Routines

Daily Phonemic Awareness
Blending and Segmenting Onset and Rime

- Read "Quack! Quack! Quack!" on page 29 of *Higglety Pigglety.*
- Play a guessing game. ***I'll say some sounds. You put them together to make words from the poem: / d /... / uck /*** (duck)***; / b /... / ig /*** (big).
- Continue with other one-syllable words from the poem.
- ***Now I'll say a word, and you take it apart:* five. *Say the beginning sound and then the ending sounds in* five.** (/ f /... / ive /)
- Continue with other one-syllable words from the poem.

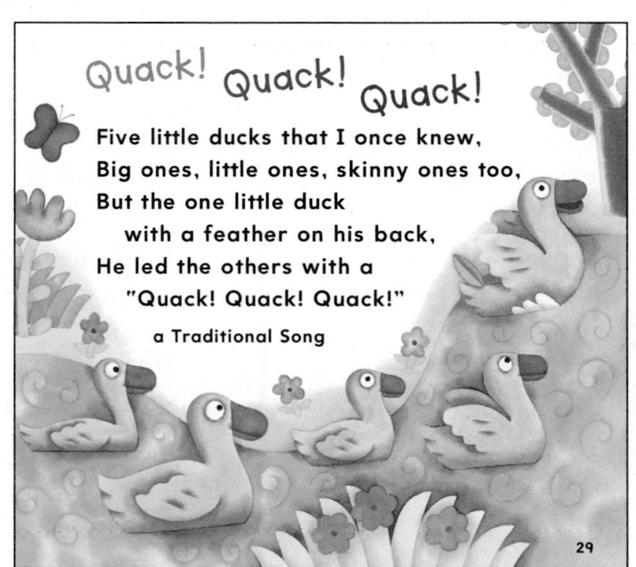

***Higglety Pigglety: A Book of Rhymes,* page 29**

Getting Ready to Learn

To help plan their day, tell children that they will

- reread the Science Link: *Checking the Weather* and the Social Studies Link: *What Can We Do?*

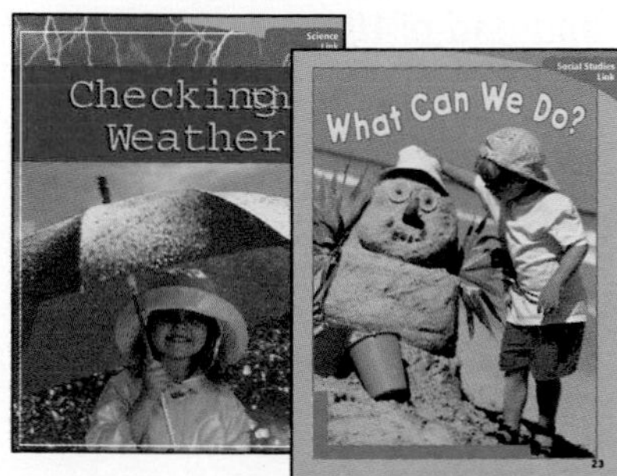

- build words with *qu* and other letters in the Phonics Center.

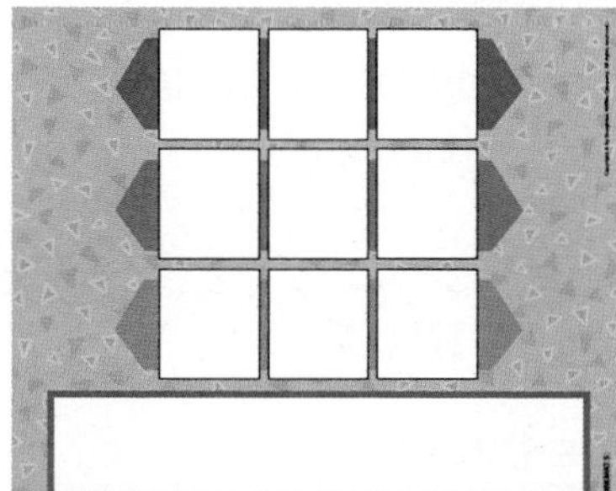

- take home a **Phonics Library** book to share.

DAY 4

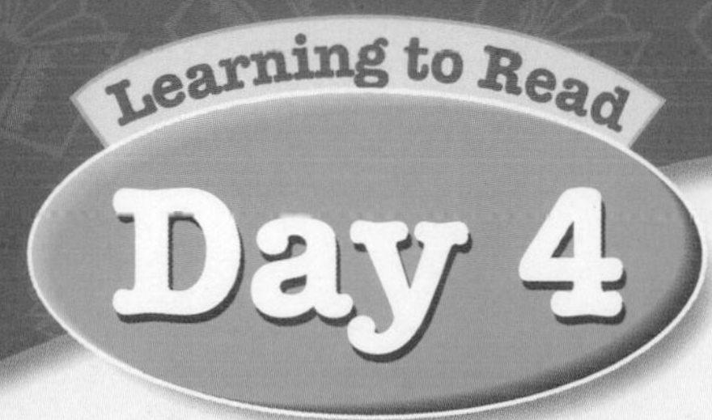

Sharing the Big Books

Science Link

OBJECTIVES

Children

- identify use of capital letter at the beginning of a sentence
- identify end punctuation

Big Book

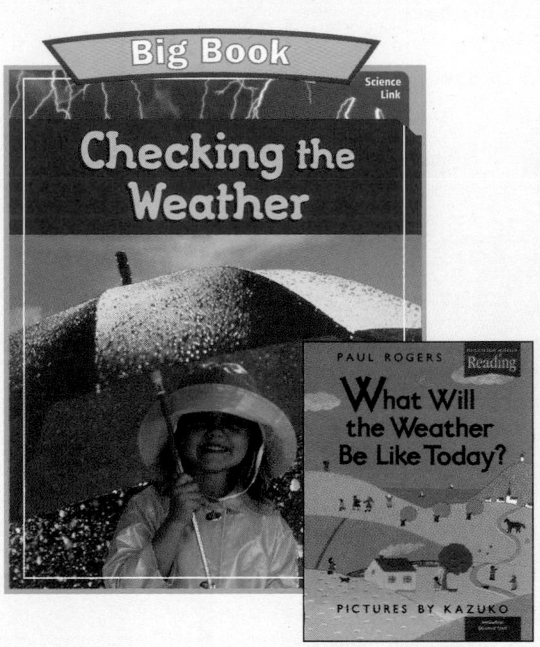

pages 33–38

Building Background

Look back at the weather symbols on your calendar. Ask children how they check the weather each day. Encourage children to use descriptive weather words.

Reading for Understanding Display *Checking the Weather* and read the title aloud. ***We read this article before. It tells about the instruments people use to check the weather. Who remembers some of them? You can use the pictures to help you remember.***

page 33

Strategy: Predict/Infer

- ***How did you know what this article would be about before we read it? What clues did you use?***

page 34

Noting Details

- ***How would you describe the weather on this page? How would you describe a foggy day?***

pages 36–37

Making Judgments

- ***Do you think wind gauges and rain gauges are useful tools? Who do you think uses tools like this?***

page 38

Concepts of Print: Capital at beginning of sentence; End punctuation

- ***What can you tell me about the beginning and end of these sentences? What do the end marks mean?***

Responding

Literature Circle Have children revisit the article to answer the questions posed by the text.

English Language Learners

Before rereading, invite pairs of children to take a picture walk through the Big Books. They can take turns sharing what they remember about the articles using the pictures as prompts.

Social Studies Link

Building Background

Reading for Understanding Remind children that they also read *What Can We Do?* Pause for discussion as you share the selection.

title page
Strategy: Infer/Predict

Does the title tell you everything about this article? Why or why not?

page 24
Evaluate

- *Is a sunny day a good day to build a sandcastle? Why?*

page 25
Drawing Conclusions

- *Why do you need a windy day to fly a kite?*

page 27
Concepts of Print: Capital at Beginning of Sentence; End Punctuation

- *How many sentences do you see? How does each sentence begin? end?*

Responding

Literature Circle Ask if children learned about a weather related-activity they hadn't thought of before reading. What would they add to the article?

Materials • newspaper weather maps • paper • crayons

Display a grouping of newspaper or magazine weather maps in the Science Center. Identify some of the symbols on the map and compare them to the ones children use for their daily calendar routine.

OBJECTIVES

Children

- identify use of capital letter at th beginning of a sentence
- identify end punctuation

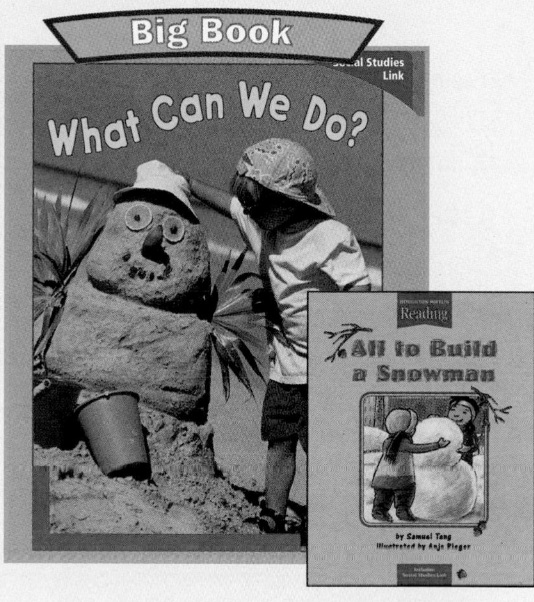

pages 23–29

DAY 4

Challenge

Some children will be able to create their own versions of *What Can We Do?* Have them draw, pictures of weather-related activities and caption them with a question and an answer.

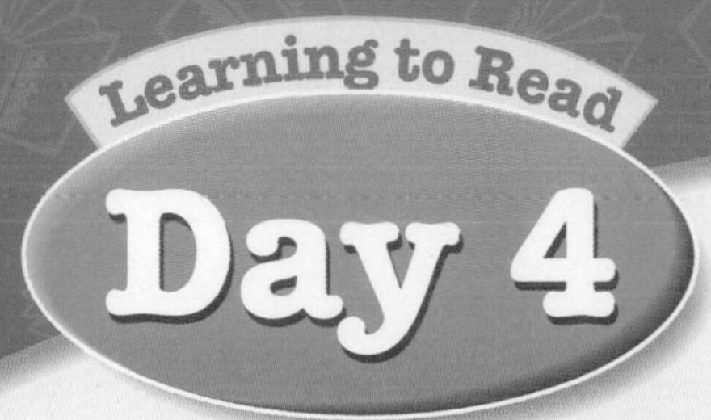

Phonics

OBJECTIVES

Children

- identify initial *qu* for words that begin with / kw /
- blend initial consonants with *-it*

MATERIALS

- ***From Apples to Zebras: A Book of ABC's,*** page 12
- **Alphafriend** *Iggy Iguana*
- **Letter Cards** *b, f, h, i, k, l, p, q, s, t, u*
- **Word Cards** *here, I, my*
- **Picture Card** *car*
- **Phonics Center:** Theme 6, Week 3, Day 4

Teacher's Note

During writing, children may ask how to spell words from the *-it* family. Help children find the word *it* on the Word Wall and substitute the appropriate initial consonant(s).

Home Connection

Challenge children to look at home for items or for names that begin with *qu*. Children can draw pictures to show what they have found.

Connect Sounds to Letters

Review *qu* Using self-stick notes, cover the words on page 12 of *From Apples to Zebras: A Book of ABC's.* Then display the page. Have children identify each picture. Ask what letter they expect to see first in each label and why. Uncover the words for children to check their predictions.

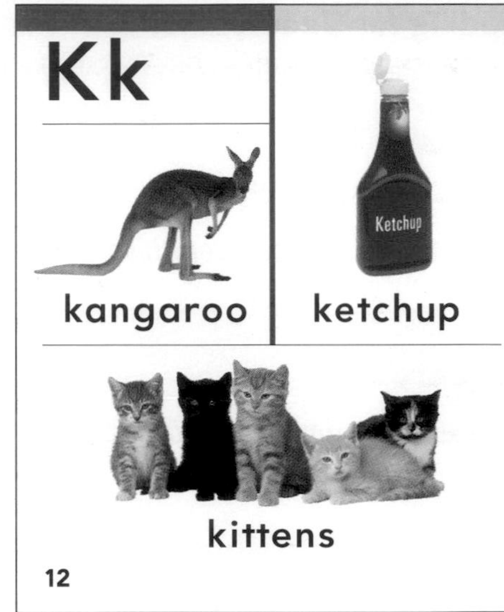

***Apples to Zebras: A Book of ABC's*, page 12**

Reviewing *-it* Remind children that every word needs a vowel. Ask which Alphafriend stands for the vowel sound / ĭ /, and then show Iggy Iguana. Some children will be able to name words that begin with / ĭ /. (*in, inside, igloo, insect*)

Hold up Letter Cards *i* and *t*. Call on a child to write *it*. ***Watch as (child's name) builds a Word Wall word: / ĭ / / t /,*** it, ***/ ĭ / / t /,*** it.

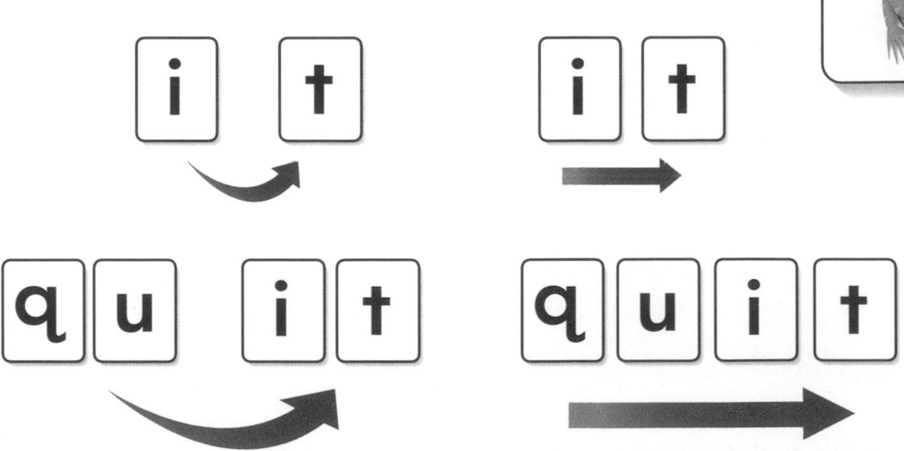

Blending *-it* Words ***How do I use*** it ***to make*** quit? ***What letters do I need? Yes,*** qu ***stands for the sound / kw /. Say it. / kw /. Now let's make a new word:*** lit. ***What letter will we need? Listen / l / / it /,*** lit. ***Think of all the words we can make with the word*** it.

Continue, choosing children to write *bit, fit, hit, kit, pit, sit* at the chart as others write at their work stations.

Apply

Focus once more on *quit*. ***Let's use the word quit in a sentence. What could you say if your car wouldn't start? Yes,*** **My car quit.** ***Let's write that.***

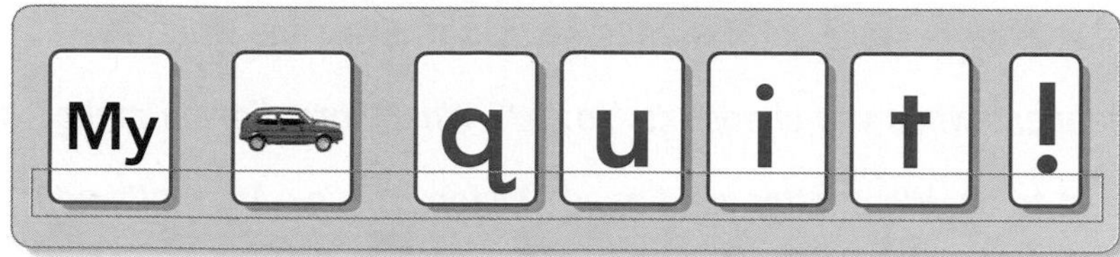

Now let's write this sentence: **Can I sit here?** ***Who will help me make the sentence? Everyone can write at your desks. Remember to blend the -it word,*** **sit.**

Tell children they will build more sentences today in the Phonics Center.

Practice Book page 191 Children will complete this page at small group time.

Phonics Library In groups today, children read *-it* words as they reread the **Phonics Library** story "Fan." See suggestions, pages T139.

Phonics Center

Use the Phonics Center Materials for **Theme 6, Week 3, Day 4**.

Practice Book p. 191

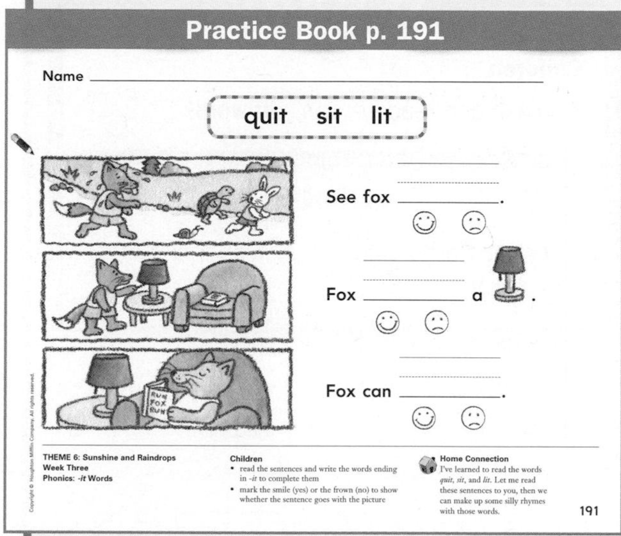

Name

quit sit lit

See fox ______.

Fox ______ a ______.

Fox can ______.

THEME 6: Sunshine and Raindrops
Week Three
Phonics: *-it* Words

Children
- read the sentences and write the words ending in *-it* to complete them
- mark the smile (yes) or the frown (no) to show whether the sentence goes with the picture

Home Connection
I've learned to read the words *quit*, *sit*, and *lit*. Let me read these sentences to you, then we can make up some silly rhymes with those words.

191

Save a few High-Frequency Word Practice Book pages to demonstrate the words children can now read.

DAY 4

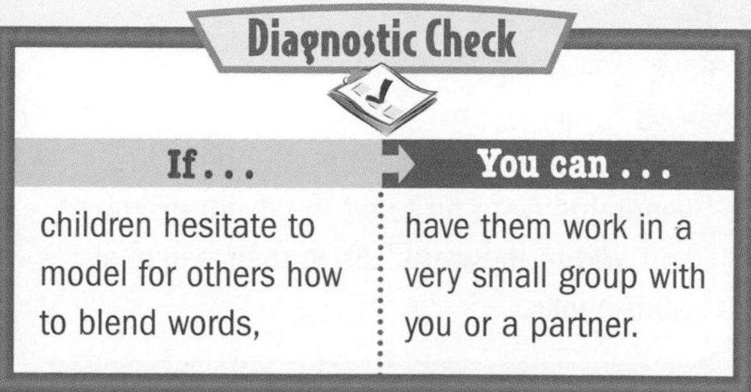

Diagnostic Check

If . . .	You can . . .
children hesitate to model for others how to blend words,	have them work in a very small group with you or a partner.

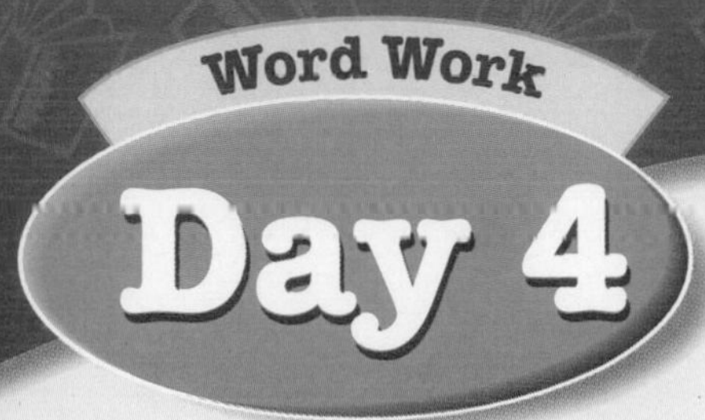

OBJECTIVES

Children

- make and read *-it, -an, -at* words

MATERIALS

- **Letter Cards** *a, b, c, f, h, k, l, m, n, p, q, r, s, t u, v*

Challenge

Children who demonstrate the ability to generalize (*it* to *hit* to *sit* to *bit,* for example) can add to the word lists in their personal word banks.

Building Words

Word Families: *-it, -an, -at,*

For children who need another review of *-it* words, do it now. Then go on to review building *-at* words. Say the sounds of the letters slowly: /ă/... /t/.

- ***How many sounds do you hear? The first sound is /ă/. What letter do I need? The last sound is /t/. Tell me what letter to choose. What word did we make? Right,*** at.
- ***Now it's your turn. Make*** sat. ***Listen:*** s-s-sat. sat. ***Everyone write.***
- ***What happens when you change /s/ to /b/? What word did you make?***
- ***Change*** at ***to*** an. ***What letter will I need? Listen /ă/ /n/.*** An, ***that's right. It's your turn. Write*** ban. ***Listen: /b/ /an/.***
- Continue making *-at* and *-an* words with other known consonants *c, f, h, m, p, r, v.*
- Note that some children may be more successful writing one word family at a time. But for others, mix them and have children listen carefully and say words slowly as they write.

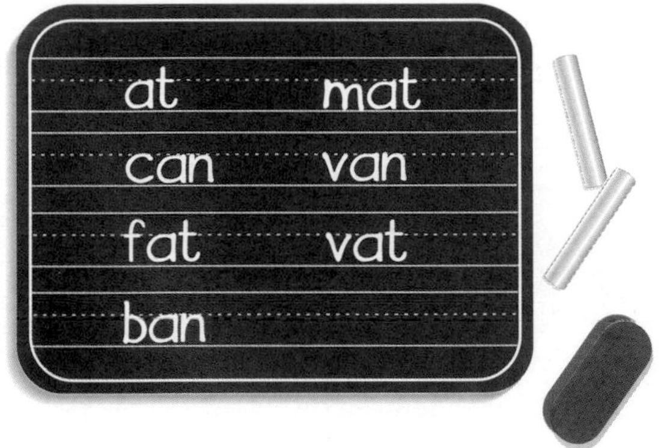

Interactive Writing

Writing a Story

Listening and Speaking Look again at the story you wrote yesterday. Does the title tell what the story is about? Ask children if they'd like to make any changes. Follow the interactive writing routine as you write together.

- *I'll change the word* fly *to* flew. *That means that we did it yesterday. Read it with me:* We flew kites. *Who will point to the word* flew? *How did you know that was the word?*
- Windy *starts with* w. *Wendy can write it for us, since her name begins with* w, *too.*
- *I like the way Nancy described the string as* long *and* red. *It helps describe the string more accurately. What marks go at the end of this sentence? How do exclamation marks help us read the last two sentences? Let's read them with excitement and expression.*
- *This ending is good. It's lively. I like it. You are very good writers!*

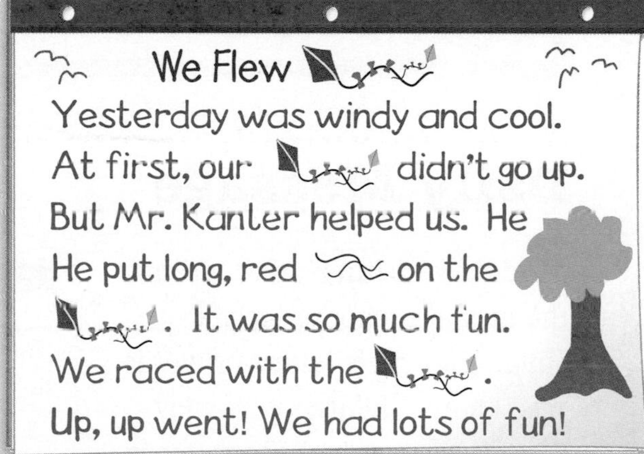

We Flew
Yesterday was windy and cool.
At first, our didn't go up.
But Mr. Kanter helped us. He
He put long, red on the
. It was so much fun.
We raced with the .
Up, up went! We had lots of fun!

At Group Time

Writing Center

Put the story in the Writing Center. Children can "read" it with a partner. Have children frame words they can read. Congratulate them for their growing understanding of reading. Encourage children to draw and write their own sentences about flying or another outdoor activity.

OBJECTIVES

Children

- participate in interactive writing

Portfolio Opportunity

Save children's writing samples to share with parents and to discuss with children at conference time.

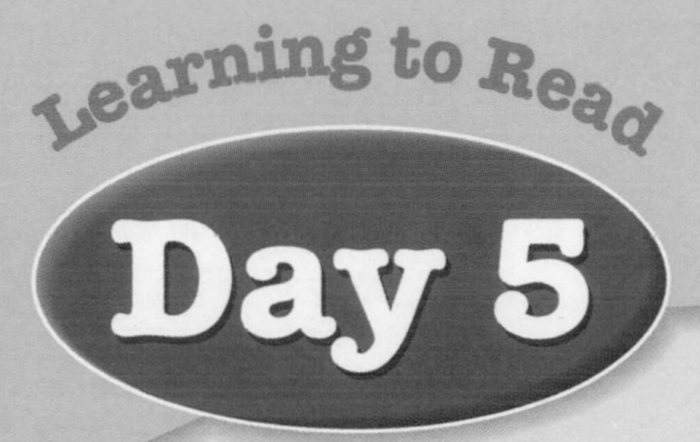

Opening

Day at a Glance

Learning to Read

Revisiting the Literature:

The Woodcutter's Cap, What Will the Weather Be Like Today? All to Build a Snowman, What Can We Do?, Checking the Weather, "Fan"

 **Phonics: Initial Consonants; *-at, -an, -it,* words; *page T154***

Word Work

Building Words, *page T156*

Writing & Language

Independent Writing, *page T157*

 **Half-Day Kindergarten**

 Indicates lessons for tested skills. Choose additional activities as time allows.

Calendar

Sunday	Monday	Tuesday	Wednesday	Thursday	Friday	Saturday
			1	2	3	4
5	6	7	8	9	10	11
12	13	14	15	16	17	18
19	20	21	22	23	24	25
26	27	28	29	30	31	

Ask children to summarize what the weather is like where *you* are today.

Daily Message

Modeled Writing After writing the message, choose specific children to circle letters or words they know. Children will enjoy seeing how much of the message they "know."

It is Friday. We will look at all the books we have read.

Have children chant the spelling of each word on the Word Wall today: **h-e-r-e *spells* here, i-s *spells* is.**

Routines

Daily Phonemic Awareness
Blending and Segmenting Onset and Rime

- Play "Pat, Pat, Clap." Remind children that in "Pat, Pat, Clap," they pat for each sound you say and then clap to say the word.
- Pat and clap with children as you say: */qu/... /it/,* **quit**; */b/... /ag/,* **bag**.
- Continue with other words from the list.
- ***Now I'll say a word. You "pat, pat" the beginning and ending sounds, then "clap" to say the word again. Listen:*** **fit.** (/f/... /it/, fit).
- Continue with other words from the list.

More Words for

Pat	Pat	Clap
pin	kid	not
sip	fun	miss
bus	top	vet
ham	hat	van

Getting Ready to Learn

To help plan their day, tell children that they will

- reread and talk about all the books they've read this week.

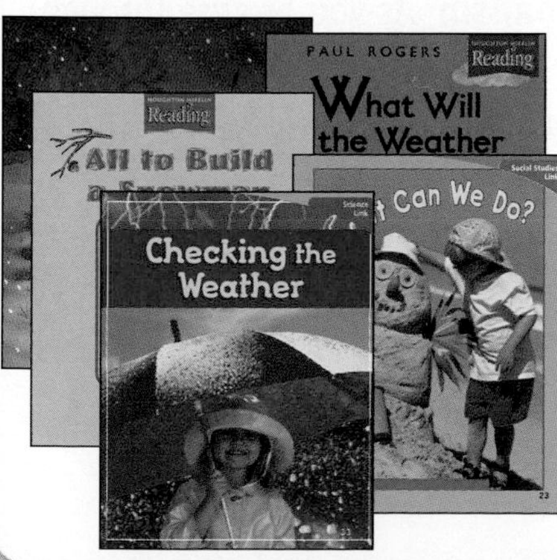

- take home a story they can read.

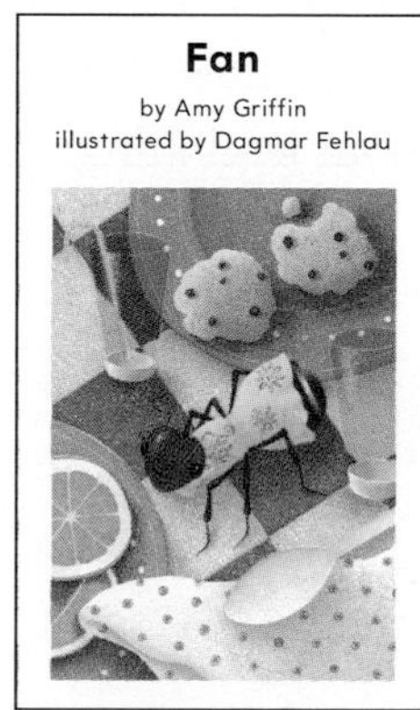

- write in their journals.

DAY 5

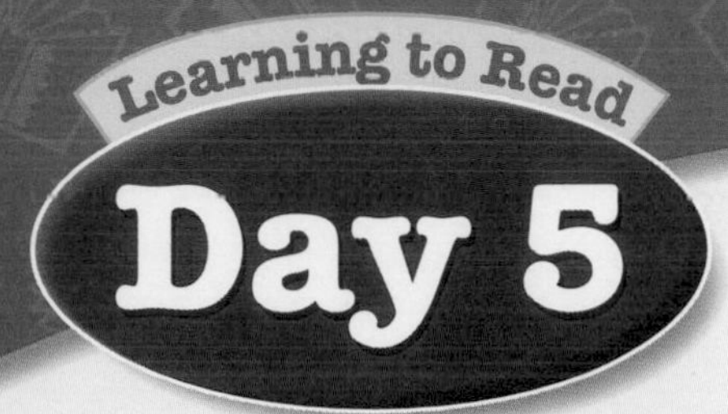

Revisiting the Literature

Literature Discussion

Compare the stories and books you've shared this week. Help children recall the selections with these prompts:

- *Who spent the winter in the woodcutter's cap? Did the animals have a good time? Why not?*
- *What is winter weather like? Show us pictures in* What Will the Weather Be Like Today? *that help describe winter where we live.*
- *Let's look at* All to Build a Snowman. *What caused all the problems in the park? What pictures tell about it?*
- *Which photographs in* What Can We Do? *remind you of something you do on a sunny day? A winter day?*
- *Let's look at "Fan" again. You can read it all by yourselves! Who will read page 17 for us? Point to the* -it *word. Read* it. *Can you find another* -it *family word somewhere in the book? Where?*
- Reread *Chicken Soup with Rice* to conclude the theme. Teach children to memorize the verse for the current month.

Comprehension: Plot In your concluding discussions, talk about the plot of the fictional story, *All to Build a Snowman.* Compare it with the Science and Social Studies Links. Explain that stories have problems and solutions. Informational articles do not.

Comprehension Focus: Fantasy/Realism As you browse through story, have children note which could really happen and which are make-believe; talk about beginning, middle, and end.

Here, Kit!

On My Way Practice Reader

Preparing to Read

Building Background Share the book's title, and have children comment on the picture. Ask them who Kit is. Invite children who have dogs to tell how they get the animals to come when they call. Do the dogs always listen?

Guiding the Reading

Walk through the pictures together. Use the ideas below to prepare children for reading on their own.

Page 1: *What are the characters doing? What is the weather like? What do you think the characters will do if it starts to rain?*

Pages 2-3: *Why are the boy and his Nan on the porch? Why is the boy calling to Kit? Where did the dog run to instead of listening to the boy?*

Pages 4-5: *Now what is Kit doing? How would you get the dog to come in out of the rain?*

Page 6: *What do the boy and his Nan try next? Do you think it will work? When you read the story, you will find out if Kit listens.*

Prompting Strategies Listen and observe children as they "whisper read," and use prompts such as these to help them apply strategies:

- *That word rhymes with* it. *Try blending the sounds*
- *You made just one mistake in that line. Can you figure it out?*
- *Try again. When you come to this word, think of a word that has the right sounds and makes sense.*

Responding

After children recall all the things the boy did to get Kit out of the rain, have them draw a picture and write a sentence to show what *they* would have done.

Leveled Books

The materials listed below provide reading practice for children at different levels.

Little Big Books

Little Readers for Guided Reading

Houghton Mifflin Classroom Bookshelf

Home Connection

Remind children to share the take-home version of "Fan" with their families.

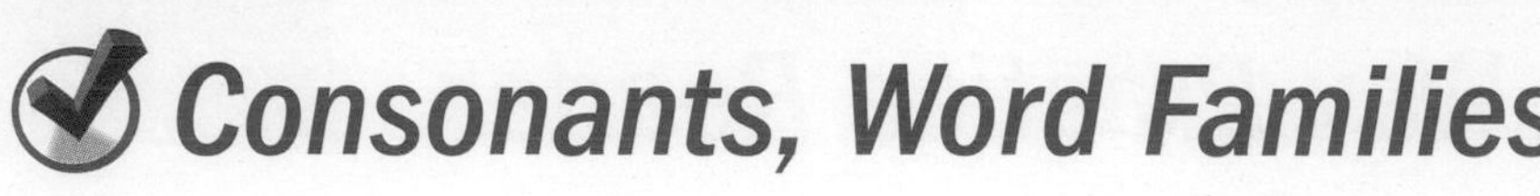

Consonants, Word Families

OBJECTIVES

Children

- build and read words with initial consonants and short *a* + *t*, short *a* + *n*, short *i* + *t*
- make sentences with high-frequency words

MATERIALS

- **Word Cards** *a, and, go, Here, I, is, it, like, my, see, to*
- **Picture Cards** assorted cards for sentence building
- **Punctuation Cards:** period, question mark

Review

Word Builders stand at the board. Word Readers work at their desks.

- ***Let's make the word* an. *Listen: /ă/ /n/,* an. *Write. Now read it together.***
- Word Readers hold up their slates or papers to show their words. Monitor progress closely. Other children come to the board. They erase the *t*, write *f*. ***What word did you make? Let's all read together. Good,* fan.**
- ***Here's a tricky one. Make* fat. *I'll say it slowly, /at/. What letter do you hear first? What letter do you hear last? Write the word. Good. Say the word with me,* fat.**
- ***Here's another tricky one! Change* fat *to* fit. *Listen /f/ /ĭ/ /t/. Remember Iggy Iguana's sound if you need help.***
- Continue until everyone has made a word at the board. Children can make: *an, tan, fan, man, can, pan, ran, van; bat, cat, sat, hat, rat, fat; it, sit, fit, hit, bit, kit, lit, pit.*

High-Frequency Word Review

I, see, my, like, a, to, and, go, is, here

Review

Give each small group the Word Cards, Picture Cards, and Punctuation Card needed to make a sentence. Each child holds a card. Children stand and arrange themselves to make a sentence for others to read. Once children read the sentence, have them change cards and make a new sentence.

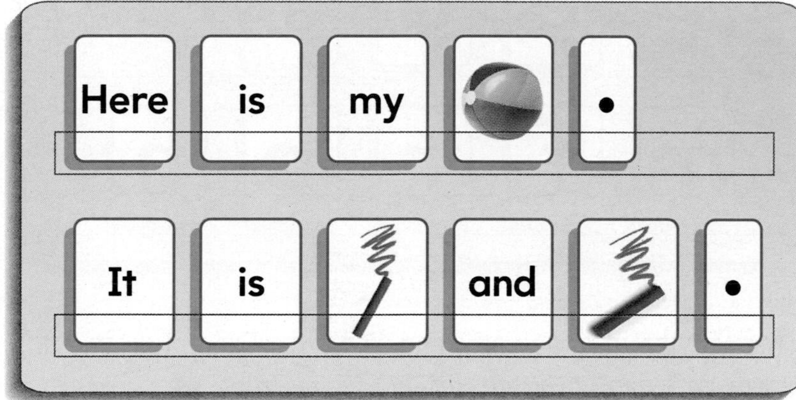

Apply

Practice Book page 192 Children can complete this page independently and read it to you during small group time.

Phonics Library Children can take turns reading a favorite part of the story "Fan." Or they might select a **Phonics Library** book from a previous theme.

Questions for discussion:

- ***What do you like about this book? Would you like to read it to a friend? Find one of our new words,* is *or* here. *Read it for us. Read the whole sentence.***
- ***Find a word that starts with the same sound as Queenie Queen's name. What is the letter? What is the sound?***

Practice Book p. 192

Portfolio Opportunity

Children may wish to save the Practice Book page in their portfolios.

Diagnostic Check

If . . .	You can . . .
children need help remembering the consonant sounds,	use *From Apples to Zebras* to review consonant sounds.
children pause at high-frequency words in **Phonics Library** selections,	have partners read words on the Word Wall together.

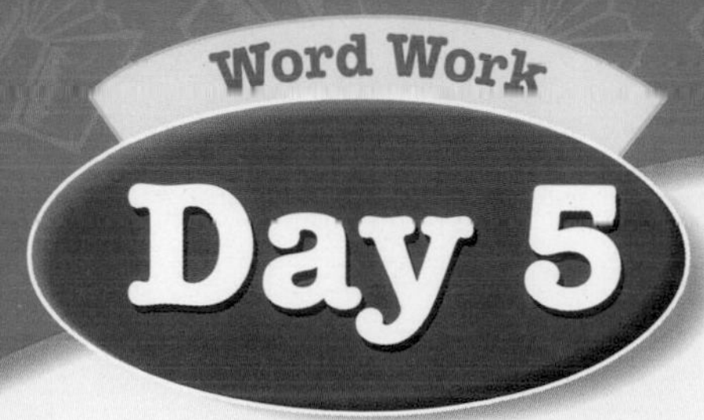

OBJECTIVES

Children

- build and read *-at, -an* and *-it* words

MATERIALS

- **Letter Cards:** *a, b, c, f, h, i, k, l, m, n, p, q, r, s, t, u, v*

Building Words

Word Families: *-an, -an, -it*

Model how to build *at.* Along the bottom of the pocket chart, line up the letters *m, f, r, b, h, s, c, v,* and *p.* ***I want to make the word* cat. *Who can tell me which letter I should take from here to make* cat?** Have a volunteer take the letter *c* and place it in front of *at.* Continue building *-at* words, using initial consonants *m, f, r, b, h, s, v,* and *p.* On chart paper, keep a list of all the *-at* words you make, and reread the list together.

Continue the activity with *-at* words and *-it* words. Examples: *an, can, fan, man, pan, ran, tan, van; it, bit, fit, hit, kit, lit, pit, quit, sit.*

Have small groups work together to build *-an, -at,* and *-it* words with magnetic letters or other alphabet blocks. Children can use their new words to create and illustrate sentences for the Word Bank section of their journals.

Independent Writing

Journals

During journal-writing time, observe children at the writing task. Do they get right to it? Or do they take a while to settle in? Do children sit comfortably? Are the mechanics of writing difficult? How do they hold their pencils? Make a special note of children who need help holding their pencils less awkwardly. See these children in a special small group session.

- ***We wrote a good story this week. Maybe you'll want to write a story too. You could use some of the weather words we learned this week. Do you remember an action word that you liked? Maybe you'll want to write more about it. Or maybe you have another idea. But remember that everyone writes carefully and quietly.***
- If time permits, allow children to share what they've written with the class.

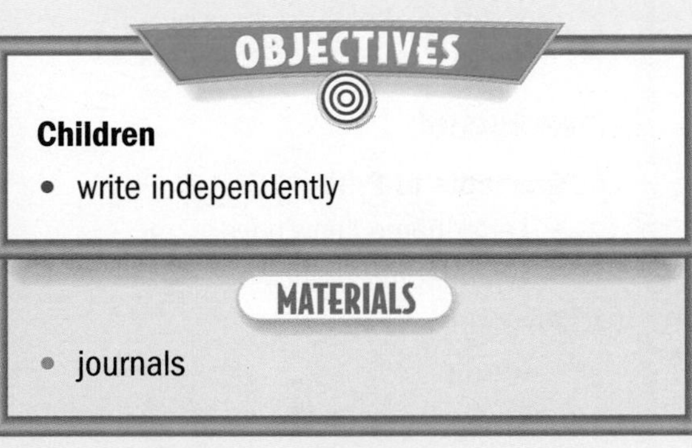

Children

- write independently

MATERIALS

- journals

Portfolio Opportunity

Mark journal entries you would like to share with parents. Also, ask children to mark their best efforts or favorite works for sharing as well.

DAY 5

English Language Learners

Have children use their journals to keep lists of new vocabulary and to illustrate those words. Pay attention to directionality and mechanics as they write words.

Theme 6

Theme Assessment Wrap-Up

Emerging Literacy Survey

Areas Assessed:

1. **Concepts of Print**
   - Letter name knowledge
   - Sound-letter association
2. **Phonemic Awareness**
   - Rhyme
   - Beginning sounds
   - Blending onsets and rimes
   - Segmenting onsets and rimes
   - Blending phonemes
   - Segmenting phonemes
3. **Beginning Reading and Writing**
   - Word recognition
   - Word writing
   - Sentence dictation
   - Oral reading

Monitoring Literacy Development

If you have administered the **Emerging Literacy Survey** as a baseline assessment of the skills children brought with them to Kindergarten, this might be a good time to re-administer all or part of it to chart progress, to identify area of strength and need, and to test the need for early intervention.

Use the **Observation Checklist** throughout the theme to write notes indicatin whether each child has a beginning, developing, or proficient understanding of reading, writing, and language concepts. (See facing page.)

Assessing Student Progress

Formal Assessment The **Integrated Theme Test** and the **Theme Skills Test** are formal assessments used to evaluate children's performance on theme objectives.

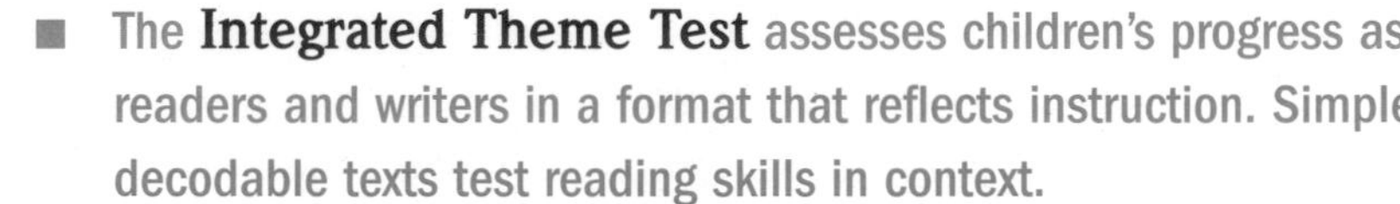

- The **Integrated Theme Test** assesses children's progress as readers and writers in a format that reflects instruction. Simple decodable texts test reading skills in context.

- The **Theme Skills Test** assesses children's mastery of specific reading and language arts skills taught in the theme.

Observation Checklist

Name ______________________ Date ______________________

	Beginning	Developing	Proficient
Listening Comprehension • Participates in shared and choral reading			
• Listens to story attentively			
Phonemic Awareness • Blends onsets and rimes			
• Segments onsets and rimes			
Phonics • Recognizes sounds for consonants			
• Builds words with word family *-it*			
Concepts of Print • Uses a capital at the beginning of a sentence			
• Uses end punctuation (period, question mark, exclamation mark)			
• Understands quotation marks			
Reading • Reads simple decodable texts			
• Reads the high-frequency words *is, here*			
Comprehension • Distinguishes fantasy from realism			
• Recognizes elements of plot (problem, solution)			
Writing and Language • Writes simple phrases			
• Participates in shared and interactive writing			

For each child, write notes or checkmarks in the appropriate columns.

Theme Resources

Resources for *Sunshine and Raindrops*

Contents

Twinkle, Twinkle, Little Star

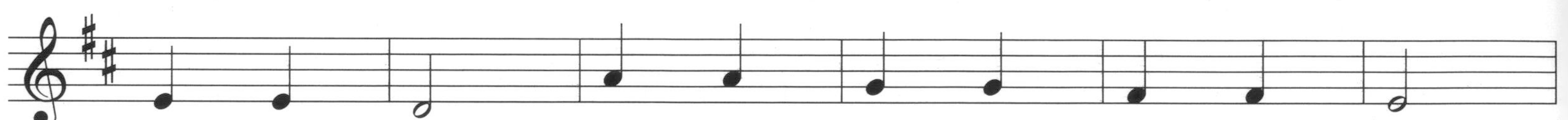

Use this music for Larry Lion's song.

The Farmer in the Dell

Use this music for Keely Kangaroo's song.

On Top of Old Smoky

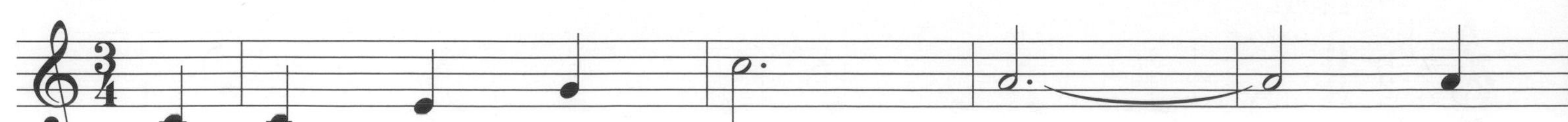
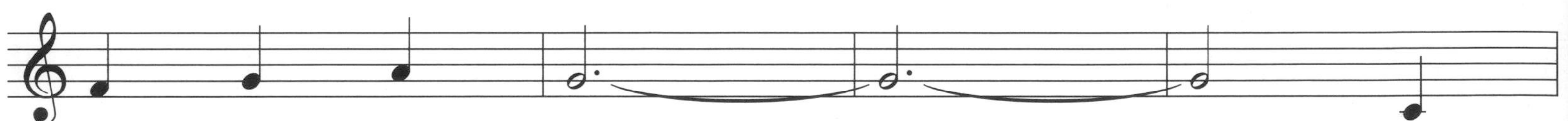
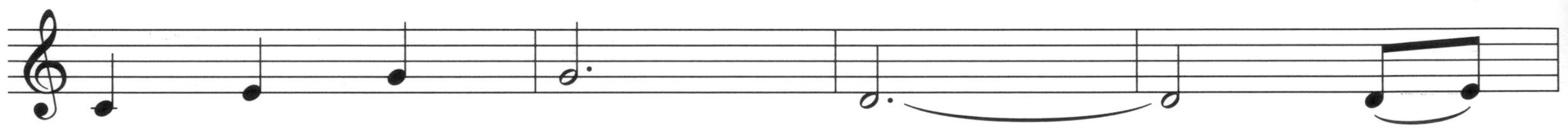
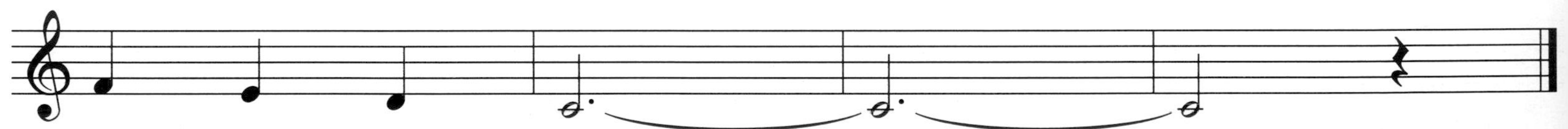

Use this music for Queenie Queen's song.

Yankee Doodle

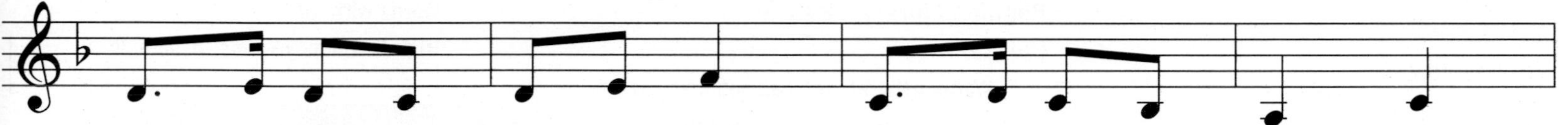

Use this music for Iggy Iguana's song.

Word List

In Themes 1 through 3, the Phonics Library stories are wordless.

Theme 1

- **Phonics Skills:** none taught in this theme
- **High-Frequency Words:** none taught in this theme

Phonics Library, Week 1:
We Go to School
wordless story

Phonics Library, Week 2:
See What We Can Do
wordless story

Phonics Library, Week 3:
We Can Make It
wordless story

Theme 2

- **Phonics Skills:** Initial consonants s, m, r
- **High-Frequency Words:** I, see

Phonics Library, Week 1:
My Red Boat
wordless story

Phonics Library, Week 2:
Look at Me
wordless story

Phonics Library, Week 3:
The Parade
wordless story

Theme 3

- **Phonics Skills:** Initial consonants t, b, n
- **High-Frequency Words:** my, like

Phonics Library, Week 1:
The Birthday Party
wordless story

Phonics Library, Week 2:
Baby Bear's Family
wordless story

Phonics Library, Week 3:
Cat's Surprise
wordless story

Theme 4

- **Phonics Skills:** Initial consonants h, v, c; words with -at
- **High-Frequency Words:** a, to

Phonics Library, Week 1:
Nat at Bat
Words with -at: *at, bat, hat, Nat, sat*
High-Frequency Words: *my, see*

Phonics Library, Week 2:
A Vat
Words with -at: *hat, mat, rat, vat*
High-Frequency Word: *a*

Phonics Library, Week 3:
Cat Sat
Words with -at: *bat, cat, hat, mat, sat*
High-Frequency Words: *my, see*

Theme 5

- **Phonics Skills:** Initial consonants p, g, f; words with -an
- **High-Frequency Words:** and, go

Phonics Library, Week 1:
Nat, Pat, and Nan
Words with -an: *Nan, ran*
Words with -at: *Nat, Pat, sat*
High-Frequency Words: *and, see*

Phonics Library, Week 2:
Go, Cat!
Words with -an: *Nan, ran, Van*
Words with -at: *Cat, Pat, sat*
High-Frequency Word: *go*

Phonics Library, Week 3:
Pat and Nan
Words with -an: *fan, Nan, ran*
Words with -at: *Pat, sat*
High-Frequency Words: *a, and, go*

Theme 6

- **Phonics Skills:** Initial consonants l, k, qu; words with -it
- **High-Frequency Words:** is, here

Phonics Library, Week 1:
Can It Fit?
Words with -it: *fit, it, sit*
Words with -an: *can, man, van*
High-Frequency Words: *a, go, I, is, my*

Phonics Library, Week 2:
Kit
Words with -it: *bit, fit, it, Kit, lit, sit*
Words with -an: *can, pan*
Words with -at: *hat*
High-Frequency Words: *a, here, I*

Phonics Library, Week 3:
Fan
Words with -it: *bit, quit*
Words with -an: *an, Fan*
Words with -at: *sat*
High-Frequency Words: *a, here, is*

Theme 7

- **Phonics Skills:** Initial consonants d, z; words with -ig
- **High-Frequency Words:** for, have

Phonics Library, Week 1:
Big Rig
Words with -ig: *Big, dig, Rig*
Words with -it: *pit*
Words with -an: *can, Dan*
High-Frequency Words: *a, for*

Phonics Library, Week 2:
Tan Van
Words with -ig: *Pig, Zig*
Words with -it: *it*
Words with -an: *can, Dan, ran, tan, van*
Words with -at: *Cat, sat*
High-Frequency Words: *a, have, I, is*

Phonics Library, Week 3:
Zig Pig and Dan Cat
Words with -ig: *dig, Pig, Zig*
Words with -it: *it*
Words with -an: *can, Dan*
Words with -at: *Cat, sat*
High-Frequency Words: *and, for, have, here, I, is*

Theme 8

- **Phonics Skills:** Consonant x; words with -ot, -ox
- **High-Frequency Words:** said, the

Phonics Library, Week 1:
Dot Got a Big Pot

Words with *-ot: Dot, got, hot, lot, pot*
Words with *-ig: big*
Words with *-it: it*
Words with *-an: Nan*
Words with *-at: Nat, sat*
High-Frequency Words: *a, and, I, is, like, said*

Phonics Library, Week 2:
The Big, Big Box

Words with *-ox: box, Fox*
Words with *-ot: not*
Words with *-ig: big*
Words with *-it: bit, fit, hit, it*
Words with *-an: can, Dan, Fan*
Words with *-at: Cat, hat, mat, sat*
High-Frequency Words: *a, is, my, said, the*

Phonics Library, Week 3:
A Pot for Dan Cat

Words with *-ot: pot*
Words with *-ox: Fox*
Words with *-ig: big*
Words with *-it: fit*
Words with *-an: can, Dan, Fan, ran*
Words with *-at: Cat, sat*
High-Frequency Words: *a, and, see, said*

Theme 9

- **Phonics Skills:** Initial consonants w, y; words with -et, -en
- **High-Frequency Words:** play, she

Phonics Library, Week 1:
Get Set! Play!

Words with *-et: get, set, wet, yet*
Words with *-ot: got, not*
Words with *-ox: Fox*
Words with *-ig: Pig*
Words with *-an: can*
High-Frequency Words: *a, play, said*

Phonics Library, Week 2:
Ben

Words with *-en: Ben, Hen, men, ten*
Words with *-et: get, net, pet, vet, yet*
Words with *-ot: got, not*
Words with *-ox: box, Fox*
Words with *-it: it*
Words with *-an: can*
High-Frequency Words: *a, I, my, play, said, she, the*

Phonics Library, Week 3:
Pig Can Get Wet

Words with *-et: get, wet*
Words with *-ot: got, not*
Words with *-ig: big, Pig, wig*
Words with *-it: sit*
Words with *-an: can*
Words with *-at: Cat, sat*
High-Frequency Words: *a, my, play, said, she*

Theme 10

- **Phonics Skills:** Initial consonant j; words with -ug, -ut
- **High-Frequency Words:** are, he

Phonics Library, Week 1:
Ken and Jen

Words with *-ug: dug*
Words with *-en: Ken, Jen*
Words with *-et: wet*
Words with *-ot: hot*
Words with *-ig: big, dig*
Words with *-it: it, pit*
High-Frequency Words: *a, and, are, is*

Phonics Library, Week 2:
It Can Fit

Words with *-ut: but, nut*
Words with *-ug: jug, lug, rug*
Words with *-ox: box*
Words with *-ot: not*
Words with *-ig: big*
Words with *-it: fit, it*
Words with *-an: can, tan, van*
Words with *-at: fat, hat*
High-Frequency Words: *a, he, see, she*

Phonics Library, Week 3:
The Bug Hut

Words with *-ut: but*
Words with *-ug: Bug, hug, lug*
Words with *-ox: box*
Words with *-ot: Dot, got, not*
Words with *-ig: Big, jig*
Words with *-an: can, Jan*
Words with *-at: fat, hat*
High-Frequency Words: *a, here, is, she, the*

Cumulative Word List

By the end of Theme 10, children will have been taught the skills necessary to read the following words.

Words with -at
at, bat, cat, fat, hat, mat, Nat, Pat, rat, sat, vat

Words with -an
an, ban, can, Dan, fan, Jan, man, Nan, pan, ran, tan, van

Words with -it
bit, fit, hit, it, kit, lit, pit, quit, sit, wit

Words with -ig
big, dig, fig, jig, pig, rig, wig, zig

Words with -ot
cot, dot, got, hot, jot, lot, not, pot, rot, tot

Words with -ox
box, fox, ox

Words with -et
bet, get, jet, let, met, net, pet, set, vet, wet, yet

Words with -en
Ben, den, hen, Jen, Ken, men, pen, ten

Words with -ug
bug, dug, hug, jug, lug, mug, rug, tug

Words with -ut
but, cut, hut, jut, nut, rut

High-Frequency Words
a, and, are, for, go, have, he, here, I, is, like, my, play, said, see, she, the, to

Technology Resources

American Melody
P. O. Box 270
Guilford, CT 06473
800-220-5557

Audio Bookshelf
174 Prescott Hill Road
Northport, ME 04849
800-234-1713

Baker & Taylor
100 Business Court Drive
Pittsburgh, PA 15205
800-775-2600

BDD Audio
1540 Broadway
New York, NY 10036
800-223-6834

Big Kids Productions
1606 Dywer Avenue
Austin, TX 78704
800-477-7811
www.bigkidsvideo.com

Blackboard Entertainment
2647 International Boulevard
Suite 853
Oakland, CA 94601
800-968-2261
www.blackboardkids.com

Books on Tape
P. O. Box 7900
Newport Beach, CA 92658
800-626-3333

Filmic Archives
The Cinema Center
Botsford, CT 06404
800-366-1920
www.filmicarchives.com

Great White Dog Picture Company
10 Toon Lane
Lee, NH 03824
800-397-7641
www.greatwhitedog.com

HarperAudio
10 E. 53rd Street
New York, NY 10022
800-242-7737

Houghton Mifflin Company
222 Berkeley Street
Boston, MA 02116
800-225-3362

Informed Democracy
P. O. Box 67
Santa Cruz, CA 95063
831-426-3921

JEF Films
143 Hickory Hill Circle
Osterville, MA 02655
508-428-7198

Kimbo Educational
P. O. Box 477
Long Branch, NJ 07740
900-631-2187

The Learning Company (dist. for Broderbund)
1 Athenaeum Street
Cambridge, MA 02142
800-716-8506
www.learningco.com

Library Video Co.
P. O. Box 580
Wynnewood, PA 19096
800-843-3620

Listening Library
One Park Avenue
Old Greenwich, CT 06870
800-243-45047

Live Oak Media
P. O. Box 652
Pine Plains, NY 12567
800-788-1121
liveoak@taconic.net

Media Basics
Lighthouse Square
P. O. Box 449
Guilford, CT 06437
800-542-2505
www.mediabasicsvideo.com

Microsoft Corp.
One Microsoft Way
Redmond, WA 98052
800-426-9400
www.microsoft.com

National Geographic Society
1145 17th Street N. W.
Washington, D. C. 20036
800-368-2728
www.nationalgeographic.com

New Kid Home Video
1364 Palisades Beach Road
Santa Monica, CA 90401
310-451-5164

Puffin Books
345 Hudson Street
New York, NY 10014
212-366-2000

Rainbow Educational Media
4540 Preslyn Drive
Raleigh, NC 27616
800-331-4047

Random House Home Video
201 E. 50th Street
New York, NY 10022
212-940-7620

Recorded Books
270 Skipjack Road
Prince Frederick, MD 20678
800-638-1304
www.recordedbooks.com

Sony Wonder
Dist. by Professional Media Service
19122 S. Vermont Avenue
Gardena, CA 90248
800-223-7672

Spoken Arts
8 Lawn Avenue
P. O. Box 100
New Rochelle, NY 10802
800-326-4090

SRA Media
220 E. Danieldale Road
DeSoto, TX 75115
800-843-8855

Sunburst Communications
101 Castleton Street
P. O. Box 100
Pleasantville, NY 10570
800-321-7511
www.sunburst.com

SVE & Churchill Media
6677 North Northwest Highway
Chicago, IL 60631
800-829-1900

Tom Snyder Productions
80 Coolidge Hill Road
Watertown, MA 02472
800-342-0236
www.tomsnyder.com

Troll Communications
100 Corporate Drive
Mahwah, NJ 07430
800-526-5289

Weston Woods
12 Oakwood Avenue
Norwalk, CT 06850-1318
800-243-5020
www.scholastic.com

Index

Boldface page references indicate formal strategy and skill instruction.

P

R

S

T

V